I firmly believe that this book could inspire members of the Body of Christ to reach that level of excellence that would please our Father's heart, as we are inspired by the examples of men and women who believe God for miracles. It will bring a revolution of faith and works that demonstrate the power and presence of God in the marketplace and in the Church worldwide.

Barbara Chan
Marketplace leader, Hong Kong, China

Rick Heeren has captured the heart of transforming a nation. He is not simply a theoretician, but also a practitioner. Be prepared to have your heart and life changed through this book—you will never be the same after reading it. You will become a radical transformer that implements real change in your life, city and nation.

Cindy Jacobs
Cofounder and President, Generals International
Red Oak, Texas, USA

The answer to Rick Heeren's constant prayer that God's will be done "on earth as it is in heaven" is masterfully revealed in the pages of *Marketplace Miracles*. The stories here are what keep Rick in a wonderful state of infectious excitement, and they prove beyond the shadow of a doubt that God is abundantly able to do more than anything we can hope or imagine.

Stephanie Klinzing
Mayor, Elk River, Minnesota, USA

We all need inspiration to think outside the box. *Marketplace Miracles* provides real life examples of men and women who have decided to believe that the Word of God is applicable to their work lives today—even when it comes to miracles! A must-read for every workplace believer who wants to go to another level.

Os Hillman
Author, *The 9 to 5 Window*
President, Marketplace Leaders and the International Coalition of Workplace Ministries
Cumming, Georgia, USA

The Church as we know it is moving very rapidly into a Kingdom expression. *Marketplace Miracles* by Rick Heeren is one of the best examples of the shift that has occurred over the last two decades. This book also serves as a model of how the Church will be seen vibrantly in societal structures rather than within the four walls where it has been contained in the past. This is an excellent read that will open you up for new vision.

Chuck D. Pierce
President, Glory of Zion International Ministries
Denton, Texas, USA

For as long as I have known Rick, he has shown a passion for the extraordinary. In *Marketplace Miracles*, Rick sets up clear road signs and guideposts for those who seek to follow the highway being forged by contemporary pioneers who have learned to position themselves as gatekeepers to usher in the extraordinary moves of God.

Graham Power
Chairman, Power Group of Companies
Transformation Africa and Global Day of Prayer
Cape Town, South Africa

My friend Rick Heeren walks in a high level of faith and trust in God. I believe that our Father in heaven is calling for all of us to walk in a higher level of faith and trust in Him. This book will encourage you to reach those levels. You are about to read stories that will introduce you to "ordinary" people who have an *extraordinary God!*

Chuck Ripka
President and CEO, Rivers International, Ripka Enterprises and Rivercenter
International Network of Christians
Elk River, Minnesota, USA

Christian leaders in the marketplace who align their thinking with God's thinking are transforming their businesses, schools, communities and nations. Rick Heeren's book shows us actual examples from around the world of miraculous transformations brought about by ordinary Christian leaders who dared to believe and obey God's direction in their spheres of influence.

Dutch Sheets
Dutch Sheets Ministries
Colorado Springs, Colorado, USA

This book may be the final tremor unleashing the spiritual tsunami that will sweep the world and revolutionize the way we do business. Business as usual will no longer hold true when we let God be God over our businesses.

Tim Tay
Business owner and CEO, Trinix Computers P/L
Perth, Australia

In this book, Rick Heeren has released what is contained in his life: faith in the God who turns the impossible into possible and the ordinary to the extraordinary. As you will see, he's still on the journey, and it's not too late for you to join him!

Dave Thompson
Senior Vice President, Harvest Evangelism, Inc.
San Jose, California, USA

Few Christian leaders would doubt that God's mandate for His people today is to take dominion over every segment of society. Can this be done? Rick Heeren, one of God's chosen workplace apostles, says *yes!* This one-of-a-kind book is not theory—it floods us with exciting news from around the world that the social transformation we have been praying for is actually happening!

C. Peter Wagner
Presiding Apostle, International Coalition of Apostles
Colorado Springs, Colorado, USA

If it sounds too good to be true, it probably means that God has been at work. It's the only conclusion you can draw when you read of the miracles in this extraordinary book from a wonderful man of God.

Ross Whitehill
COO, Thomas Murray, Ltd.
London, England

RICK HEEREN

MARKETPLACE MIRACLES

Extraordinary Stories of Marketplace Turnarounds
Transforming Businesses, Schools and Communities

Regal

From Gospel Light
Ventura, California, U.S.A.

Published by Regal
From Gospel Light
Ventura, California, U.S.A.
www.regalbooks.com
Printed in the U.S.A.

Library of Congress Cataloging-in-Publication Data
Heeren, Rick.
  Marketplace miracles / Rick Heeren.
     p. cm.
  ISBN 978-0-8307-4396-4 (hard cover) — ISBN 978-0-8307-4386-5 (international trade paper)
  1. Businesspeople—Religious life. 2. Evangelistic work. 3. Miracles. I. Title.
  BV4596.B8H44 2007
  269'.2—dc22

                                                                              2007000042

1 2 3 4 5 6 7 8 9 10 / 10 09 08

Rights for publishing this book outside the U.S.A. or in non-English languages are administered
by Gospel Light Worldwide, an international not-for-profit ministry. For additional information,
please visit www.glww.org, email info@glww.org, or write to Gospel Light Worldwide, 1957 Eastman
Avenue, Ventura, CA 93003, U.S.A.

DEDICATION

I dedicate this book to my nephew Justin Herbst and his family. Justin was born with cerebral palsy (CP). Even though he is a relative and I have been aware of his disability, it wasn't until I interviewed his mother for a chapter in this book that I really understood the extraordinary miracles that have taken place in their family.

First, I dedicate this book to Justin, who has made up his mind to live a victorious life. I attended his high school graduation party and watched him wheel his wheelchair out onto the patio where all his guests were gathered. Without notes, he addressed every person in the audience and told each one, in a very personal way, how his or her life had encouraged him. I had tears in my eyes as I realized how much about each person's contribution Justin had stored in his memory. Near the end of his talk, he said the following: "I have embraced my disability. My disability has helped me to understand the world in a bigger way. I have begun to understand that it is so difficult to achieve what you want. You could give up. But you just have to keep going. You have got to keep striving."

Second, I dedicate this book to his sister, Kacie, and his brother, Clay, who have lived in a home where their disabled brother received an enormous amount of attention. In the backyard speech, Justin told his sister and his brother how much he respects them.

Third, I dedicate this book to Justin's mother, Patti, and his father, Chuck, who have not only learned how to contribute to their son's success, but have also helped other children with CP through the Center for Independence, which they founded. I now understand why Patti was named one of the top eight citizens in Chicago.

CONTENTS

ACKNOWLEDGMENTS

Thanks to Bill Greig III, who encouraged me on a bus in Hong Kong to consider having Regal Books publish this book, and thanks to Dr. Gary S. Greig, Bill's brother, for being the champion for it as it moved from a concept to a reality within Regal. It is also an extraordinary miracle that Gary was available when I needed the assistance of an Old Testament scholar—he was formerly a professor of Old Testament Theology at Regent University. Thanks also to Jerry Gramckow, who edited the book and challenged me to push for a higher level of excellence within it. And, finally, thanks to all of the people who allowed me to tell their stories.

FOREWORD

Ed Silvoso

To see what you haven't yet seen, you need to do what you haven't yet done, because if you keep on doing what you have always done, you will continue to see what you have always seen.

In his book *Marketplace Miracles*, Rick Heeren shows with eloquent persuasiveness that miracles—those rare divine interventions into human affairs—shouldn't be so rare. We should expect to see them regularly. And we should expect more than just run-of-the-mill miracles—we should witness extraordinary miracles in the marketplace, where the need is greatest.

In my book *Anointed for Business*, I define "the marketplace" as the combination of business, education and government. These are the three arteries through which the life of nations and cities flows daily. Like clogged arteries in a sick patient, the immense and complex problems prevalent in the marketplace today defy ordinary solutions. Miracles are needed, and miracles require God's intervention.

But does God really care about what goes on in the workplace, holding office hours on days other than Sunday? Is He in on Mondays? Or on Tuesdays, Wednesdays, Thursdays, Fridays and Saturdays, for that matter? Is He as interested in human affairs as we are told He is in eternal matters?

How trustworthy is 1 John 4:4: "He who is in [us] is greater than he who is in the world"—especially when we are way down on the scoreboard and time is running out?

Does He really care?

In this book, Rick Heeren answers these questions with a resounding *yes*. God cares so much that He is willing and eager to perform extraordinary miracles in the marketplace, and to do it again and again, as He did in Ephesus through Paul, who introduced the term "extraordinary miracles" in the Bible (see Acts 19:11, *NIV*).

This book will shift your paradigms in the most inspiring way. You will begin to believe what you never believed before, and as a result you will attempt things you never tried before. And when you do, you will begin to rely on God's power to see what you haven't yet seen.

Ed Silvoso
Author, *Anointed for Business*

GOD IS ABOUT TO START A REVOLUTION

I am part of a team at Harvest Evangelism that has been urging marketplace Christians (those who work in business, education or government) to be ministers when they go to work each day. Over the years, the feedback I have received from many successful marketplace Christians has been startling. Some successful Christians have told me that their experience with some marketplace Christians has been so negative (breaking covenants, expecting better-than-average financial arrangements, poor quality of work, and so on) that now they would rather do business with non-Christians.

As a result of their substandard work, some marketplace Christians have been forsaken and hated by the public. However, I believe that this drought of excellence is about to end. God is about to make marketplace Christians the very definition of excellence. He is about to distinguish marketplace Christians as people who perform at a level of excellence that abundantly exceeds their non-Christian marketplace peers. God is indeed raising the standard of excellence in the marketplace. God is calling marketplace Christians to work at their jobs with the highest level of integrity and the greatest quality they can achieve.

I believe the Lord is about to start a revolution in which marketplace Christians will stand out because of their relationship to the Lord. Marketplace Christians will be known not only for having a living relationship with the Lord and meeting people's needs through prayer but also for the high quality of their work. As marketplace Christians commit to aligning their thinking with God's thinking and to obeying Him in the way they perform at work, God will use them to transform their spheres of influence.

Whereas you have been forsaken and hated, so that no one went through you,
I will make you an eternal excellence, a joy of many generations.
Isaiah 60:15

CHAPTER 1

THE REVELATION OF GOD'S DEFINITION

In November 2003, I attended the final banquet for that year's Harvest Evangelism Institute in Mar del Plata, Argentina. I was sitting near the back of the dining hall when I heard Ed Silvoso, the founder and president of Harvest Evangelism, announce my name and ask me to come to the front of the room. When I got to the platform, Ed asked me to kneel and then spoke these words over me: "Rick, the Lord is releasing a mantle of extraordinary miracles upon you."

I quickly told the Lord that I welcomed His new anointing, but that I really did not know what He meant by "extraordinary miracles." When I got back to my room, I searched my Bible, and as I did so the Holy Spirit led me to Acts 19:11, which states, "God did extraordinary miracles through Paul" (*NIV*). Yet I still didn't know what this phrase meant. I thought to myself, *Aren't all miracles extraordinary?*

For two years I cried out to the Lord, asking Him to help me understand His perspective about extraordinary miracles. Then, in August 2005, as I was flying from Minneapolis to San Francisco to attend Harvest Evangelism's twenty-fifth anniversary celebration, the Lord revealed to me that my next book would contain a chapter about Valley Christian Schools (VCS). I had first met Dr. Clifford Daugherty, the president of VCS, 10 years earlier, but I had not seen him for about 5 years. I knew, however, that VCS had turned around dramatically under Dr. Daugherty's leadership.

At one of the first events at Harvest Evangelism's anniversary celebration, amazingly, there was Dr. Daugherty. I rushed over and explained to him that the Lord had told me I would write a new book and that one of the chapters would be about his school. Clifford said he had just documented the turnaround of Valley Christian in a manuscript he hoped to publish. He had a copy of the manuscript with him and asked if I would like to read it. I had assumed I would have to follow Clifford around with a pad of paper, making notes for my book, but now I had his manuscript that contained all the details. This confirmed what the Lord had told me on the plane.

I studied Clifford's manuscript intensely, which eventually became the foundation for chapter 3 in this book. But the Lord also used Clifford's manuscript to help me understand the concept of "extraordinary miracles."

A TRIP TO ARGENTINA

As I read Clifford's manuscript, the Lord reminded me of an extraordinarily miraculous breakthrough I had experienced several years earlier. I used to pray once a week with Frank, a Native American pastor, who served a congregation on the north side of Minneapolis. One day after we had finished praying, I asked Frank if he and his wife would accompany me on a trip to Argentina. He talked it over with his wife, and they decided they would like to go. However, the cost of the trip was beyond their budget. I didn't have the money either, but we agreed to cry out to God together for the resources for Frank and his wife to take this trip.

God pushed this prayer request to an even higher level by giving me the boldness to ask other ethnic pastors and their wives to make the trip with us. In addition to Frank and his wife, 28 others joined us in believing that God would make it possible for the entire group to make the trip to Argentina. At $3,000 each, the cost for 30 people to go to Argentina was $90,000. Believing the Lord for $90,000 stretched me far beyond what I had ever experienced before.

Frank and I began praying that the Lord would make it possible for all of these friends to go to Argentina. We prayed that prayer every week thereafter, listened to the Lord, did what He told us to do and trusted Him to provide what was needed. Then miracles began to happen. I suddenly started receiving financial commitments from marketplace

Christians. Amazingly, people began pressing checks for $25,000 into my hands. Eventually, I had the $90,000 we needed to take 30 people to Argentina.

Most of these people did not have passports, so I began helping them get their paperwork together to submit applications. I don't want to minimize this step, because many of these leaders had never had a passport before, and some were in the United States as temporary residents on green cards. The Lord challenged me to believe Him for even more miraculous breakthroughs in order to overcome these difficulties.

I had to book nonrefundable airline tickets for the entire group prior to their receiving their passports. During this process I discovered that Frank didn't have a birth certificate. Despite this apparent problem, I booked airline tickets for him and his wife as an act of faith in and obedience to the Lord.

The Passport Problem

When I talked to my own pastor about the challenge of obtaining a passport for Frank, the Lord moved miraculously again and provided me with strategic contacts. My pastor suggested we enlist the services of one of our U.S. senators. We contacted the senator's office, and his Minnesota staff began to assist us in exploring ways in which we could get a passport for Frank. After several weeks, the senator's staff did not see any way they could help. No birth certificate, no passport! The situation seemed impossible.

On the day before the trip to Argentina, my pastor and I met in his office to pray that God would give us wisdom about how we could help get a passport for Frank. Surely God would make a way for Frank to make the trip to Argentina, since He had already provided the funds to send him.

I made one last call to the senator's staff person in Minnesota. Then the Lord worked another miracle: Remarkably, the staff person had just discovered that Frank's birth certificate was in a sealed legal file in Montana! I immediately contacted a Christian lawyer friend and told him what we had discovered. He sprang into action and contacted the agency in Montana that had jurisdiction over the file and asked them for the name and telephone number of a local lawyer who had excellent rapport with that agency. He then called that lawyer and hired him to get a court order to open the sealed legal file. Within an hour, the lawyer had the birth certificate and had hired an overnight messenger service to send it to the Seattle passport office. At the same time, I hired another messenger service to arrive at the Seattle passport office when that office opened the following day.

Perhaps the most amazing part of this miracle was that one messenger service delivered the birth certificate while a second messenger service stood and waited for the passport office to process the birth certificate and create the passport. Everything went as we had hoped. The passport office created the passport, and the second messenger service rushed it to the airport and put it on the next flight from Seattle to Miami.

The Lord continued to accomplish miraculously what had seemed impossible, given all the different—and essential—steps involved in the process. At the beginning of that same day, Frank and his wife boarded the airplane with their 28 teammates and flew from Minneapolis to Miami. We waited several hours at the Miami Airport, hoping to receive the passport from Seattle prior to the departure of the plane that would take us from Miami to Buenos Aires, Argentina.

We soon learned that the Seattle-to-Miami flight was a bit delayed and that it would arrive just after our flight to Argentina was scheduled to depart. Although this looked like another impossible situation, I decided that it was not a cause for discouragement. God had taken us this far, and He would see this through to completion. I told Frank and his wife about the delay and that they would have to stay overnight at the Miami Airport hotel. They would receive the passport and depart for Argentina the following day.

At this point, the Lord did something special to bless this couple. When their 28 teammates heard that Frank and his wife would have to stay overnight at the hotel, they took up an offering to pay for their hotel room. They raised enough money for the couple to have an extraordinary dinner in addition to covering the cost of the very expensive hotel room at the airport hotel.

Two days after I arrived in Argentina, I returned to our hotel to find Frank and his wife waiting on a bench just outside the front door. They told us that they had enjoyed a wonderful dinner as they waited in Miami—an extravagant date. They also had a very nice room in the hotel. When they arrived at the airline ticket office the next day, the passport was there and they were able to fly to Argentina. God had indeed made a way when there seemed to be no way.

The Bus Ride of Reconciliation

But God wasn't done yet. At the end of our visit to Argentina, another extraordinary event occurred on the bus ride from Mar del Plata to the airport in Buenos Aires. About two hours into the bus ride, one of the African-American leaders stood up and proclaimed in a loud voice that the Lord had told him revival would not come to his congregation unless he repented for the sins that African-Americans had committed against representatives of other people groups. A representative from one of the other people groups jumped up, forgave the African-American leader, and then proclaimed that his people group was guilty of similar sins. He confessed these sins and asked to be forgiven. Then a representative of another people group extended the same forgiveness and also confessed and repented for the sins of his people group. This process went on for two hours.

The presence of the Lord rested upon that bus in a tangible way. At one point in the journey, I was sitting toward the front of the bus and became aware of loud talking behind me. I noticed that Pastor Napoleon Meynard, a Nicaraguan pastor from the Twin Cities, was talking loudly to the driver. I thought to myself, *Wow, they're making a lot of noise. Can't they see that we're holding church here in the back of the bus?* Imagine how embarrassed I was to learn that Napoleon was leading the bus driver to the Lord. Napoleon later told me that the driver had initiated the conversation, saying, "If this is what it is like to be a Christian, show me how to become one. I want to experience this kind of love on a regular basis."

It didn't even end there. When Rachel and I arrived at the airport to check in, we turned to our left to see two Hispanic couples leading their ticket agent in a prayer to receive Jesus Christ as his Savior and Lord.

Then, when we went into the restaurant, several of the waiters allowed us to lead them in a prayer to receive the Lord.

Since this time, many of the leaders who were with me on that trip have expressed their opinion that a change in the spiritual climate surrounding ethnic relations in the Twin Cities took place on that day as we interceded and made reconciliation on our bus ride through Argentina.[1] Through this experience, I realized that God's power is always far greater than the problems that may confront us. He showed me that when we surrender the circumstances to Him, ask Him for His direction, align our thinking with His thinking and then do what He says, He is able to do much more than we ever could ask for.

WHAT IS NECESSARY FOR AN EXTRAORDINARY MIRACLE

The Lord left me wondering for two years before He finally gave me an idea of what an extraordinary miracle looked like and the process I needed to go through in order for such a miracle to take place. Specifically, He revealed to me that extraordinary miracles always (1) *start with a revelation of God's extraordinary goal* that should be (2) *written down and shared with others*. Such miracles require us to (3) *align our thinking to God's extraordinary goal*, (4) *realize that God will do the miracles through our hands* and (5) *understand that God's grace will take us from where we are to where He wants us to be*. Once we have done this, we then simply (6) *wait for God's grace to take effect*. In the following section, I will explain each of these steps in greater detail.

1. Seeking Wisdom About God's Goals
For an extraordinary miracle to occur in our lives, we must first ask God for wisdom as it relates to His goals. This whole concept is based on being able to hear the Lord's voice. If we are not accustomed to hearing His voice, we will not know where He wants us to go.[2] When I read Clifford Daugherty's manuscript, I noticed that the Lord told Clifford that VCS was simply trying to survive, which was not His will for the organization. God told Clifford that VCS needed to align their goals with the higher standards of excellence He had for them.

As I reflected on this idea of receiving God's higher standard of excellence, the words of Ephesians 3:20 came to mind: "Now to Him who is able to do exceedingly abundantly above all that we ask or think, according to the power that works in us." This is the first component that is necessary for an extraordinary miracle to occur: The Lord must give us a revelation that is "exceedingly abundantly above all that we ask or think."

2. Writing the Vision and Sharing It with Others
Once we have received a revelation from the Lord, the next step is to write the vision down and share that document with other interested parties. Habakkuk 2:2 forms the foundation for this component: "Write the vision and make it plain on tablets, that he may run who reads it." In the case of VCS, the vision the Lord had given to each department head was written and combined in a document that became known as *A Quest for Excellence.*

3. Aligning Our Thinking to God's Goal
The next step requires us to align our thinking to the revelation we have received from the Lord. This is often where the problems occur: Our thinking is often the ceiling that limits the Lord's ability to bring about transformation in our lives. However, when we hear the Lord and are willing to change our thinking in response to what we hear, this barrier is removed and He can do the extraordinary through us. In Colossians 3:2, Paul writes, "Set your minds on things above, not on things on the earth." In other words, we shouldn't try to figure out how God's goal will be accomplished in human terms alone. We should just align our thinking with His revelation.

In 1 Chronicles 28:19, King David told his son Solomon that he had received the written revelation of the blueprints for building the Temple. "'Every part of this blueprint,' David told Solomon, 'was given to me in writing from the hand of the Lord'" (*TLB*). Then David told Solomon that he should not let the size of the Lord's revelation overwhelm him but that he should align his thinking with the Lord's revelation. If Solomon did, God would perform extraordinary miracles through his hands. "Then he continued, 'Be strong and courageous and get to work. Don't be frightened by the size of the task, for the Lord my God is with you; he will not forsake you. He will see to it that everything is finished correctly'" (1 Chron. 28:20, *TLB*).

If anyone in the Bible had a right to be frightened by the size of a revelation, it was Mary. Imagine how she must have felt when the angel Gabriel told her that through the power of the Holy Spirit, she would conceive the Son of God. "Let it be to me according to your word" was her response (Luke 1:38).

So the third factor in releasing God to work extraordinary miracles in our lives and in the marketplace is to adjust our thinking to agree with His revelation.

4. Realizing God Will Do Extraordinary Miracles Through Our Hands

Once we have aligned our thinking with God's revelation, we need to realize that God will do these miracles through our hands. In Acts 19:11, Luke states that "God did extraordinary miracles by the hands of Paul" (*RSV*). God was doing the miracles, but He was doing them through the hands of a human named Paul.

The same thought is reflected in Ephesians 3:20: "[God is] able to do exceedingly abundantly [that is, extraordinary miracles] ... according to the power *that works in us*" (emphasis added). Most of us don't realize—or believe, perhaps—that we can be the vessels through whom God can do the extraordinary and even the impossible. We limit God by focusing only on what we can do by ourselves. We leave God's power out of the picture. But if we take the first steps in obedience to the Lord's direction, rely on His extraordinary power and repent of all fear and anxiety and doubt, He can catapult us forward to achieve things we never thought possible.

My friend and colleague Ted Hahs once made a comment that stuck with me. He said, "Everybody believed that God could kill Goliath. But David was the only one in Israel who believed that God could use *him* to kill Goliath."

Exodus 34:10 reveals that God gave Moses a very similar message. God told Moses He would display the miraculous through his hands, not in some ethereal vacuum out in the desert: "The Lord replied, 'All right, this is the contract I am going to make with you. I will do miracles such as have never been done before anywhere in all the earth, and all the people of Israel shall see the power of the Lord—the terrible power I will display through you'" (*TLB*).

5. Understanding God's Grace Will Take Us Where He Wants Us to Be

Next, we need to understand that God's grace will take us from where we are to where He wants us to be. Look at Zechariah 4:6-7:

> Then he said, "This is God's message to Zerubbabel: 'Not by might, nor by power, but by my Spirit, says the Lord of Hosts—you will succeed because of my Spirit, though you are few and weak.' Therefore no mountain, however high, can stand before Zerubbabel! For it will flatten out before him! And Zerubbabel will finish building this Temple with mighty shouts of thanksgiving for God's mercy, declaring that all was done by grace alone" (TLB).

Look especially at the phrases "you will succeed because of my Spirit" and "all was done by grace alone." If the Holy Spirit leads us, His grace will be sufficient for everything we need.

6. Waiting for God's Grace to Take Effect

In order for an extraordinary miracle to take place, we must take the final step: to wait upon the Lord for His grace to take effect. Habakkuk 2:3 states, "For the vision is yet for an appointed time; but at the end it will speak, and it will not lie. Though it tarries, wait for it; because it will surely come, it will not tarry."

EXPECT A MIRACLE

Extraordinary miracles are miracles the Lord does through people in order to take them from where they are to where He wants them to be. In the case of the trip to Argentina, the Lord worked five extraordinary miracles when I aligned my thinking with His thinking and did what He led me to do.

First, He helped me find 30 ethnic leaders who would agree to go to Argentina, even though no funds were available at the time they agreed to the trip. Second, He enabled us to raise $90,000 to finance the trip for 30 people. Third, He intervened in obtaining passports for 29 people. Fourth, He intervened in obtaining a birth certificate and then a passport for Pastor Frank, all within 24 hours of departure. Fifth, He transformed ethnic relations in the Twin Cities through the spiritual reconciliation of the 30 participants during their bus ride to the airport at Buenos Aires.

All of this—and the stories of marketplace miracles you're about to read—took place as people got a revelation of God's extraordinary goal, wrote down their vision, shared it with others, aligned their thinking with God's goal, realized that God would do the extraordinary miracles through their hands, understood that God's grace would take them where He wanted them to be, and trusted Him as they waited for that grace to take effect.

Notes

1. Rick Heeren, *Thank God It's Monday! How to Take God to Work with You* (San Jose, CA: Transformational Publications, February 2004), pp. 50-51. Copies may be ordered at www.citymiracles.com.
2. To learn how to hear and listen to God's voice, I recommend *The Beginner's Guide to Hearing God* by Jim W. Goll (Regal, 2004) and *Hearing God's Voice* by Henry T. Blackaby and Richard Blackaby (B & H Publishing Group, 2002).

CHAPTER 2

GOD: THE SOURCE OF OUR PROVISION

If you have the Holy Spirit and your competitors don't, shouldn't you have an advantage? Of course you should. As I stated in the previous chapter, if we are led by the Holy Spirit, then His grace is sufficient for everything we need. If we have faith, we will trust in God to meet our needs—and more. His grace will be the wellspring of amazing things—including extraordinary miracles in the marketplace.

COMING FROM BEHIND, GETTING AHEAD

So often in our lives—and especially in our careers—we fall prey to discouragement. We can't see how God can possibly use our professional life to accomplish great things. Perhaps we even feel that our Christian faith puts us at a disadvantage when it comes to doing business. But nothing could be farther from the truth.

Consider 1 Kings 18:44-46, a passage I heard preached on by a pastor in Argentina in October 2005:

> Then it came to pass the seventh time, that [Elijah's servant] said, "There is a cloud, as small as a man's hand, rising out of the sea!" So [Elijah] said, "Go up, say to Ahab, 'Prepare your chariot, and go down before the rain stops you.'" Now it happened in the meantime that the sky became black with clouds and wind, and there was a heavy rain. So Ahab rode away and went to Jezreel. Then the hand of the LORD came upon Elijah; and he girded up his loins and ran ahead of Ahab to the entrance of Jezreel.

As I listened to the preaching and began to study this Scripture, I could see how the Lord was using it to tell us that He desires to bring a revolution in the marketplace. I see a small cloud—and that cloud is growing bigger and bigger. It's going to rain! God is going to deliver us from the drought and famine that have plagued the world of business, education and government. We are about to experience marketplace excellence that has eluded us in the past.

Furthermore, as the Argentine pastor highlighted, as Elijah started out behind but arrived at Jezreel before King Ahab did, so we will finish ahead of our secular competitors—if we'll cling to God's vision and run forward in faith. This is a promise, not merely a possibility: "And the LORD will make you the head and not the tail; you shall be above only, and not be beneath, if you heed the commandments of the LORD your God, which I command you today, and are careful to observe them" (Deut. 28:13). Like Elijah, if we are doing something God's way, we will always finish ahead, never behind.

CLAIMING THE PROMISES

Yet the promise that we'll finish ahead of the game is just one of the many blessings God has promised to His people. In fact, if we look at Deuteronomy 28, we see that it is a list of blessings that will come to those who love and serve the Lord.

1. The Lord will set you high above all nations of the earth (see v. 1).
2. You will be blessed in the city (see v. 3).
3. You will be blessed in the country (see v. 3).
4. Your offspring will be blessed (see v. 4).
5. Your land will be productive (see v. 4).
6. Your herds will increase (see v. 4).
7. Your basket will be blessed (see v. 5).
8. Your kneading bowl will be blessed (see v. 5).
9. You will be blessed when you go in (see v. 6).
10. You will be blessed when you go out (see v. 6).
11. Your enemies will be defeated (see v. 7).

12. Your storehouses will be blessed (see v. 8).
13. You shall prosper in everything that you attempt (see v. 8).
14. Your land shall be blessed (see v. 8).
15. You shall be blessed with holiness (see v. 9).
16. People will see the favor of the Lord upon you (see v. 10).
17. People will be afraid of you (see v. 10).
18. The Lord will grant you plenty of goods (see v. 11).
19. The Lord will grant you plenty of offspring in your family (see v. 11).
20. The Lord will grant you plenty of offspring in your flocks (see v. 11).
21. The Lord will grant you plenty of increase in your crops (see v. 11).
22. The Lord will grant you plenty of increase in your land (see v. 11).
23. The Lord will give you access to His treasure in the heavens (see v. 12).
24. The Lord will bless the work of your hands (see v. 12).
25. You will lend, but you will not borrow (see v. 12).
26. You shall be the head and not the tail (see v. 13).
27. You shall be above and not beneath (see v. 13).

Are these promised blessings of Deuteronomy 28 still relevant for New Testament believers? The answer is yes. God's promises are eternal. In His Word He is speaking to those who have loved and obeyed His commands in the past—and to those who love Him and obey Him in the here and now.

Some evangelicals unfortunately believe that the Old Testament has little bearing on New Testament faith. But such a view hardly reflects the attitude that Jesus, the apostles and the Early Church had toward the Old Testament, which was their Bible. We should be careful not to hold such a view, either. The well-known evangelical New Testament scholar F. F. Bruce made this point about the Old Testament:

Some readers even today find difficulties in the acceptance of the Old Testament as part of the Church's canon. The Old Testament was the Bible of our Lord and His apostles, and its authority was fully acknowledged by them. . . . The Old and New Testaments, in fact, cannot be dissociated. . . . We cannot understand the New apart from the Old. The Old Testament is to the New as the root is to the fruit. It is a grave mistake to think that the fruit of the Spirit in Christianity will grow and ripen better if the plant is severed from its roots in the Old Covenant.[1]

In fact, the Old Testament was the only Bible—the only canon of authoritative Scripture—that the New Testament Church had before the New Testament documents began to be collected in the late first century A.D.[2] When Paul wrote in 2 Timothy 3:16 that "All Scripture is God-breathed and is useful for teaching . . . and training in righteousness" (*NIV*), he meant that all *the Old Testament* "is God-breathed and is useful for teaching . . . and training in righteousness" (*NIV*, emphasis added).

Although the New Testament makes it clear that we are saved not by keeping Old Testament law but by faith in Christ and the atonement of His blood for our sins (see Rom. 6:14; Gal. 2:16; 5:6), this does not mean that the deeper principles of Old Testament law, which include the promised blessings of Deuteronomy 28, are nullified by faith in Christ. Paul emphatically teaches this in Romans 3:31: "Do we, then, *nullify* the law by this faith? *Not at all!* Rather, we *uphold* the law" (*NIV*, emphasis added). In fact, New Testament faith fulfills or establishes the deeper principles of Old Testament law embodied in the Ten Commandments and the blessings of Deuteronomy 28:

Let no debt remain outstanding, except the continuing debt to love one another, for he who loves his fellowman has fulfilled the law. The commandments, "Do not commit adultery," "Do not murder," "Do not steal," "Do not covet," and whatever other commandment there may be, are summed up in this one rule: "Love your neighbor as yourself." Love does no harm to its neighbor. Therefore love is the fulfillment of the law (Rom. 13:8-10, *NIV*).

And finally, the admonition in Deuteronomy 28:1 to listen to and obey the voice of the Lord is echoed in the New Testament in Jesus' words in John 10:27-28: "My sheep listen to my voice; I know them, and they follow me. I give them eternal life, and they shall never perish" (*NIV*). Different words, yes, but the same God, the same promise.

AVOIDING IDOLATRY

What does this mean for us today? That we as followers of Christ can access all of these blessings as long as we are obedient to God's commandments and especially the commandment "not to go after other gods to serve them" (see Deut. 28:14). This last phrase is very significant. Let's look at what the Lord says about other gods in the Ten Commandments:

> And God spoke all these words, saying: "I am the LORD your God, who brought you out of the land of Egypt, out of the house of bondage. You shall have no other gods before Me. You shall not make for yourself a carved image, or any likeness of anything that is in heaven above, or that is in the earth beneath, or that is in the water under the earth; you shall not bow down to them nor serve them. For I, the LORD your God, am a jealous God, visiting the iniquity of the fathers on the children to the third and fourth generations of those who hate Me, but showing mercy to thousands, to those who love Me and keep My commandments" (Exod. 20:1-6).

In the Ten Commandments the Lord states very clearly that we are to worship Him alone, that idolatry is strictly forbidden. And we shouldn't think that just because we're not worshiping a golden calf we're "in the clear." False gods come in many shapes and forms. Consider Hosea 2:5:

> For she said, "I will go after my lovers,
> Who give me my bread and my water,
> My wool and my linen,
> My oil and my drink."

In this passage, Hosea gives us a broader definition of "idolatry," illustrating how anything that takes the place of God in our lives is, in fact, an idol. In the second part of Hosea 2:5, Hosea's wife, Gomer, is going after other lovers, thinking they are the ones who give her sustenance and provisions (bread, water, wool, linen, oil and drink). Yet the first part of Hosea 2:8 makes it clear that God is the real source of her sustenance and provision:

For she did not know
That I gave her grain, new wine, and oil,
And multiplied her silver and gold

Hosea's wife had lost sight of the fact that the Lord was her source for everything. He reminds us that all good things come from Him.

"It shall come to pass in that day that I will answer," says the LORD; "I will answer the heavens, and they shall answer the earth. The earth shall answer with grain, with new wine, and with oil; they shall answer Jezreel. Then I will sow her for Myself in the earth, and I will have mercy on her who had not obtained mercy; then I will say to those who were not My people, 'You are My people!' And they shall say, 'You are my God!'" (Hos. 2:21-23).

Look especially at the phrase "They shall answer Jezreel." *Jezreel* means "God sows." In other words, God is the source of our provision. He is the one who sows blessings in our lives. We need to trust Him with all of our hearts and lean not on our own understanding.

Even as I thought about this, I remembered three bestselling secular marketplace books I read this year. I reflected upon the fact that there was not one word in any of those books about God being the One who sows blessings in our lives. The essence of each of these books was, "If you do X, Y and Z, you will be a success." Doesn't that seem like idolatry? Doesn't that seem like looking to something other than God for provision in our lives?

Of course, there are consequences for such idolatry.

My people are destroyed for lack of knowledge. Because you have rejected knowledge, I also will reject you from being priest for Me; because you have forgotten the law of your God, I also will forget your children (Hos. 4:6).

Considered in context, this verse means that people *who fail to understand that God is their provider* are "destroyed for lack of knowledge." Consider a story I share in my book *The Threshing Floor*. In 1906, leaders of the flour-milling industry in Minneapolis donated to the city a statue called the "Father of Waters," symbolizing the Mississippi River. In the dedication ceremony, the donors explicitly stated that it was the "river god" who gave them their prosperity. They had lost sight of the fact that the Lord was their source for everything. They had lost sight of Jezreel. What was the result? The Lord removed His hand of blessing, and that was the end of their prosperity![3]

CASE IN POINT

We don't have to look very far to see that God's Word is true—that He alone sows blessings in our lives. Consider Graham Power, CEO of The Power Companies in South Africa, who spoke in Elk River, Minnesota, on December 14, 2005, about his experience of God's blessings.

According to Graham, before he became a Christian, he behaved as if it were in his power to gain wealth—and he sought to accumulate a lot of it. He sought to build his company bigger, to amass profits, to purchase bigger homes, to get more "stuff." He was clearly a living example of the essence of idolatry: "Then you say in your heart, 'My power and the might of my hand have gained me this wealth'" (Deut. 8:17).

But his story didn't end there.

One day he gave his life to the Lord—and he experienced a paradigm shift. He came to see that all he is and has comes from God alone. He began to live in God's grace and power—not his own. He now quotes Deuteronomy 8:18 often: "And you shall remember the LORD your God, for it is He who gives you power to get wealth"—and puts it into practice by donating 10 percent of the profits of each of his 12 companies to help those in need. He has also set a cap on his personal income and donates 100 percent above that cap to the work of the Lord. Clearly, Graham Power now understands Jezreel!

Let's follow Graham's lead and seek God alone for our sustenance. Once we're willing to step out in faith, we'll step into the promised blessings of God—and watch the marketplace miracles begin!

Notes
1. F. F. Bruce, *The Books and the Parchments* (Westwood, NJ: Revell, 1950), pp. 81-82.
2. M. Müller, *The First Bible of the Church. A Plea for the Septuagint* (Sheffield, England: Sheffield Academic Press, 1996), p. 1.
3. Rick Heeren, *The Threshing Floor: Minnesota, God's Threshing Floor for the Nation* (San Jose, CA: Transformational Publications 2004), pp. 124-134. Copies can be ordered at www.citymira cles.com.

CHAPTER 3

STAYING TRUE TO THE VISION

Maybe you're still skeptical about the whole concept of marketplace miracles. Maybe you still wonder if God intervenes in the life of Christian businesses. You've probably seen plenty of Christian companies fail miserably—despite talented leadership and grand beginnings. But maybe those businesses forgot that God is our CEO—that He calls the shots. And that He can bring victory from defeat.

Nowhere is this truth more clearly illustrated than in the life and times of Valley Christian Schools (VCS), which I recently visited. On a trip to meet with Ed Silvoso in San Jose, California, he took me to see VCS's new Skyway Campus. Ed's car wound up the curved driveway that led to the top of the hill, where a stunning panorama of the city of San Jose lay below us. Reaching the top of the hill, a sense of awe came over me as I took my first look at the magnificent Skyway Campus.

A number of years earlier, Ed had introduced me to Dr. Clifford Daugherty, president of VCS. Ed and Clifford had become friends, and Clifford had asked Ed to become VCS's chaplain. Once on the inside, Ed discovered that this organization desperately needed help. It had been losing large sums of money, making it impossible to pay their teachers competitive wages.

The school was getting bounced around from facility to facility, because it lacked a permanent home. Ed told me that in the midst of these crises, he had met with Clifford Daugherty and the board and that they had implemented prayer evangelism together within the school. The result? God had responded by bringing spiritual transformation to the organization.

AN EXTRAORDINARY ORGANIZATION

Now here we were on top of this hill, looking at facilities that would have made many colleges envious—symbols of prosperity were everywhere. "Wow, this is a high school?" I asked. "Look at that football stadium! Look at that swimming pool!"

In 2003, the approximately 200,000 square feet of facilities of the Skyway Campus were valued at $80 million. They are now valued at over $100 million. According to their annual report for 2004, VCS generated approximately $420,000 in surplus from operations. The 2005-2006 school-year budget was about $25 million.

In addition to having some of the finest facilities of any high school in America, VCS has also achieved an extraordinary level of excellence in both academic and athletic endeavors. Here is a summary of those achievements from Dr. Daugherty's book *The Quest for Excellence*.[1]

- In 2002 the VCS high school was selected by Cal Hi Sports as the California State Athletic School of the Year (Division IV).

- Valley Christian High School athletes have won 76 league championships and 10 Central Coast Sectional (CCS) championships.

- VCS boasts the highest-ranked high school football team in the San Francisco Bay and San Jose areas. On the morning of December 3, 2005, after VCS won its fourth consecutive CCS championship, www.Calpreps.com ranked the Valley Warriors as the number one high school football team in California (all 995 high school football teams in California were included in the rankings).

- VCS teams won back-to-back CCS basketball championships for 2003 and 2004.

- The girls' soccer team won the CCS championship title in 2004 and 2006.

- The girls' softball team was ranked fourth in California in 2006 among all high schools.

- Splash, VCS's U.S. Olympic preparation swim team, placed first in competition at the Santa Clara International Swim Center in 2004.

- VCS's field show competition band claimed the state championship for AA/AAA class at the Western Band Association field show competition in both 2003 and 2004, along with many sweepstakes trophies in the band competitions.

- VCS's symphonic band took first place in the Disney World band competition sweepstakes in the spring of 2005.

- Seven students were selected for the All-State Honor Band in the 2004-2005 school year.

- VCS's dance, theater, orchestra and vocal departments produce some of the most amazing amateur theater productions imaginable. The theater won the prestigious award for best staging from the Center for Performing Arts in 2005.

- Students manage and produce programming for KVCH, the world's first high school radio station to broadcast live on the Internet 24 hours a day.

- Among schools in the Association of Christian Schools International, the VCS yearbook has been a first-place winner in many categories for years.

- The high school newspaper, *The Warrior*, received a first-place ranking for three consecutive years in the American High School Newspaper Awards.

- Sixty-eight percent of Valley Christian high school's 2004 graduating class of more than 280 students qualified for admission to the University of California. Another 28 percent qualified for California State University. More than 95 percent of graduates enroll in college, and many are accepted into some of the top universities in the nation.

- The 2005 graduating class boasted two National Achievement Scholars, four National Merit Scholar finalists and well over $5 million in college scholarship offers.

- In the 2005-2006 scholastic year, 15 advanced placement (AP) college-level courses were offered, in many cases with more than one class period per course. During 2005, a total of 337 students, many of whom took multiple AP courses, enjoyed pass rates for college credit at more than double the California high school average.

- The Junior High Jazz band won the 2006 Western States Reno Jazz Championships.

In 2004, the United States Department of Education bestowed the "No Child Left Behind" Blue Ribbon Award on Valley Christian High School, the only private high school in California and one of only four in the nation to receive the prestigious Blue Ribbon Award that year. Among many other requirements, VCS was able to show evidence that student scholastic achievement scores were among the top 10 percent in the nation. Not too shabby!

AN EVEN MORE EXTRAORDINARY TRANSFORMATION

Given their recent accomplishments, it might surprise you to learn that Valley Christian Schools hasn't always been at the top of the heap. In fact, the state of affairs at VCS in 1987 was downright dismal. Here are the stats—they aren't pretty.

- $420,000 projected deficit
- Enrollment at just over 800 students, down from 1,400
- Constant displacement from rented facilities
- Constant moves to new rented facilities
- Inability to pay teachers competitive salaries
- Lack of academic achievement
- Oppressive legalistic culture on campus

How did such an extraordinary turnaround happen? It began when VCS redefined their organizational goals. Instead of just trying to survive, they decided to set an extraordinary goal for themselves—a goal defined by the Lord. Here is what Clifford Daugherty has said regarding their primary goal, namely, *excellence*: "The key to the success of the Quest for Excellence is in the definition of 'excellence.' We began to understand that the definition of 'excellence' at Valley Christian Schools involves the nature, character, and works of God. The word 'quest' communicates the idea that we are on a journey toward God's excellence."[2]

Once the goal had been redefined and the school had once again made God the center of their business, Dr. Daugherty began challenging all of the teachers and administrators to ask God to give them the desires of their hearts—that is to transplant God's desires into their hearts. Clifford challenged his team to ask God for His definition of excellence for each area. He told them that he dreamed of a day when the public would value Valley Christian's capabilities above those of all other schools. The Lord then stretched each department head at Valley Christian to dream big dreams about what his or her department could become (the resulting mosaic of testimonies became the basis for Valley Christian's *Quest for Excellence*).

Once the leadership of VCS began to seek God's vision for their school, amazing things began to happen. God performed a series of miracles to close the gap between where they were and where He wanted them to be. These extraordinary miracles came in the following categories: (1) solving the financial crisis, (2) solving the spiritual crisis, (3) solving the crisis of low teacher salaries, and (4) solving the facilities crisis.

Solving the Financial Crisis

The projected deficit for the year ending June 1992 was $280,000. When Clifford Daugherty asked God what to do, the Lord gave him a three-step action plan. First, the Daugherty's would sell their home and donate the equity—about $70,000—to VCS. Second, the board of directors would agree to match the $70,000 donation. Third, parents and friends would be asked to match the $140,000 donated by the Daugherty's and the board. Intercessors connected with VCS and began praying for this turnaround strategy to be successfully implemented. As a result of prayer and the financial sacrifices made by the Daughertys and the board of directors, the hearts of others were moved to give, enabling VCS to fully cover its deficit.

Valley Christian Schools ended its next fiscal year, in June 1993, with a surplus of $50,000. This surplus resulted from successive and substantial tuition increases. Parents were willing to pay a higher rate of tuition because they, too, bought into the *Quest for Excellence*. They perceived that, given the new vision and goal of VCS, the education their children were now receiving had extraordinary value. In fact, they became part of making that vision a reality by giving financial contributions to the school above and beyond their tuition payments.

At the same time, VCS's enrollment increased as they promoted their *Quest for Excellence* program to new parents. As enrollment increased, the school administration was able to selectively register outstanding students.

Solving the Spiritual Crisis

But there was more to VCS's transformation than money—that "more" was prayer evangelism. As a result of Dr. Clifford Daugherty's sharing with Ed Silvoso about the challenges VCS faced, Ed volunteered to serve as chaplain for the organization. Ed and his wife, Ruth, already met on a weekly basis for prayer and Bible study; now Ed shared an action plan for implementing prayer evangelism that could transform VCS.

In August 1992, Ed and all seven board members and five administrators met to rededicate themselves and VCS to the Lord's purposes. They also committed to implementing prayer evangelism in their own lives—and to model prayer evangelism for the students. In November 1992, Clifford and his wife, Kris, attended the Harvest Evangelism International Institute in Buenos Aires and learned more about prayer evangelism. It was there that God gave Dr. Daugherty a vision for transforming the spiritual climate at VCS through prayer evangelism.

Two months later, on January 13, 1993, the senior high students gathered in a chapel service where Clifford introduced Pray Valley. This strategy called for a group of student intercessors to volunteer to pray daily for every VCS high school student—by name. By March of that same year, 58 student intercessors were praying for 90 percent of the 410 high school students.

On Friday, March 12, 1993, the high school held another chapel service, which was to end at the 11:30 A.M. lunch bell. With the entire high school student body in attendance, the Holy Spirit moved on the gathering, causing several teens to repent publicly for sinful behaviors and rededicate themselves to the Lord. The first lunch bell rang, but no one left; then the second lunch bell rang, and again, no one left. Ed Silvoso, who was scheduled to speak, gave an altar call instead—and almost every student gave or recommitted his or her life to Christ. The spiritual transformation was total—and complete.

Solving the Crisis of Low Teacher Salaries

Just as the solutions for the facilities crisis began to come into view, the VCS teachers complained to Dr. Daugherty that they were still paid poorly compared to public school teachers. They told him that with significant new money being directed toward facilities, they felt that it was only fair that they receive a pay increase. Clifford had planned to solve the facilities crisis first and then take on the project of increasing teachers' salaries. The teachers did not understand, and Dr. Daugherty took the matter to the Lord.

He asked the Lord for $1 million more per year for teachers' salaries. In answer to that prayer, an individual stepped forward and donated $1 million per year for 10 years. During the 10 years of this donation, VCS set aside funds that then allowed them to continue supporting more competitive faculty salaries for decades to come.

Given the improved salaries at VCS, great teachers did not want to leave, and teachers with the best credentials began applying for employment. Eventually, this resulted in a significant upgrade in the quality of the teachers. Now VCS had the best physics teachers, the best chemistry teachers, the best math teachers, and so on.

One can only imagine how thrilled the parents were to see that the school's *Quest for Excellence* was working. I can envision how a parent might have reacted to tuition increases: "Of course, I will pay the higher tuition. Where else can my child have access to Christian teachers with these credentials?" In short, solving the problem of low teacher salaries in such a dramatic fashion contributed mightily to solving the school's financial problems on a permanent basis.

Solving the Facilities Crisis

Perhaps the most dramatic miracle that took place at VCS involved God's provision of a home for the school, which had been without permanent facilities since its inception.

In 1987, Valley Christian tried to purchase Camden High School, where its high school was holding its classes. But the skyrocketing land values in Silicon Valley inspired a developer to outbid VCS for the campus. The developer allowed the school a lease extension, but eventually, in the spring of 1989, he sent an eviction notice.

In 1988, school leaders prayed about where to locate permanently. A woman stepped forward and volunteered to sell VCS 25 acres on top of a hill at the intersection of Skyway Drive and Monterey Highway. Her offer to sell at $1 per square foot was considerably below market rates in Silicon Valley, where prices for land were as high as $23 per square foot. The school made an initial assessment of the woman's land and found that, by itself, it was big enough for the campus they envisioned.

The board and administration then began looking for other potential land acquisitions in addition to the Skyway property. They learned that 32 acres of adjacent land belonged to a developer. As it turned out, that developer was not interested in selling his land to the school. VCS did not let the developer's reluctance dissuade them from pursuing their objective. They began to pray and took positive steps, assuming the Lord would make a way where there seemed to be no way. As an act of faith, they purchased the woman's Skyway property.

With the woman's property in hand, they then offered the developer $1 per acre for 23 of his 32 acres. They also told the developer he could recognize the difference between $1 per acre purchase price and the market value of the land as a charitable (read "tax deductible") contribution to VCS. They got their extraordinary miracle—the developer changed his mind and agreed to the sale.

VCS acquired this second Skyway property in February 1989. Valley Christian knew they had to perform an environmental impact study before they could build on this land. They hired an outside firm to perform the study, with a particular emphasis on assessing the impact of their plan on an endangered, protected species of butterfly. The outside firm stated that the project would not endanger the protected butterfly, but that it would endanger two rare, protected species of plants that were growing on the property. They estimated it would cost $200,000 to $300,000 to move the endangered plants from the Skyway property. This news caused the Skyway property development planning process to grind to a halt.

Dr. Daugherty cried out to the Lord for assistance. Still, the Skyway property development process lay dormant for five years until a solution could be found for the endangered plants. Eventually, God led VCS to an expert in the endangered plant species. Amazingly, he was the person who had originally presented the case that convinced the government to put these plants on the endangered list. He said he could solve this problem for just $10,000—not $200,000 to $300,000, which were the earlier estimates. The consultant was able to resolve all the regulatory issues and showed the school how to dig up and relocate the endangered plants.

But VCS hadn't faced the last obstacle by far. Now neighbors were outraged when they heard that the school was moving forward with the re-zoning application for the Skyway property. They feared the VCS campus would increase traffic in their community. As a result, the San Jose Planning commission unanimously voted against granting permission for re-zoning. But the city council had ultimate authority over the decision, so VCS leaders and families prayed for God's help to influence the city council. A city council woman representing the district that included the Skyway property declared her support for the school's re-zoning proposal. With her support, VCS appealed, and on May 17, 1994, their re-zoning application was approved.

While touring the Skyway property one day, Dr. Daugherty and his wife discovered that occultists were performing witchcraft there. In 1996, one of the parents, a prayer intercessor—along with his son—built a 20-foot cross and installed it on the Skyway property. A Bible was buried in the concrete at the base of the cross. On Sunday, June 9, 1996, VCS dedicated the cross and the ground it was on to the Lord. On that day the Lord took possession of the hill.

As VCS began to move forward with their building plans, significant neighborhood opposition to the Skyway project again arose. A community meeting was scheduled for May 12, 1998, to provide an opportunity for the neighbors to voice their concerns. Just prior to the community meeting, the Lord led Dr. Daugherty to meet with one of the neighbors. Then, at the meeting, that neighbor ended up defending the Skyway campus. With that neighbor's testimony, the tide turned; the other neighbors had a change of heart and decided to support the Skyway campus.

But yet another obstacle soon threatened to derail the building project. A male Burrowing Owl—a protected species—took up residence on the Skyway site. This discovery led to another season of prayer. A couple months later, the owl died of natural causes and VCS received permission to proceed with their building plans.

Then there was the problem related to the girls' softball program. Upon review, it was apparent that the development plan did not provide enough space for a girls' softball field. In order to resolve this problem, Valley Christian wanted to buy two-and-one-half acres known as the "donut hole." Again a season of prayer ensued, and the Lord instructed VCS to offer the owners 110 percent of the land's market value. The owners agreed and the sale closed on May 20, 1998.

Then they faced the giant of financing the construction. Valley Christian needed $28 million. An expert was hired to pursue a tax-exempt, low-interest municipal loan. The initial reaction of firms that could provide the financing was that VCS would have to modify its mission and drop its Christian focus. That was unacceptable to Dr. Daugherty and the board.

Meanwhile, VCS's municipal bond counsel, a partner in a San Francisco law firm, offered to help obtain the tax-exempt construction loan of $28 million, which a recent Supreme Court ruling allowed them to pursue. The VCS board approved this approach, and a financial services firm signed a term sheet and agreed to lend the school the $28 million.

Then another setback occurred. The San Jose city attorney was convinced that having the city serve as a conduit for a $28 million bond issue for a Christian school would violate the First Amendment clause regarding government "establishment of religion." The Santa Clara County Counsel held the same opinion. After a presentation by the VCS bond counsel, the county counsel changed his opinion and gave a favorable recommendation to the Santa Clara County Board of Supervisors. The board of supervisors approved the VCS application. Then the nine-county Association of Bay Area Governments (ABAG) had to ratify the decision. The ABAG approved the VCS application, even though one of the board members was adamantly opposed to it.

Then there was the problem of how to construct a fire-defense system on top of a huge hill. The San Jose Fire Department recommended a water tower that had a capacity of more than a million gallons and that was able to deliver 4,500 gallons per minute for four hours. The City of San Jose Planning Department, however, vetoed such a huge and unsightly structure on top of the hill. Dr. Daugherty began to pray and eventually got a unique idea: *What about a water reservoir rather than a water tower?*

When he spoke about the idea to his consultants, one of them inquired, "Do you mean a swimming pool?" The consultant began plans to build such a pool. VCS submitted the plans in October 1998 to the San Jose Fire Department for its approval, but the fire captains unanimously rejected the plan. So VCS submitted an appeal, which was also rejected.

Dr. Daugherty went back to prayer, and finally a new impression formed in his mind: *Find out which consultant has such credibility that when he speaks, every fire chief in America listens.* VCS received the name of an engineering firm that had that kind of reputation. Their report dated January 11, 1999, was positive, but the fire captains again rejected it. Miraculously, the fire chief made an executive decision and reversed the ruling, and the pool-based fire system was approved. Now I understand why VCS has such an enormous swimming pool.

VCS wasn't home free yet. Before the loan closed, the executive general counsel of the lender refused to finance the loan. Again more prayer ensued; VCS stormed heaven! Eventually the lender's senior management overruled its legal counsel and agreed to the deal.

Finally, in the last months of 1998—hundreds of obstacles, mountains of paperwork and countless prayers later—VCS received their loan and were able to proceed. The road had been long and difficult, but VCS stayed true to their God-given vision. And God did not disappoint them, proving that marketplace miracles *do happen*.

Notes

1. Dr. Clifford Daugherty, *Quest for Excellence* (Mustang, OK: Tate Publishing, 2006), pp. 219-221.
2. Ibid., p. 51.

CHAPTER 4

FULFILLING THE DREAM

My next encounter with a marketplace miracle was in Cape Town, South Africa. In early October 2006, Dr. Niel Stegmann (a brilliant and faithful man God is using to transform the world's healthcare system, see chapter 9) drove me from Cape Town to a nearby fishing village called Kalk Bay, where Media Village is located. My daughter Arleigh had been studying in the Media Village Video School and had just graduated in late September 2006. Though I had been leading a conference in the Twin Cities at the time, I was now able to visit Media Village and see where Arleigh had studied.

Kalk Bay's magnificent beauty struck me immediately. From where Media Village sits, right across the road from the beach, a vast panorama of blue ocean and white breakers crashing against the shore can be seen. Looking farther out, I saw whales breeching and fishing boats plowing through the waves to exit the harbor.

Media Village's training center is a large, old building, with a tall fence and gate surrounding the building and its parking lot. You have to know the gate's lock code or identify yourself to the receptionist, in order to gain access. On the walls, just inside the front entrance, hang 62 award certificates Media Village has received for its excellent video productions. There is also a collection of old equipment, such as tripods and cameras. These old pieces of equipment fit right in with the old building that houses them, and provide a dramatic contrast with the state-of-the-art communications work taught and practiced within the building.

Arleigh introduced me to her classmates and teachers, who hailed from all over the globe. We also spent some quality time with the school's directors, Graham and Diane Vermooten. In getting to know them, I learned their extraordinary story as they shared their encounter with God—and their experience of the miraculous.

THE EARLY YEARS

More than 25 years ago, the Lord laid on the hearts of Graham and Diane Vermooten a passion for communicating His purposes to this generation of young people. At that stage of their lives Graham and Diane were newlyweds and worked for Youth For Christ (YFC) in South Africa, which involved training up and leading teams of young people in sharing the gospel in South Africa through music and drama.

The 1980s were turbulent years there—the nation was at the peak of its apartheid regime and touring with mixed-race teams was not socially acceptable. There were times when host families did not want to accommodate young Christians of color. This resulted in Graham having to make difficult decisions regarding YFC's willingness to minister in certain communities. On one occasion, when a young black girl was told she could not sleep in a white family's home, the entire team slept on the garage floor as a sign of solidarity and unity. The Vermootens swam against the current and stood for righteousness when others would not.

Graham and Diane had always been passionate about communicating the gospel, and now these YFC teams allowed them to share their passion with young people. When they visited high schools and youth groups across the nation, presenting gospel-centered musicals and dramas, their enthusiasm was infectious as they shared stories of hope, reconciliation and peace with South Africa's young people.

Although Graham and Diane were always on the road—they slept in more than 60 beds in their first 2 years of marriage—they were undaunted by these challenges because they loved their ministry. And the fruits of their labor were evident—not only were young people coming to know the Lord, but their team members were also beginning to grow in their understanding of what it meant to trust God to provide for them in every area of their lives.

Though they enjoyed their work with YFC, after two years Graham and Diane felt a clear prompting from the Lord to take a youth pastor position in the largest evangelical church in their city. Again, they quickly found ways to express their creativity through music and drama to communicate the message of God's love—a message they knew and loved so well. Over the next five years they received recognition for their creative youth programs and the high quality of their musical and drama presentations. Their youth rallies were jam-packed; teenagers literally climbed up onto window ledges to get a good view.

God was preparing them for the next step He had planned for them. In every piece of theater or musical they performed, and in every innovative youth program and discipling method they developed, God was honing new skills in them. Years later, these skills would be put to use in the creative environment of Media Village.

Leaving a thriving youth ministry was not an easy decision to make, but in the early 1990s, Graham felt he needed to improve his business skills and moved into the corporate world for several years. Financially, things had just started booming; Graham bought Diane her dream house. They had two young sons, and life was beginning to get very comfortable. Then one day, a friend and colleague named John Higson took Graham to lunch. John's agenda was clear: He had come with a specific question on his heart. He reminded Graham about his passion for young people and his desire to be innovative—to think outside the box in providing young people a platform to be heard, and a safe place to hear the salvation message. He then asked Graham the burning question: "How long before you fulfill your dream?"

When Graham returned home and repeated the conversation to Diane, she did not need to wait for the answer, because the Lord had already been speaking to her about the very same issue. Within weeks, Graham and Diane had joined Youth With A Mission, sold their beautiful five-bedroom home overlooking Table Mountain, took their children out of preschool and moved into a small cottage on Fish Hoek beach. Their journey of living by faith and walking in simple obedience had started anew—they were once again daring to live life on the edge with God.

YOUTH WITH A MISSION

Upon joining YWAM, the Vermootens completed their Discipleship Training School (DTS) in Muizenberg, South Africa. These three months were indeed God's gift of time to the family. They were able to look back over their lives and see the way the Lord had been weaving all the threads of their experiences into a new tapestry.

Their hearts were stirred by Martin Luther's statement that a gospel that does not deal with the issues of the day is not the gospel at all. The South African issues of the day were clear, but how to deal with them was not that obvious. They cried out to God to ask Him how they could use their talents and gifts to serve Him and contribute toward the fulfillment of the Great Commission.

Then, with only one week to go before the end of their DTS, they heard international speaker Landa Cope teach about discipling nations. Presenting what she called "the Old Testament Template," Landa encouraged her listeners to rediscover a vital, relevant and effective strategy to discover God's purposes for every sphere of society.

Graham and Diane both experienced the "aha!" moment during her lectures. This was what they had been looking for; this was the method that would allow them to use their skills and move into the field of communications with confidence. Within days, their vision became clear; they surrendered their lives to God, that He might use their mass media expertise to clearly communicate the gospel. God had equipped them, and now it was time to use their labor as an act of worship.

MEDIA VILLAGE

Their first step was to create a training center that would equip students to disciple nations through mass communications, acknowledging that the media gives Christians a platform from which to be salt and light. Thus began Media Village. They believed it was the combination of faith and skill that would enable their graduates to thrive in a very competitive industry. The world needs such Christians—people who are respected for their skills as well as known for their faith and integrity.

The cornerstone of Media Village was the concept that training and production needed to go hand in hand. The idea that students could live and learn in an interactive and dynamic production facility resulted in the development of two separate expressions of the ministry: Media Village Training (MVT), a ministry of YWAM and a registered nonprofit company, and Media Village Productions (MVP), a for-profit business. All of MVP's video production work, promotional videos, corporate projects and business transactions generate profits, which are then channeled directly into scholarships, administrative funding and logistical assistance for Media Village Training. This model allowed the Vermootens to create a self-sustaining ministry in which students from Africa's underprivileged nations have an opportunity to get quality communications training.

Although the vision had begun taking shape, Graham and Diane soon discovered that even when God plants a dream, the gestation of that vision is totally His timing. God is never in a hurry and will wait until the time is right to give birth to His purposes and plans.

After completing their DTS, the Vermooten family spent seven months on the University of the Nations Campus in Hawaii, getting equipped to run YWAM communication schools in Africa. Upon their return, the entire leadership team of the local ministry had changed, and the new leader was not eager to embrace the Vermootens or their vision. They had to wait nearly two years to start growing the ministry. They knew, however, that their vision was what God wanted. As they waited on His timing, they served on the local YWAM base, sold books, copied tapes and simply prayed and waited more. They were determined not to be the maidens who got tired of waiting and let their lanterns go out (see Matt. 25).

Two years later, their first School of Video Production was finally in the works. Diane was responsible for the curriculum development and logistical preparation for the school. Graham was responsible for raising the finances—a difficult task at the time, as the only tool they had was the vision God had planted in their hearts. Despite numerous presentations, hundreds of letters and lots of prayer, Diane and Graham still waited for a breakthrough. The vision was great, but the resources were nonexistent.

With only two weeks to go before the commencement of the first class in 1995, the Vermootens walked through the empty building and wondered how they would train the soon-to-arrive students. Sitting on the wooden floor in the proposed editing suite, they looked at the empty wooden console and prayed for a miracle.

When the first overseas students began to arrive, the classroom was ready and the text books were prepared, but the technical equipment wasn't there yet. Those were difficult days, yet the Vermootens dared to get out of the boat and walk on water—though they felt they were drowning. Graham held on to Ephesians 3:20 with all his might, firmly believing God wanted to do far more than he could ever dream or imagine. They wanted to equip world-changers, yet they had nothing from which to begin. The days of waiting seemed to be endless; Graham and Diane spent a great deal of time in the presence of the Lord. They cried and waited and refused to give up.

Then on June 19, 1995, with only a few days to go before the opening of their very first School of Video Production, Diane was home, praying and crying before the Lord. The pressure had almost become too much. But then, through her tears, Diane read the words of 1 Kings 20:13. Diane saw words jump from the page: "Do you see this vast army? I will give it into your hand today, and then you will know that I am the LORD" (*NIV*). Through her tears Diane claimed that prayer for herself and determined to believe God that there was a breakthrough in the battle.

Within 15 minutes, their treasurer called and said that an anonymous donor had just deposited $50,000 into their account. Suddenly they saw the release of Kingdom finances upon the ministry.

The following weekend they had a burglary at their home. This misfortune turned into a blessing, as they were able to take the insurance payout and put it into the startup fund. Diane surrendered a family insurance plan, and they mortgaged their home. Whatever God told them to do, they did.

The school commenced on time, with nine students in the first class. These students continuously experienced the Lord's blessing, and despite having no equipment only one week prior to the school's start date, they lacked nothing throughout their course.

After three years of successful ministry, however, the Vermootens had to move Media Village. They could only afford a dark, musty, two-room office. It was even too small for Graham to hold business meetings.

Could they really impact the nations from this place? In their discouragement, they called the place the Hole in the Wall.

At the time, the ministry was barely afloat financially, so the staff brought their own supplies to work to avoid ministry debt. They were determined to be generous and honor the Lord in every little detail of starting a ministry. When the vision seemed to be fading, they determined once again not to give up but to hold on to the vision God had given them, confident that He would provide a better home for them.

INNISFAIL HOTEL

Taking another step in faith, they moved Media Village into another rented house. Conditions were far from ideal, but one day, several months later, their landlord, a delightful Jewish friend and real estate agent, called to say she had found the perfect place for Media Village: the old Innisfail Hotel. This majestic hotel was the oldest residential hotel on the False Bay coast. It had been built in the early 1900s by the Dalebrook sisters, Christian women who built a hospital, church and orphanage all in the small Kalk Bay community. Their heart had been to use their financial resources to alleviate the plight of the poor.

When Graham and Diane visited the site, they looked across the beautiful False Bay coast and felt a stirring in their spirits. Could this be Media Village's new home? Could this be their opportunity to restore this building to its spiritual roots? It seemed their moment had arrived—that they were meant to take possession of new land. But do such opportunities ever come easily? Not usually. The asking price of the hotel was $2.2 million.

This was a daunting amount of money, and seemed completely unattainable. Was this really what the Lord wanted? The faith challenge was large, and Graham and Diane needed clear direction from the Lord. So they often drove to the building late at night, sat outside in the dark and simply asked God for a miracle. They stood on the seashore with their backs to the ocean and stretched their hands out toward the building, trusting the Lord for favor.

Negotiations began, and Graham informed the building's owners that even though he and Diane didn't have the necessary funds, they still believed God wanted them to have the building. At this stage the building was held in trust by an international board and was administered in Ireland. All communication regarding selling conditions with this board had been strictly legal and impersonal. Then one day the board chairman added this postscript to a letter: "Should you manage to get this building, I would personally like to contribute toward it."

That was the confirmation Graham needed; he called the chairman, Robert Quale, and heard an amazing story of God's providence. Quale had two children, both of whom had gone on YWAM outreaches, and Loren Cunningham, YWAM's founder, had recently been a guest in their home. What were the odds of an Irish attorney having links with YWAM *and* wanting to stand in the gap for people he had never met? Mr. Quale explained that he would need to administer the trust with his client's best interest in mind, but he would be willing to present the Vermootens' case to them and to speak on their behalf. This was very important in light of the fact that the Vermootens still had no finances.

After prayer-walking the property, Graham and Diane boldly produced their first brochure and declared to the world that this was to be Media Village's new home. After much negotiation and several contracts, Media Village purchased the building for $1.3 million, *almost $1 million less than originally asked.*

But that's not the whole story: Several months into their negotiations to buy the Innisfail Hotel, an American donor, wanting to invest in South Africa, suggested he would be willing to purchase the building and sign a 10-year contract that would effectively lease the facility to Media Village for $1 per year. Staff and students rejoiced and celebrated. It seemed God had answered their prayers in a miraculous way. Legal contracts were drawn and then, with only two weeks to go, the donor went silent and then never communicated with Graham again. Everyone was devastated, and it seemed Media Village would lose the building.

After spending hours in prayer, however, it became evident that this was not about Media Village *losing* their building but rather about them *owning* it. Miraculously, they received the funds needed for a down payment and suddenly found themselves owners of their own facility.

At first the small staff seemed to rattle around this spacious building, but now that four years have passed, they are outgrowing the place. Another move is imminent. God has provided over and over, enabling Media Village to pay off this building and get into an economic position to confidently face the challenges of growth and a new move.

VISION ACHIEVED: TODAY'S MEDIA VILLAGE

Today Graham serves as CEO of Media Village and is responsible for the leadership, strategic planning and financial accountability of the entire ministry. Diane is executive producer and is responsible for the productions undertaken by Media Village. Graham and Diane are accountable to a board of directors—but they are not the only ones held accountable for the ministry. Students are considered missionaries and are required to raise funds to pay the cost of tuition and accommodation. Because so many students come from underprivileged communities, this is almost always a challenge. Graham and Diane remain totally committed to training African students, so a large percentage of the fees they charge their corporate clients are used to cover the training expenses.

Courses

And what exactly does this training involve? Primarily, courses that give the students a theoretical understanding of the media industry, such as the following:

- *Discipleship Training School* is the entrance requirement for all students who desire to study through the University of the Nations.
- *Video Production* provides students with skills required to produce documentaries and redemptive stories through video and TV broadcasting.
- *Radio Broadcasting* equips students to present, on air, various styles of radio programs and to manage the administration of

a radio station. In Africa, where more people have access to radio than running water, this course plays a vital role in presenting the gospel in underserved countries.

· *Communication Foundations* teaches the basics of written and verbal communication.

· *Digital Photography and Story Telling* explores the use of photography in telling redemptive stories. Students also learn how to use various digital photography software programs.

· *3-D Animation* equips students to work on Myia and to create 3-D stories and communication.

· *Writing for Mass Media School* teaches students to write for a variety of media formats, ranging from feature film to magazine inserts and newspaper journalism.

Goals

The fundamental goal of Media Village is to communicate stories of personal transformation from around the world. Every project, assignment or promotional piece Media Village produces is measured through this lens. With a commitment to excellence, Media Village Productions creates documentaries for ministries and nongovernmental organizations (NGOs), helping them effectively communicate to the world that which might otherwise go unnoticed. The Transformation Africa movement, Global Day of Prayer and Harvest Evangelism are a few of their first-priority clients.

But producing materials for other organizations is only part of what the staff and students of Media Village are up to. They also have a passion to discover and explore the message that God has for *them* to share with others. In 2005, when a tragic tsunami hit the shores of Indonesia, Media Village sent a film crew to document survivor stories and the work of rebuilding. This project raised more than $1 million! Churches then distributed that money throughout the region.

Other projects include a movie about the persecuted church in Nigeria and a partnership with Ed Silvoso and Harvest Evangelism to document the transformation of nations through marketplace redemption. Such opportunities allow Media Village teams to travel the globe and be scribes of God's mighty moves around the world.

Impact

With a vision to impact the nations, it became inevitable that Media Village graduates would need to return to their own nations and begin to take their skills into the mission field of mass media.

Eight of Media Village's South African students have gone on to develop their own media production studios. Many Media Village graduates have returned to their home nations and have been offered influential media positions, allowing them to influence governments and key leaders. While the stories of influence are many, some are especially worth noting.

After his training, Andriana Andriamanantena returned to his home country of Madagascar and accepted an influential role in his nation's media—selecting the content to be aired on Madagascar's national television.

Anne Samson, a Nigerian, is a Media Village graduate who has a passion to rebuild her ravaged nation and pioneer Media Village Nigeria. Anne's exceptional track record in training and production has already drawn attention from the local government. Today this relationship with the Nigerian government has given her a voice in the national media, providing her with a legitimate platform for addressing government corruption issues.

Another graduate, Deborah Manguet, is serving as a member of the Nigerian government film-and-media board. She is currently developing media-training curricula that are being used to inspire young people to tell the stories of their nation.

Joseph Kebbie, the School of Radio Broadcast leader at Media Village, has a vision to use radio broadcasting to improve communication in his country. Joseph's uncle is the vice president of Liberia, and after he watched Media Village's *Transformations* videos, he invited Graham to bring a delegation of influential South African and American business professionals to Liberia. Their goal is to establish partnerships with Christian companies that can pave the way for ethical transactions in business and government. In a nation known for corruption, this is a strong move toward transformational leadership and increased levels of accountability.

Joseph Bubahase Ndereyimana walked the vast distance from Rwanda to South Africa to enroll at Media Village. Joseph completed several media courses and today is editor of a national newspaper. He plans to run for government office.

Sarel Pretorious, a South African student, studied and worked at Media Village for several years. He excelled as a videographer, and after leaving Media Village, he pursued a career as a stedicam operator in the city (a stedicam is a type of camera that is used to shoot action shots on movie sets). Using his stedicam, Sarel recently shot a portion of the feature film *Tsotsi*—which won an Oscar in 2006.

Not only are individual lives being changed, but also communities around the globe are being impacted as Media Village has opened locations in Cypress, India, Nigeria and Northern Ireland. To date, Media Village Productions has received 62 National Television and Video Awards. They were also nominated for two Avanti Awards (South Africa's equivalent to the Oscar).

Mark 8:18 asks, "Do you have eyes but fail to see, and ears but fail to hear?" (*NIV*). Media Village has eyes that have seen the potential of mass media as a powerful tool to extend the Kingdom. They have heard the stories of God at work around the world and are willing to record those stories, using the pen of modern media.

As Graham and Diane demonstrated their willingness to follow His lead, God increased their faith, their vision and their harvest. Given all the obstacles in their way, only divine intervention can explain where they—and Media Village—are today . . . and where they are headed!

CHAPTER 5

KINGDOM ROCKER

Maybe the testimonies shared so far haven't surprised you much. You probably think it's not such a big deal for God to take care of His own franchise—namely, Christian schools. But what if you could see the miraculous transform an industry that's famous for being everything that Christianity *isn't*? Think the music industry is beyond redemption? Think again.

In the late 1990s, a singer-songwriter named R.J. was leading a highly successful contemporary Christian group that had a few number-one singles. After a number of years with this group, R.J. grew frustrated, feeling that he was "preaching to the choir," and decided to leave the band and wait on God for direction. He had no idea what God was preparing to do in his life.

In 2000, R.J. started to record an album of art-worship songs with some friends and local musicians, but it just didn't feel right. Every time he played, he felt as if something was missing. As he continued to pray about his destiny, God began to speak to R.J., not about his career, but about the purpose of music and art. R.J. was struggling to see how the pieces were supposed to fit together when, a few days before Christmas, a representative of a major secular record label called. Apparently, someone had given this music producer a copy of R.J.'s album of art-worship songs, and one of the company's artist development gurus really liked what he heard. He invited R.J. to come to Los Angeles to play his music for some record company executives.

R.J. was excited, but he still did not have a clear vision of where God was leading him. Regardless, he decided to go to Los Angeles to play his music. As R.J. stood on the stage preparing to perform in front of a nightclub audience filled with record executives as well as the regular bar patrons, God spoke something to him very clearly: "The world does not need another rock band." The Lord began to show R.J. the faces of each person in the audience, reminding him how he had started playing music as a teenager in nightclubs just like this. "The world doesn't need to be entertained any more than it already it is—what they need is Jesus." R.J. understood that God was calling him back into the secular industry, and God was doing it through these worship songs!

At first, R.J. thought God was going to open doors and get things moving quickly, but that turned out not to be the case. R.J. remained diligent through the ups and downs and continued to write and record. Record label after record label came to listen, and he developed some great relationships, but a contract never materialized. After more than two years of hard work with seemingly little to show for it, R.J. went to God in prayer, wondering if he should quit. God said, "You are thinking too small. You are worried about getting a record deal, but I want you to disciple an industry."

THE VISION

God began to show R.J. a vision that went far beyond anything he could have imagined. Since its inception, the music business has been all about the greedy exploitation of artists and the public through corruption, manipulation and control, and an appeal to the flesh (think sex, drugs and rock and roll). God told R.J. he was to counter these spirits operating behind the industry scenes with the work of the Holy Spirit. He was to disciple the music business by modeling the kingdom of God. He would do this through not only the lyrics of the songs, but also through his business practices: by honoring relationships before money, by living morally in an immoral environment and by caring for the poor. God told R.J., "I want to do more than transform individuals—I want to transform the entire industry!"

This word from God gave R.J. new strength to continue. In the next year, a record company offered him a deal. At the contract signing, R.J. stopped the proceedings and told the record company executive that he intended to give away 50 percent of all the band's royalties—this money would go to a fund that would be "controlled" by fans of the band.

Fans would be able to email the band names of organizations that were making a difference in the world around them. Once every four months, the band would pick five causes from the list, and then fans would vote through the band's website to decide which cause would get that quarter's distribution of funds.

What was the reaction? R.J.'s manager and the record company executive were blown away. Sure, people had occasionally given away small percentages of their earnings, but 50 percent was unprecedented. The record company executive was so moved by R.J.'s commitment that they offered him an even split on profits from the record, something almost unheard of (most major artists only receive between 8 and 11 percent of profits). At last it seemed that huge doors were opening for R.J.'s band. But God was preparing a test.

THE TESTING

With the record ready to come out in only a few months, everyone was riding high and excited to see the results of years of hard work. Then, only weeks before the release, R.J.'s keyboardist, Len Johnson, had a clear sense from the Lord that things were not going to go as planned. The word he was sensing was that God was going to "cause" the record to fail—He was not just allowing it, but was actively leading the record into a season of defeat. The purpose of this failure was so that only God would get the credit for the success of the project. God would resurrect it in a miraculous way and it would bring Him glory, but that could not happen until human efforts had fully "died."

By the time R.J.'s record was released, the record label was in serious financial trouble, having gambled on other artists' records. Only a couple months later, R.J. fired the publicist, then the booking agent, then the manager. Just five months after the record hit stores, it was certifiably "done," according to industry standards. The band had no financial tour support, no advertising support, no manager—and any buzz there had been about the band had since disappeared.

The biggest blow came when R.J. went to release the first distribution from the fund that had been collecting 50 percent of the royalties from the record sales. R.J. discovered that due to a technicality in their distribution contract, the record company wasn't going to reimburse R.J. or the fund until the band had sold 40,000 records. This meant that R.J. was going to have to give more than $50,000 to the fund before he would ever see a dollar from the record company!

Emotionally, spiritually and financially this was a devastating blow, and again R.J. went to the Lord, wondering whether he should just give up. After much prayer, he decided to pay for the first distribution of the fund from the proceeds resulting from the sale of his house, but he began to wonder if a resurrection of the album was even possible at this point.

The week after the voting began on the band's website, Len had another clear word from the Lord about the circumstances. God had been testing R.J. to see if he would be faithful to the vision he had received, even when it cost him personally. The word also said that R.J.'s faithfulness had won him a new level of spiritual authority. R.J. was about to begin to walk in a season of amazing favor and victory, and it would begin when his check for the fund cleared the bank.

R.J. heard the word and, by faith, he booked a couple shows in Los Angeles the following weekend. Just R.J. and Len would do the shows, without the rest of the band. As they drove to Los Angeles, R.J. expressed his fears and doubts, and openly questioned whether he should give up after this next trip. In the middle of the conversation, R.J.'s ex-manager called, saying some company had asked to meet with him before the show that evening. Apparently the company was so new that it didn't even have a website yet, so he wasn't sure the meeting would be worth their time. Still, R.J. half-heartedly agreed, not expecting much, and called the company back to schedule the meeting.

THE EXTRAORDINARY MIRACLE

When R.J. and Len arrived at the company buildings, Len had a deep sense that God was going to do something huge. Rather than go inside, he stayed in the parking lot and prayed while R.J. met with whoever was inside. When R.J. came out 10 minutes later, his eyes were the size of dinner plates, and he told Len, "You've *got* to come to the second half of this meeting! This is unbelievable." As they climbed into the car, Len asked, "Where's the second half of the meeting?" R.J. answered, "It's on the other side of the street—and get this, they own the whole street!"

As they drove, R.J. told him that when he had walked into the building, a vice president had met him and asked him to come into their board meeting. As R.J. entered the room, the entire board and the CEO had stood up and begun to cheer. All of them had pumped R.J.'s hand, telling him how excited they were to meet him, and how much they were looking forward to working with him. After some short introductions, the CEO had asked if he could personally show R.J. around the facilities.

On the other side of the street, the CEO explained that this new company had purchased the largest sound stages in all of Los Angeles. Their stages were large enough to simulate playing arenas the size of the Staples Center. All of these rehearsal facilities were outfitted with dozens of remote control digital video cameras that were embedded in the walls; each rehearsal could be videotaped and recorded with the highest quality gear. The CEO casually mentioned that this company had one of the largest digital video storage networks in the world, second only to CNN.

Next, the executive team took R.J. and Len to a screening room and showed them some videos of bands that had been testing out the rooms during the previous week. They were some of the largest acts in music, including Fiona Apple, Fleetwood Mac, Eminem, Babyface, Tony Bennett, and more. When the screening was over, the CEO walked over and told R.J., "God put you on the face of the earth to play music, and don't you ever doubt that again! I know you are God's man. I knew it from the first two bars of your music I heard. That's why I want you in this company."

R.J. almost began to cry—it was as if this CEO was prophesying his destiny. Then the CEO explained how he believed that his company was going to be different. He believed that music shouldn't be about exploiting the public for money or even entertaining them, but it should be about lifting them to new heights at every level of their existence.

His company was going to be about helping people, especially the poor. R.J. and the keyboardist looked at him in shock and said, "You are preaching to the choir here!"

The CEO then asked if they had seen the room where the company wanted R.J.'s band to play that weekend. R.J. and Len looked blankly at him. The CEO then explained that several bands were there rehearsing for the Grammy Awards that weekend—bands and musicians like U2, Paul McCartney, Christina Aguilera and Faith Hill. The company believed so much in R.J. and his music that they wanted him to come and rehearse there with the rest of the Grammy Award artists, with the hope that they would be able to videotape R.J. meeting them. Then, on a cable TV channel that reached 44 million homes, the company would broadcast these videos of R.J.'s band rehearsing and interacting with these megastars. The CEO reaffirmed that his company wanted to introduce an unknown band to the world—and they had decided that it would be R.J.'s band!

The CEO led R.J. down the hallway to a huge auditorium where they found a band rehearsing. As they watched, they realized they were watching Prince's backup band in action! The CEO stopped the rehearsal and introduced Prince's people to R.J. and Len as if they were huge stars.

Later, when they were in the CEO's personal office to finalize details, R.J. looked around the room and noticed that on the bookshelf were a *New International Version* Study Bible and a copy of *The Purpose Driven Life* by Rick Warren. These two books stood between an MTV music award and a Grammy Award. A poster of all the names of God through all the books of the Bible hung on the wall. This CEO was a believer. After shaking hands with him to seal the deal, R.J. and Len left to go play their evening show, rejoicing in God's goodness!

But God's goodness didn't stop there. When R.J. checked his email later that night, he found a message from the Starbucks Corporation asking him to provide a quote to be used on the side of tens of millions of coffee cups around the world. Most bands would do anything to get this kind of publicity, but to get it for *free* was absolutely the favor of God.

A week later, R.J. was rehearsing next to Paul McCartney, TV shows were calling and asking to use his songs, and the most successful manager in the music business was begging R.J. to work with her! God rocked R.J.'s world, and now He's using R.J. to rock the music world.

If God can work these kinds of miracles in the music industry, what kind of amazing things do you imagine He can do in your life—and in your place of business? Dream big. Pray hard. Wait on His timing. Then expect the unexpected.

CHAPTER 6

RECLAIMING AMERICA

Genesis 13:17 recounts a conversation God had with Abraham: "Arise, walk in the land through its length and its width, for I give it to you." Basically, He's saying, *Abraham, go for a walk.* And what is Abraham's reaction: "But, Lord, me . . . ? You are calling me to do this?" A surprising reaction? Well, hardly. In fact, I think we can all relate. The real question is not how you'd feel, but what you would do if God gave you the command to get up and go for a walk. Pastor John Halvorsen had to sort that one out.

You see, he had been praying about what God wanted him to do with the ache in his heart to reach America. He had expected to be released into a fairly normal evangelism ministry, but try as he might, he could not get away from this dramatic call. He read that Genesis passage in different Bible versions. He sought the counsel of others. He continued to talk with God—and the answer was always the same: *Arise, walk the length and breadth of the land.*

John had always known that God uses ordinary people to accomplish extraordinary things. God had used John prophetically during his ministry in different parts of the world, but being asked to walk across America was much more than he was expecting. Yet he knew that was exactly what God was calling him to do. He just didn't know *why* he was supposed to do it.

His first thought was that he was supposed to use it to raise money for missions. Like others have done, he could take pledges for each mile walked, and perhaps God would use the money for the outreach ministry he had been seeking. When he and his wife, Sandy, prayed about it, God emphatically said, "No!" In fact, God did not allow them to do any fundraising, but He did ask them for total reliance on Him for their daily needs.

What other purpose could there be? Was he to use the walk as a way to attract people to meetings in churches along the way? Was he supposed to write a book about it? There were lots of good ideas, but there were no answers until God spoke to him again.

God wanted this to be a prayer walk, a step of faith—well, many thousands of steps—called Prayer Walk America.

God was calling John to use this walk to pray for America and to lift up prayer for this country among believers throughout the nation. Indeed, the message was twofold. To the Church in America, the message was that it was time to unite and pray like never before. To those outside the Church, it was a warning that difficult times were coming to the country, and Jesus Christ is the only answer.

John's heart leaped with excitement as he accepted and embraced the task God had laid before him. Now it was time to get to work.

PREPARATION

John and a soon-to-be friend, Ron, were both members of Antioch Christian Fellowship in Eden Prairie, Minnesota. Pastor Alan Langstaff, then senior pastor of that congregation, called Ron and asked him to meet with John to discuss his plans and give him any advice on communications and handling the media. Ron had known John as a missionary from their congregation and was happy to talk with him, fully expecting that this would be a one-time meeting. He didn't realize that God was about to turn his world upside down, too.

As Ron listened to John share this crazy idea, God spoke to him about His heart for the U.S. and His desire to see it return to Him. Before Ron knew what was happening, he found himself joining John in Prayer Walk America, beginning a journey that would not only touch a nation, but would also change the course of his life.

Immediately, the two began preparing for the walk. John prepared by walking around his city, trying to get in shape for the 20 to 22 miles a day he would walk once he got started. Ron prepared by plotting John's route and contacting intercessors, churches and the media all across the country.

The enormity of the task was almost too much to comprehend, and they had no idea what to expect on the road. They did know, however, that to accomplish everything God wanted them to do they would need to rely on Him and His leading every step of the way.

And lead them He did. Whether it was across arid desert terrain, over the Rocky Mountains, through vast stretches of farmland in the Midwest or into cities of every size, God went before them and made a way where there seemed to be no way.

GOD'S GAME PLAN REVEALED

The first leg of the walk began at the Canadian border, in International Falls, Minnesota, and followed the course of the Mississippi River to the Gulf of Mexico. Ron had contacted media outlets, both Christian and secular, and on day two of the walk he received a call from a DJ at a country-western station in International Falls. They talked for three or four minutes, and the DJ grew more and more excited about what they were doing. He told Ron he would like to interview him on his radio program. Ron offered to get in touch with John so that the DJ could interview him from the road. He shocked Ron with his next comment.

"You don't understand, Ron. We've been on a news break, and I'm going to put you on the air with me in 45 seconds." Ron's heart began to pound. They were just two days into the walk and hardly understood what they were doing themselves, and now Ron had just a few seconds before he was going to be interviewed on the radio! He prayed an urgent prayer for wisdom about what he should say.

As soon as Ron opened his mouth to speak, the anointing of the Holy Spirit filled him and gave him the words he needed. For 15 minutes, he shared the story of Prayer Walk America and the reality of the love of Christ with the audience of this secular radio station. As he closed the interview, the announcer told his listeners that he felt Prayer Walk America could be one of the most significant events taking place in the country. He urged them to stay tuned for updates. When he got off the air that morning, the DJ drove down the highway until he found John and conducted what would be the first of his weekly interviews during the walk, allowing John to share what God was doing in the lives of people across the country.

Clearly this walk was part of God's plan to bring His message to America. Everywhere John went, the secular media came out to meet them or brought them into their studio for interviews. People read about them in the headlines of their morning paper, they heard radio interviews, and when they got home at night they saw John on the television news—walking through their community. And through it all, the media allowed John and Ron to freely share with America God's message of hope and love for them.

The prophetic nature of the walk cannot be overlooked. The discovery of the Mississippi River took place from south to north; John reversed that flow, walking from north to south along the river. The path of U.S. migration went from east to west; John reversed that flow walking from west to east. For a portion of the trip, John followed part of the Oregon Trail in the West, retracing the steps of the pioneers, just as Isaac walked the path of Abraham and dug again the wells that had been stopped up (see Gen. 26:18-22). Ultimately, the prayer walk covered about 5,000 miles, and with every step he took, John reclaimed the land for Jesus Christ.

Even though John did the actual walking, Ron joined him along the path for meetings in churches of every size and denomination. This gave them an up-close look at America's churches and its people. From small, storefront churches to modern megachurches, from a cattle auction barn in Oregon to the Oval Office in Washington, D.C., God not only revealed Himself in powerful ways, but also released His heart of compassion for the people of this nation.

WAITING ON A MIRACLE

Perhaps the most definitive revelation of God's power came when Ron went to Washington, D.C., to lay the groundwork for the final leg of the walk. He talked to his friend Dan, who lived there, about John's plans to walk across the Chesapeake Bay Bridge. "I don't think they let people walk across that bridge," the friend replied.

This was not the response Ron had expected. Up to that point, they had seen God do extraordinary things as they followed His direction during this journey. In fact, He had spoken clearly to Ron a month earlier, telling him to change the final route of the walk to make sure the walk went through Washington, D.C., across the Chesapeake Bay Bridge, and on into Delaware. Yet, here he was, being told that the route God had chosen was closed to them.

Oh, well, Ron thought. *Dan must be wrong about the bridge. I'll call someone and get permission when I get back to Minnesota.* It wasn't going to be that simple. When Ron returned home, he called the head of the Maryland Department of Transportation, who told Ron, "We don't allow anyone to walk across that bridge." Ron tried to explain in more detail what Prayer Walk America was all about, but the official didn't seem to care. The bridge was the main corridor across the Bay, the official explained, and it would cause tremendous traffic problems if they allowed pedestrians on the bridge. The official went on to say that recently a major Hollywood celebrity had organized a charity walk across the bridge. But neither charity nor celebrity mattered; the group was rounded up and arrested. It just couldn't be done.

As Ron thanked the official for his time and hung up the phone, he was already working on other ways to get permission to cross that bridge. They had about seven months before they would reach that point, and Ron was sure God would get them over it somehow. So Ron rallied his intercessors.

About a week later, Ron called one of his senators in Washington. He explained to one of the staffers who he was and what he wanted to do; he then asked if there was anything the senator could do to help. When Ron mentioned walking across the bridge, the staffer blurted out, "You must be joking. Nobody walks across the Chesapeake Bay Bridge." Ron assured the staffer he wasn't joking, and the staffer asked Ron to explain everything again. When he finished, the man asked him to send him a letter stating who they were and what they wanted to do, and he would see what could be done. Ron told the staffer he would have the letter by the end of the week. He then contacted the intercessors and asked them to pray harder.

For the next month he and his family joined John on the road. He heard nothing in response to his letter, though he'd left a number of messages at the senator's office. Finally, when he got back to the office at their church, he received a reply.

It seemed Ron's letter had indeed reached the senator, who passed it on to the governor of Maryland, who forwarded it to the head of the Department of Transportation, who sent it to the Maryland state highway patrol, who controlled access to the bridge. All of them gave the same reply: "You can't walk across the Chesapeake Bay Bridge."

With just four months remaining, they were no closer to getting across the bridge. In fact, it appeared every possible avenue had led to a dead end. They continued to pray.

For the next couple months, Ron divided his time between the office and the RV, on the road with John. Ron would occasionally call some of the same people he had already spoken to, just to see if anything had changed, but to no avail. People began to suggest different ideas, like taking a boat across the Bay, driving across the bridge or walking around the Bay, but John and Ron still believed they were supposed to *walk across the bridge*.

It was now about a month before they reached Washington, D.C., and Ron was preparing to hit the road for the final time. He needed to bring press releases, maps and timelines for everywhere John would be walking. The problem he had was this: If they had to walk around the north end of the Bay rather than across the bridge, it would add days to the walk and change the cities they went through. Ron's solution was simple. When he got in the RV for the last month of the walk, he carried two sets of everything with him, one for the bridge route and another for the north route. The intercessors, meanwhile, never quit praying.

The days on the road were always busy and went by quickly. Soon they were walking through Gettysburg and heading for Washington. They had continued to discuss the options for the Bay, but time was running out: They were just four days from reaching the bridge, and they needed to make a decision. Shortly after supper Ron's cell phone rang.

"Do you still want to walk across the bridge?" a man's voice asked Ron, who then had to ask the man to repeat himself just to make sure he was hearing correctly. As it turned out, the caller was the head of the Department of Transportation. "It just so happens that we are going to shut down one side of the bridge next Monday for some repair work. If you will agree to five requirements, we will let you walk across the Chesapeake Bay Bridge."

This was a miracle! Transportation officials were going to close the eastbound lane of the bridge on the very day John and Ron had scheduled to walk across it. The official, though, had five requirements that Ron had to agree to:

1. The walk had to be at night, so no one would see them.
2. John had to walk alone; no one could join him.
3. The event had to remain secret.
4. The news media could not be informed. If the official even thought the media might find out, the walk was off.
5. It couldn't rain. If it rained, transportation workers wouldn't be able to do their work and they wouldn't close the bridge.

Ron quickly agreed before the official could change his mind. Ron walked into the RV and told John about the phone call. John's jaw dropped, and his wife, Sandy, began to thank God. The two men just looked at each other and shook their heads in amazement at what God was about to do. Ron sent word to the intercessors, and they began to praise God and ask Him to hold back the rain.

The bridge crossing was set for Monday night. They decided that it would be best if John ended his walk at the bridge on Saturday and then not walk at all until 10:00 P.M. Monday. That way, no one would be with him.

John walked his standard 20 miles on Saturday and reached the police station located at the beginning of the bridge. He decided he would go in and introduce himself and see if the police had any instructions for him. He was not prepared for what he heard. He approached the desk sergeant and told him who he was and that he was going to walk the bridge on Monday. The officer looked at him incredulously and declared, "You're not walking my bridge." John explained that he had been given permission, but the officer wouldn't listen. "We are the ones in charge of the bridge," he said. "And we haven't received any orders about you or anyone else walking this bridge. No one is allowed to walk the Chesapeake Bay Bridge."

John wasn't sure what to think of the exchange. He talked to Ron about it when he got back to the RV. Ron assured John that everything was going to be fine (although Ron wasn't sure how). Ron had been given the name and telephone number of a woman who'd been assigned the job of making sure that John got across the bridge. She told Ron that he and John should still plan to be at the bridge on Monday.

That Sunday they parked the campers along the Bay and took some time to rest. Early in the afternoon a policeman drove up and began to talk with them. At one point he looked over his shoulder, then quietly asked, "There's a rumor going around that someone is going to walk the bridge on Monday. Is that you?" Even the police were getting curious.

On Monday morning, a park ranger asked them the same question. Apparently, no one could believe that somebody was going to walk across the bridge. Ron and John were a little concerned that word was getting out, but they didn't think anything was going to stop this walk now.

Monday night finally arrived, and Ron went with John and Sandy to the police station. A different officer was at the desk that night and Ron handed him his card. "This is John Halvorsen," Ron said as he motioned to John. "And he is going to walk your bridge tonight." The officer looked at Ron, then at John and then at Ron's card again. A smile crossed the officer's face and he said, "We're going to have a police car escort you across the bridge. We'll be ready for you in five minutes."

Everyone breathed a sigh of relief. Apparently the transportation authorities had been so concerned over publicity about the walk that they informed the police only about an hour before John and Ron arrived. Now Ron grew a bit bolder. "This is John's wife," he explained. "I know she can't walk with John tonight, but can she ride with the policeman in the escort car?"

"Of course she can," he replied. "Why don't you go down to the bridge and wait."

They walked to the end of the bridge and took some pictures with the sign that read, "No pedestrians allowed." In a few minutes a police car drove up and they had another surprise. Who do you suppose was driving the escort car? It was the desk sergeant from Saturday who had told John he wouldn't allow anyone to walk his bridge! Sandy climbed into the car and talked to him about Jesus as they drove over the bridge and into the darkness, the headlights of the car illuminating every one of John's footsteps as he crossed the Chesapeake Bay Bridge. God is so great!

At last, the prayer walk was drawing to a close. John had walked 104 days to complete the north-south route, and the west-to-east walk took over seven months to finish. Ron and the intercessors had been with him every step of the way. Now it was time to finish the task they had started—and entrust the outcome to God.

On the final day of the walk, just as John was about to step onto the shore of the Atlantic Ocean, John and Ron were connected by satellite to an estimated 2 million believers around the world who were participating in Bill Bright's Prayer and Fasting Conference. As the voices of these saints rose as one to heaven, John led them in a prayer of repentance on behalf of America, and a cry to God to once again bring revival to our land.

Ron believes that prayer continues to shake the heavens and the earth today. Believers everywhere echo the cry for revival as they seek to bring His kingdom into their homes, workplaces and cities. More importantly, it is being heard by a God who loves beyond measure and who is able beyond imagination to do such great things.

As they were driving back to Minnesota after the end of the prayer walk, Ron thought he should call the senator's office and let his chief of staff know what had happened. The chief of staff had no idea John had been allowed to walk the bridge, and when Ron asked him to pass along his thanks to the senator, the staffer felt he needed to confess something: "When you first called, I didn't think you had any chance of getting across that bridge," he said. "I'll let the senator know you called, but we really didn't have anything to do with this. This was all God."

PERIMETER DRIVE

When the prayer walk was complete and John, Ron and the entourage were making their way back home in three tired RVs, they began to pray and ask God, "What now, Lord?" It did not take Him long to answer.

They had mobilized intercessory prayer for each state, and God led them to ask the intercessors to seek Him for a Scripture verse regarding the state for which they were praying. About the same time, John felt God was calling them to perform a prophetic act that would not only lay out His claim to this land, but would also form a framework for a canopy of prayer to be raised over the nation.

God directed them to take the Scripture verses the intercessors had received and write them on 50 gold stakes, along with the name of each state. They were then to travel around the perimeter of the United States, driving each stake into the ground wherever God would direct, proclaiming His lordship over America and calling for revival in each state.

Now they were faced with a familiar question: How were they going to do this? One of the obstacles they had to overcome was their lack of a reliable vehicle for the trip. Still, they continued with their planning, trusting that God would make a way.

During a church service a couple weeks before their scheduled departure, their pastor told the congregation what John and Ron were about to do and invited the congregation to help them if they felt they should—but he didn't take an offering for them. John and Ron weren't sure what to think of this, but John thought he should go and stand by the door when the service was over in case anyone wanted to talk to him about their need for a vehicle. As he stood up to go, the Holy Spirit spoke to him very clearly. "Do you want to take up this offering, or do you want Me to take up the offering?"

At those words, John not only walked away from the door, he walked all the way downstairs so that he wouldn't get in God's way. He was standing alone in the basement when a woman from the congregation approached him.

"I was looking for you upstairs. God told me you needed a car, and I want to let you use my van for the trip."

With that, she handed John a set of keys to a brand-new Toyota van that she had owned for less than a month. God was on the move again!

John and his wife, Sandy, left the following week and drove to Duluth, Minnesota. There they drove the first stake into the ground. They then began to drive along the Canadian border toward New England. Ron flew to Boston and joined them for the rest of the trip.

They drove from there down the eastern seaboard to Florida, went west along the Gulf of Mexico to Texas, followed the Mexican border to California, went north up the Coast Highway to Washington and skirted the Canadian border back to Minnesota. They drove about 10,000 miles in 19 days.

In addition to having them pound stakes into the ground whenever He told them to stop, God also told John to call for revival from the four corners of the country. So, at the water's edge in New York City, on the Miami Beach shore, on the beach in Los Angeles and at the Seattle waterfront, they blew a shofar and called for the four winds to blow revival into this land.

As they reached home, having literally come full circle, they realized that God wants revival in America even more than they do. He's simply watching and waiting for those who are willing to obey Him wholeheartedly in order to see it happen.

John and Ron had listened in awe to that first, gentle whisper of the Holy Spirit that breathed their ministry into existence—and then they walked in obedience to His will, trusting that He would lead them. What was the fruit of their labor? They wept with joy as Jesus' love touched the lives of people everywhere.

What they gave to God is what He wants from us: listening hearts and lives lived in obedience to Him. When we are willing to be used mightily by God, as Ron and John were, then He will do amazing things through us.[1]

Note

1. For a number of years, I had been asking the Lord to send me an associate to assist with the ministry He has called me to. One day in 2005, Ron Olson called me and invited me to a meeting in his hometown of Chanhassen, Minnesota. When the meeting was over, I looked at Ron and said, "I don't know why I haven't thought of it before, but I am thinking it now. Would you have any interest in joining me as a missionary in the Central USA Region of

Harvest Evangelism?" After Ron and his wife, Linda, discussed the idea with Rachel and me, I introduced them to Dave Thompson and Ed Silvoso of Harvest Evangelism. Everyone was satisfied that the Lord had answered my prayer to bring an associate to work with me. As I read this testimony, however, I realize that the Lord has done more than simply increase the size of our staff. As Ron and Linda join our team, they bring all the experience, all the spiritual authority and all the anointing that they attained during Prayer Walk America.

CHAPTER 7

GOD PROVIDES

After reading about an amazing journey, perhaps you've been inspired to seek God's will for your own walk of faith. But maybe you're feeling that you're not "up" to the task—that you're not gifted enough, not "holy" enough. Have no fear. God doesn't expect you to work in your own power. In fact, as you follow His lead and seek to do His will, He will provide the abundance you need for bringing the extraordinary grace of God into the ordinary tasks of life.

WHEN GOD IS YOUR BUSINESS PARTNER

This has certainly been the experience of Ken Beaudry, founder and CEO of the Beaudry Companies, which have four divisions: propane, commercial diesel, transportation of petroleum products, and lubricants. He hasn't always made the right decisions in business, but God has provided the increase nevertheless.

Recently, I was in Northfield, Minnesota, leading a discussion about city and national transformation; Ken Beaudry and Mayor Stephanie Klinzing were also there to tell what the Lord is doing in Elk River, Minnesota. Ken and his wife, Carrie, are intercessors for the project Pray Elk River. They have mobilized and trained intercessors in Elk River, and they have led citywide strategic intercession for the city. In addition, Dr. Paul Cox has trained them in the ministry of generational deliverance.

Yet, Ken, who—together with his wife—has been in business for 24 years, has a vision that reaches far beyond his local community. The Lord has given him a heart for the nations. So, as Ken learned about tithing and the principle of sowing and reaping, the Holy Spirit encouraged him to have faith for the transformation of a nation (at that time, no one was talking about national transformation). Ken prayed for two years for the Lord to give him a nation.

AN ANSWERED PRAYER: UKRAINE

One day in the winter of 1999, Ken got a call from John Matthews of Scarlet Thread Ministries, headquartered in the Twin Cities. John wanted Ken to go to Ukraine to teach new Christian businessmen about Christian integrity and ethics. He told Ken that he and his wife, Jackie, had become part of a church plant called Churches of Praise in the city of Krivoy Rog in 1993. Churches of Praise had grown to a dozen or so by that time. The Holy Spirit was now moving powerfully in the church: People were embracing the gift of salvation, and experiencing physical and emotional healing, as well as deliverance. Many were set free from drug addiction and involvement in the mafia.

In May 1999, Ken and Carrie went to Ukraine and taught local businessmen how to respond to God's call to be ministers in the marketplace. Ken used examples from the Bible to show how God used businessmen to do extraordinary things for His kingdom—and how He still desires to work through them today.

When Ken first arrived, Pastor Gregory, head of the Churches of Praise, asked him to speak to the Bible school they'd started for the purpose of training pastors to do church planting. While teaching this class seemed like a fairly straightforward assignment, when Ken arrived at the Bible school, the most amazing thing happened. As the Holy Spirit visited the class, Ken stood but could not speak—he just hung on to the podium. Those in the room at the time experienced extraordinary manifestations of the Holy Spirit for at least an hour and a half. As the Holy Spirit came upon them, many experienced the joy of the Lord; some fell out of their chairs, overcome by God's presence. The translator could not translate because she also was so overcome by God and the joy of the Lord.

Pastor Gregory was not present in the class at the time. Ken distinctly remembers thinking, *When Pastor Gregory finds out what had happened, I will be kicked out of the church.* He didn't know whether Pastor

Gregory would be open to the move of the Holy Spirit.

Well, Pastor Gregory *was* open! He asked Ken to preach at his church the following Sunday—a church with about 1,200 members and probably the largest church in the city of Krivoy Rog. When Sunday arrived, the church was packed! Ken went to the podium, and again he could not speak. Ken could see a haze of God's glory over the whole congregation as the Holy Spirit fell on the entire congregation. People experienced the joy of the Lord and fell out of their chairs; and many reported physical healings. Still others reported receiving visions from the Lord and experiencing greater revelation of the love of God for them. Later, when Ken could speak, he spoke about the glory of God.

That was the first of many trips to Ukraine. The Lord performed signs and wonders and healings in many of the meetings. Eventually Ken realized that Ukraine was God's answer to his prayer for a nation.

As a result, the Beaudry Companies financed a team of apostolic overseers in the United States to work with the team in Ukraine. They sowed thousands of dollars per month into the project. By the spring of 2001, they were planting one church a month in Ukraine.

One day while Ken was sitting at his office desk in Elk River, Minnesota, the Holy Spirit told him, "You can do more." At that time, there was a request for a prison ministry. Ken began sowing $700 a month for the prison ministry in addition to what he was giving for Bible distribution, food for the poor, church building and planting projects.

Prior to this experience, Ken could not have imagined that one could invest in the expansion of God's kingdom and see such a tremendous return on investment. In every area that Ken invested in Ukraine, he saw increase—an increase in prison ministry and an increase in church planting. Ken and Carrie stand on the truth of Luke 6:38:

Give, and it will be given to you: good measure, pressed down, shaken together, and running over will be put into your bosom. For with the same measure that you use, it will be measured back to you.

At home, Ken's business also experienced supernatural increase. At that time they were franchising various brands of gasoline—Shell, Connoco, Phillips and Marathon. As Ken worked very closely with his salesperson, God brought in new customers as fast as they could write up sales contracts! They put a lot of new construction into convenience stores through an alliance with Shell Oil. One day Shell called Ken's area representative and asked, "What are those guys in the Elk River area doing? You've got more deals going than anyone else in the country!" Beaudry Oil's growth rate increased from 7 to 10 percent per year to 25 percent per year.

REAPING A HARVEST

In February 2002, Ken and Pastor Gregory had a strategy meeting regarding their work in Ukraine. They prepared a strategy to go into major cities across Ukraine to plant churches and build bible schools. They knew it would take a long time and be very expensive, but they knew God was in it. They didn't realize then that the Holy Spirit intended to move rapidly.

Later that year, after a pastors' conference, the Holy Spirit came with fire and brought increase upon revival. Everything Beaudry Oil invested into Ukraine caused increase for the company and for the Ukrainians. For example, the $700 per month the Beaudrys had invested in the prison ministry multiplied to the point that the Churches of Praise now minister in 23 different prisons—even in some in different countries. In one prison near the city of Dnepetroske, revival hit in such a marvelous way that 300 prisoners came to Christ! They started a church in that prison. When prison authorities, who were former Communists, saw what was happening, they gave the prisoners a large room in the prison to have as their church building. Some of the toughest criminals in the prison have been set free by Jesus and are now training for full-time ministry!

Meanwhile, the Holy Spirit was firing up the church planters. Churches of Praise's strategy had always been to go into Ukraine's major cities, which are easier to penetrate than the villages. Most of

Ukraine's 23,000 villages are dark places, where witchcraft is prevalent and some of the country's worst poverty exists. But this is where the Holy Spirit sent the church planters, and He sent them with signs and wonders. Miracles and salvations occurred, just like those recorded in the book of Acts. People were hearing of Jesus for the first time and receiving Him as their savior, being baptized and experiencing physical and emotional healing. Within a little over a year, 300 churches were planted, and within 3 years the number had grown to 500. The Holy Spirit told some of the participants to take the revival fire to other nations.

The Churches of Praise Network is presently in four other nations (Ken cannot reveal the names of these because they are predominantly Muslim). The Lord has given the Ukrainians a supernatural ability to reach the Muslim nations. Westerners seem to have little success in bringing Muslims to Jesus, but when the Ukrainians preach the gospel to them, the Word of God penetrates their hearts and they come to Jesus. One of the nations they are in is 98 percent Muslim. Within a short period, 40 churches had been planted in that nation. Praise the Lord! This is what God does when people believe Him for national transformation.

Ken likes to say, "If you will ask our Father, He can take you places you've never dreamed, do things beyond what you could ever expect." Ken often prays, "My God shall supply all of my needs according to His riches in glory by Christ Jesus exceedingly, abundantly beyond whatever I can ask, think or imagine until I have an abundance for every good work" (see Phil. 4:19; Eph. 3:20 and Matt. 13:12).

God is looking for marketplace people who will go beyond the ordinary. Doing the extraordinary starts with having faith and asking for His abundance. Will you ask? Will you believe? Will you obey? He will do the rest.

CHAPTER 8

A TALL ORDER: BRINGING PEACE TO UGANDA

When we think of marketplace miracles, I wonder how many of us think about the ability of God to bring peace from war. Perhaps we tend to think that ending bloodshed is beyond God's power—after all, human nature is human nature. But isn't that what miracles are all about: God transforming the natural through His power and grace? My encounter with just such a miracle began with a dinner party.

In August 2005, at the twenty-fifth anniversary of Harvest Evangelism, I had the opportunity to meet and have dinner with Julius Peter Oyet and Joshua Lwere, two of the top three leaders of the 10,000-pastor network in Uganda. During dinner, Julius told me about how the Lord had used him and others to end Uganda's 20-year-long civil war. As I thought about writing this book, I knew that this story had to be a part of it. Julius Oyet believes God is able to do exceedingly, abundantly above all that he can ask or think, because of the power that works within him.

Julius is from northern Uganda, in the very place where the civil war was most intense. The rebel leader, a man named Joseph Kony, kept his headquarters in Sudan, just north of Uganda, and entered northern Uganda to raid and bring destruction to the people who lived there. Then he retreated back into his safe-haven in Sudan. Kony called his organization the Lord's Resistance Army (LRA). The LRA was not a Christian organization. Far from it! In fact, Kony was deeply involved in traditional African spiritual practices and occultism. For more than two decades, the LRA destroyed millions of innocent lives, wrecked the economy and left thousands of homesteads burned and destroyed.

Eventually, Julius made his way back to his motherland, the Acholiland in the northern part of Uganda, to hold a Redeeming the Land crusade. Acholiland is his home province—he grew up in this area—and he knew the territory. During the crusade, he noticed uniformed military were observing his ministry. Obviously, they weren't sure if Julius was legitimate or somehow connected to the LRA. Prompted by the Lord, Julius told the crowd that he knew how to end the civil war and that he needed to meet with the president of Uganda to tell him how. Amazingly, President Yoweri Kaguta Museveni was also in the same town of Gulu at that time, taking stock of the destruction the LRA had wrought there. When word reached him that Julius wanted to see him, the president cheerfully arranged a meeting.

After introductions, President Museveni asked Julius to talk about how he would end the country's civil war. Julius responded that the civil war was a spiritual battle. He said that a spiritual war must be fought with spiritual weapons. He told the president it is impossible to kill demons with bullets. The president seemed interested in this new perspective, so he encouraged Julius to continue. Julius said demonic altars were the source of the rebels' satanic power. The president responded that the country had fought this war for nearly 20 years using conventional warfare methods—nothing had worked. They needed a new approach.

OPERATION GIDEON

Julius's approach was not only new—it was also radical. But in order for the president to understand its significance, Julius needed to explain to him the unholy trinity behind the war.

So Julius then told the president that the LRA had been formed in 1948 by a man named Sibirino Lukoya Kibero, who at that time referred to himself as "god the father." Eventually, when Joseph Kony teamed up with him, Kibero referred to Kony as "god the son." When Alice Auma-Lakwena joined him, Kibero referred to her as "god the holy spirit." This unholy trinity constructed satanic altars all over Acholiland. They used human sacrifices to enhance the spiritual power of these satanic altars.

Julius then told the president that the Lord had led him to the following verses from Judges 6:25-26:

> Now it came to pass the same night that the LORD said to him, "Take your father's young bull, the second bull of seven years old, and tear down the altar of Baal that your father has, and cut down the wooden image that is beside it; and build an altar to the LORD your God on top of this rock in the proper arrangement, and take the second bull and offer a burnt sacrifice with the wood of the image which you shall cut down."

Julius told President Museveni that the Lord used these verses from the life of Gideon to lead him to form a strategy called Operation Gideon. President Museveni was impressed with Julius's proposal and introduced him to the key generals in the Ugandan Army. He instructed them to put soldiers, helicopters, trucks and tanks at Julius's disposal.

Now it was time for Julius to get to work—and for God to lead the way. The first target of Operation Gideon was Pabbo Camp.

Pabbo Camp

On Saturday, March 1, 2003, Julius led an Operation Gideon team of 22 people to Pabbo Camp, which was the largest displaced people's camp in northern Uganda. At the time it had a population of 62,000 people living in small grass-thatched huts in overcrowded neighborhoods. Conditions in the camp were deplorable. Most of the villagers had no clothes; some wore rags. The malnourished, diseased children ate only once a day, while their parents ate only once a week! It was a heartbreaking experience for the team.

In the midst of this abject poverty was a demonized woman named Margaret Akello. The demonic power in this sorceress was so strong that whenever she looked at and pointed to a hut, it would catch fire and burn to ashes. By the time the Operation Gideon team caught up to her, she had burned some 3,000 huts in the camp. This added greatly to the misery of the displaced people in the camp. She also torched any who criticized her.

When the team encountered Margaret, they observed how tall and fat she was. This huge woman walked with an air of arrogance and self-confidence. When Julius approached her, he told her to describe the number and kinds of demons that inhabited her body. She bragged about the many principality-level demons that controlled her life. She also displayed a variety of paraphernalia she used in her witchcraft.

Julius told the woman, just like the Prophet Elijah told the false prophets of Baal on Mount Carmel, to summon all of her demons because there was going to be a confrontation between the spiritual forces of wickedness that inhabited her and the Lord Jesus Christ. In response, her body became stiff and her eyes became as big as saucers. Julius grabbed a gourd that was part of her witchcraft paraphernalia and crushed it under his feet on the ground. He told the demons they were wicked spirits, and the power of Jesus Christ would destroy them.

The crowd that had gathered drew back and held their breath as they watched this confrontation. To the crowd's amazement, Julius's clothes did not catch fire, and no other harm came to him. The Ugandan army personnel with him were also amazed. Julius used the name of Jesus Christ to command the demons to come out of the woman. The rest of the Operation Gideon team interceded for him while he carried out this extraordinary act of deliverance.

The demons left the woman at once, and she confessed that she felt very good after their departure. She then allowed Julius to lead her in a prayer to invite Jesus Christ to be her Savior and Lord. (Margaret Akello is now a strong Christian and she is a member of the intercessors in one of Julius' churches in Gulu Town.)

When the crowd saw that the power of God was stronger than the demonic power in the woman, many asked to be led in prayer to receive Jesus Christ as their Savior and Lord. Then the team burned all the witchcraft paraphernalia and prayed over the remaining possessions belonging to the woman.

When I heard this story, I thought of Paul's statement in 1 Corinthians 2:4-5:

And my speech and my preaching were not with persuasive
words of human wisdom, but in demonstration of the Spirit
and of power, that your faith should not be in the wisdom of
men but in the power of God.

Agwengtina Altar and the Awere Hills

On Sunday, March 2, 2003, Julius led an Operation Gideon team of
32 people to Joseph Kony's home in Agwengtina in the Gulu District.
They were escorted by Ugandan soldiers.

The team's first stop was at the Odek Primary School, where a local
official told them Kony had repeated the seventh grade three times.

Then the team met Kony's stepbrother, who led them to Joseph
Kony's home, where they met a number of Joseph Kony's relatives.
Julius explained the Operation Gideon mission to the family. Then the
team led the family members in prayer. The family denounced all the
evil covenants they had made. They asked God to deliver Joseph Kony
from the evil spirits that had been leading him to do unspeakable evil.
They asked forgiveness for their entire family. Julius then led the family in a prayer to accept Jesus Christ as their Savior and Lord, and
requested that Major Olivia Sempa of the Ugandan Army share Holy
Communion with Kony's family.

In seeking to know more about Kony, Julius discovered that evil
spirits had entered the young man in 1984. They had forced him to
abandon his studies and become a witchdoctor. Other evil spirits had
entered him in 1987 (they called themselves the holy spirits), com-
manding him to fight for the overthrow of the government and restore
the Ten Commandment rule in Uganda.

These same spirits gave Kony extraordinary power to fight against
the government. Kony and his leaders would often summon the power
of these demonic spirits at Awere, a subcounty in Aswa County, northeast of Gulu District. The hills at Awere are very steep and almost
impossible to climb. The tops of these hills are flat, with stagnant,
demonized water in the middle. This site served as an occultic altar
from which the rebels obtained demonic power. Kony's rebel leaders
carried water from this altar in a white jerry can and sprinkled it on the

battlefield so that the evil spirits would appear and fight against the Ugandan Army.

Mysterious things happened on the Awere Hills altar. For example, strange lightning, killer bees and huge, hideous snakes appeared suddenly and afflicted people living nearby. The people around the area were so afraid, they did not want to go near the Awere Hills altar. A local official informed the team that a couple days earlier a soldier who tried to reach the Awere Hills altar fell dead at the foot of the hill.

That very Sunday, Julius and several other pastors led the Operation Gideon team to the Awere Hills altar. A 13-vehicle convoy of Ugandan soldiers escorted them. Despite the difficulties, the team managed to climb the hills to the altar. They found the names of Joseph Kony's spirits written on the hills. There were also signs posted that featured the names of rebel commanders.

The Operation Gideon members prayed, repented for, denounced and canceled all the sacrifices and covenants made at the altar. As they prayed, a strange wind blew on top of the hill. Julius and another member of the team rebuked the wind in the name of Jesus Christ and it subsided. Then the team read a variety of Scriptures at the site. Afterward, they took Holy Communion together. They pleaded the blood of Jesus Christ for redemption, grace, peace and forgiveness in Acholiland and in Uganda. They also prayed for churches to worship freely and for righteousness to return to the land. Their objective was to reverse the curse brought on by the pagan altar Kony had built for his demonic spirits. As they ended the day, having demolished the powers of Satan from Awere hills, 42 of the soldiers who escorted the team gave their lives to Jesus right there on the hill!

Awach Altar

Awach altar is in Awach Subcounty, in Aswa County, some distance northeast of Gulu Town, in the Gulu district of northern Uganda. Built on the banks of the Abera River, it was the second altar Kony erected for the purposes of making sacrifices and demonic covenants. When Kony "dedicated" the Awach altar in 1987, he sacrificed a young man and a bull there as part of the ceremony.

The Operation Gideon team visited the Awach altar on Monday, March 3, 2003. Again they were escorted by soldiers to the site.

The team began by praying prayers of individual and corporate repentance on behalf of Awach people, religious leaders, cultural leaders and the entire population of Acholis. They also read verses from the Bible. They sanctified the River Abera, according to 2 Kings 2:19-22.

> Then the men of the city said to Elisha, "Please notice, the situation of this city is pleasant, as my lord sees; but the water is bad, and the ground barren." And he said, "Bring me a new bowl, and put salt in it." So they brought it to him. Then he went out to the source of the water, and cast in the salt there, and said, "Thus says the LORD: 'I have healed this water; from it there shall be no more death or barrenness.'" So the water remains healed to this day, according to the word of Elisha which he spoke.

They also poured anointing oil and salt into the water to reverse the curse. Then, using 12 stones, the team erected "God's altar." Once again, the Ugandan soldiers present—including the commander that led the army to Awach altar—gave their lives to Jesus Christ.

Agwee Altar in Kilak County

Agwee altar was built on the Agwee River in Kilak County, deep in the mountains. Located about three miles from Mount Kilak, it can be reached only by plane. Still, Joseph Kony, Sibirino Lukoya Kibero and Alice Auma-Lakwena visited the place to draw the satanic powers and water for rituals.

On Tuesday, March 4, 2003, the Operation Gideon team arrived at the Agwee altar, having flown in an army helicopter to get there. They found that Ugandan soldiers had been deployed earlier in the area for their protection. While attempting to land near the site of the demonic water, the helicopter almost crashed. The pilot had to try several times before landing the helicopter safely. The Operation Gideon team prayed in the air and God intervened!

The Operation Gideon team arrived at the site and held hands and prayed. Julius interviewed the Ugandan soldiers, who testified about the Agwee River. They said that for many generations the people could not drink the water because it was cursed. They told how they had found a guinea rat that had drunk the water and died at the spot. They skinned it and dried it, but the blood from the rat was green instead of red. The meat became green after cooking it. They ended up throwing it away. They also learned that other animals had died at the spot. Even the honey that was in a nearby beehive was inedible. Furthermore, pregnant women who touched the water suffered miscarriages. People were warned not to drink or touch the water because anything with blood that touched the water would die instantly!

Julius led a first Operation Gideon team to the top of the rock to the Agwee altar. The team continued with prayers, worship, praise and songs. They were joined later by a second team of 16 people led by Bishop Tom Okello. The Ugandan soldiers provided protection for the team during the ceremony.

The teams repented of sins and denounced alliances with the resident evil spirits. Julius poured anointing oil and salt into the Agwee River to cleanse it and reverse the curses. He amazed the onlookers when he washed his face in the water. The Operation Gideon team and the Ugandan soldiers then drank the water. Bishop Tom Okello led the team in Holy Communion. Then Pastor Experito dipped his foot into the water. One brother amused the team by washing his shirt in the water!

Twelve Ugandan soldiers who witnessed the healing of these waters gave their lives to the Lord. They were also baptized in the Agwee River immediately. Then, before the team departed back to Gulu, another 15 soldiers invited Jesus Christ to be their Savior and Lord. Even the helicopter crew that took the team to the Agwee altar got saved.

The bees in the hive beside the river had been deadly, but after prayers, the team feasted on the honey without any negative consequence. The military detachment commander then told Julius they had wanted to transfer or relocate because of lack of water in the area, but changed his mind after this event, seeing that there was now plenty of water in the Agwee for the soldiers.

The Main Roundabout Gulu Town Altar

The main roundabout is in the center of Gulu town. It is especially dangerous because the rebels have turned it into a demonic altar. As a result, there have been an unusually large number of traffic accidents, many of which have been fatal. There is a three-foot high steel pan in the center of the roundabout where rebels have made sacrifices of sheep and goats and made covenants with evil spirits.

The Operation Gideon team visited the place on the last day of their trip, on Tuesday, March 4. The team surrounded the area and Julius, Bishop Tom Okello and Pastor Macho led prayers and read a number of Scripture verses at the site. The team turned, facing north, east, west and south, and proclaimed healing, peace and restoration of land, people, the neighboring districts and the entire nation of Uganda. Then Julius poured salt and anointing oil to sanctify the land and reverse the curses, pleading the blood of Jesus Christ. They also prayed for new life, redemption of the land and peace to all of Uganda as Julius blew the trumpet.

VICTORY IS THE LORD'S

Julius concluded his story by sharing with us that these events resulted in a great diminishment of the demonic powers of the rebel leaders. While Joseph Kony and his team still hide out in southern Sudan, many of his closest supporters now serve as his surrogates to UN-led peace talks in Juba, Sudan, in an effort to end the 22-year war! Most LRA fighters and commanders have turned themselves in.

The cessation of hostilities has resulted in the Lord giving Julius great favor with the president. Julius shared with us that the pastors' association of Uganda had decided that Harvest Evangelism should come to Uganda to assist them in rebuilding their country economically. The first major visit to Uganda by Harvest Evangelism was held in September 2006. A significant delegation from Uganda also participated in the Harvest Evangelism Institute in Argentina in November 2006. That delegation included the First Lady of Uganda and a number of prominent business leaders and pastors from that country.

Sounds incredible, doesn't it? From civil war to rebuilding. From bearing arms to bearing the love of Jesus. Incredible but not impossible. Not for God. With God, all things are possible (see Luke 1:37).

CHAPTER 9

INFOCARE: THE KING'S COMPANY

Some might say that to find a healthcare company more interested in people than profits is a marketplace miracle in itself. But what if I told you that such a company does exist—and that you haven't even heard the miracle part yet? Keep reading. It gets better—and you won't believe what God is up to this time around.

I didn't have much of an idea myself in the beginning, when, in Buenos Aires I hosted a table at the Welcome Dinner at Harvest Evangelism's International Institute on Nation Transformation Through Marketplace Redemption. As our guests were arriving, I invited a number of close friends to sit at my table. Then I spotted Dr. Niel Stegmann and Johan du Preez from Cape Town, South Africa. As the founder of a South African company named InfoCare, Niel had developed an information system for hospitals, physicians and pharmacies. Johan was the CEO of Innofin, a retail investment company for affluent investors. I invited them to join our table, and they took their seats at the table, right across from me.

A NEW BUSINESS PLAN

During the course of the evening, I learned that Niel was interested in transforming his company into a Kingdom business as a result of reading Ed Silvoso's book *Anointed for Business*. Inspired by Ed's vision, Neil experienced a paradigm shift and was beginning to see his work as his ministry. He dreamed of a day when he could cap his income and give 100 percent above that amount to the expansion of God's kingdom.

Niel said he had begun the development of his information system with his own resources; those resources were insufficient to finish the task, so he took on partners. "Were these Christian partners?" I asked. "No, they are not Christians," was his reply. "Then you are unequally yoked with nonbelievers," I told him, referring to 2 Corinthians 6:14: "Do not be unequally yoked together with unbelievers. For what fellowship has righteousness with lawlessness? And what communion has light with darkness?"

Over the next few days, the Holy Spirit convinced Niel to find a way to buy out his non-Christian partners. When he learned that I had spent 18 of my 25-year business career in the healthcare industry, Niel asked me if I would come to South Africa to help him evaluate his company and devise a strategy to buy out his non-Christian partners. I asked him if I could bring my good friend Bob Wood to help me. Bob and I had worked together some 12 years earlier and had enjoyed an extraordinary synergy working together—our gifts were complementary. Niel agreed to hire Bob and me for the task, but he urged us to make the trip prior to December 15, just a month later. Apparently everyone goes on vacation in South Africa after December 15. Niel's request was also urgent because his company was completely out of cash; his back was against the wall.

So Bob and I made the trip to South Africa, and although I had taken long international flights before, somehow the journey to South Africa seemed unusually difficult. After a day and a half of travel—and losing our luggage along the way—we finally arrived in Cape Town.

Bob and I conducted an initial evaluation and concluded that the InfoCare system was technologically sound. Together with Niel and Johan, however, we broadened InfoCare's mission of simply selling software to improving the operational and financial performance of the healthcare systems throughout developing nations. The software would still be involved but would be merely one component of a much larger plan for improving healthcare systems. We also determined that, in addition to generating more working capital, InfoCare would need to raise $250,000 to buy out the non-Christian stockholders.

On Saturday, December 11, we had breakfast with Graham Power, the CEO of the Power Group of Companies, a South African construction business. During breakfast, I briefed Graham on our positive assessment of InfoCare. I also told Graham that we would be working with Niel and Johan to raise the necessary funds, both for the working capital and for the buyout. From there we went to Graham's office, where he told us he had decided to give InfoCare a gift of $42,000, which we applied to the company's working capital needs.

Shortly after, Bob and I flew back to the United States. Just after our departure from Cape Town, Niel and Johan began negotiating a buy-out agreement with Niel's non-Christian stockholders. This agreement was finally signed in March 2005. The buyout would cost $250,000, if it was accomplished on or before June 30, 2005. On July 1, 2005, the price would increase by $50,000. The deal was in God's hands now.

DIVINE APPOINTMENT

For our part, instead of returning to our homes in Minnesota, Bob and I flew to San Francisco for a strategic planning meeting for Harvest Evangelism. Before the meetings began, Bob and I had lunch with Ed Silvoso and summarized our six-day visit to Cape Town. That was when I told Ed that I thought that we should help Niel Stegmann market his InfoCare software in Argentina. José Sanz, from Córdoba, Argentina, joined us in these meetings, so Bob and I had a chance to brief him on our thoughts about transforming the healthcare industry in his country.

Then, in February 2005, Rachel and I attended Harvest Evangelism's Apostolic Transformation Network (ATN) meeting in Honolulu, Hawaii. Niel Stegmann and Johan du Preez also attended. Just prior to the meeting, Ed Silvoso and I had lunch with Niel and Johan to discuss how to deploy the InfoCare software in Argentina.

After the conference, Rachel and I flew to Kona, Hawaii, to take a much-needed vacation. While there, I got a phone call from a doctor named Randy Peck. I didn't know how he knew me or how he had found my cell phone number. He told me he was a physician who lived in Culpeper, Virginia, a city I'd never heard of before. Within seconds, however, I thought to myself, *This is a divine appointment!*

We talked about our faith; in fact, we prayed together several times during our phone conversation. Although I did not understand the significance at the time, he told me that the 400-year anniversary of the founding of Jamestown, Virginia, would take place in 2007 and that the whole world would focus its attention on his state (more about that in chapter 13). Then we discussed the need to transform the healthcare industry throughout the world. Suddenly, my thoughts turned to Niel Stegmann. I told my new friend about the six days Bob Wood and I had spent with Niel in Cape Town the previous December. I told him our assessment was that the InfoCare system is well constructed and could serve as the basis for transforming the healthcare industry. I gave Randy Niel Stegmann's email address and suggested that he contact him.

A couple months later I learned that Niel Stegmann and Johan du Preez had traveled from Cape Town to Culpeper to meet Randy Peck and his friend Michael Stay. Niel, Johan, Randy and Michael began talking about building a strategy to market the InfoCare software system in the United States. That strategy eventually became known as TKC-InfoCare. "TKC" stands for "The King's Company"—the King, of course, being the Lord Jesus Christ.

In June 2005, Niel and Rina Stegmann traveled with Rachel and me to Culpeper to discuss the presentation of a business plan for TKC-InfoCare to prospective investors. During this trip to Culpeper, Rachel and I first met Randy and Julia Peck and their two children, Caran and Robbie. It was also during this trip that we met Michael and Cindy Stay.

We were all aware that Niel Stegmann had to exercise his option to buy out his non-Christian stockholders before June 30, 2005. During a meeting in a conference room in the Culpeper Business Center, Randy and Julia Peck announced that they would take $300,000 from their retirement account and lend it—interest free—to Niel and Rina Stegmann so that they could buy out their non-Christian stockholders prior to June 30, 2005. Everyone in the room was stunned by this extraordinary offer—Rachel wept as she contemplated the Pecks' enormous compassion. Within 24 hours the $300,000 was wire transferred to the InfoCare bank account in Cape Town. Then the bank made the

$250,000 payment to Niel's non-Christian stockholders, thereby terminating their ownership of InfoCare stock. At last, Niel owned 100 percent of InfoCare. The other $50,000 was available as working capital for InfoCare.

ENLARGING THE VISION

As I mentioned earlier, in December 2004, Bob Wood and I recommended to Ed Silvoso and José Sanz that we should help Niel Stegmann bring his software system into Argentina. These discussions continued into 2005 without a conclusion. Finally, in March 2005, Niel Stegmann and his wife, Rina, flew from South Africa to Buenos Aires. Once in Argentina, they contacted José Sanz, who agreed to meet with them in his hometown of Córdoba.

The Lord blessed this meeting: José listened as Niel told him about the InfoCare software and how he wanted to implement a performance improvement strategy for hospitals using InfoCare software. Niel's presentation impressed José; he contacted friends with business and medical backgrounds and arranged for them to meet with him and Niel in Buenos Aires. Later, José called Ed Silvoso and said, "Rick was right! Niel Stegmann does have the software system and hospital performance improvement expertise that will bless Argentina." Ed called me right after that phone call and said he and José both believed Niel Stegmann's system should be brought to Argentina.

In June 2005, I was in Argentina for the Harvest Evangelism Short Term Mission Trip. Niel and Rina Stegmann were also in Buenos Aires—they were meeting with Dr. Alfredo Stern, the city's Secretary of Health. Niel invited me to join them. The IT leader for Buenos Aires' healthcare system was also involved. As we discussed installing the InfoCare system in a prototype hospital, Niel told Dr. Stern of his great optimism that the InfoCare system would be a blessing to the city's healthcare system. But Dr. Stern told Niel he had been around this healthcare system too long to be optimistic.

Just then I sensed that it was time for me to speak up. I said, "If we have to depend on human solutions, I wouldn't be optimistic either.

That is why we want to dedicate this project to the Lord." Dr. Stern asked what I meant. I replied, "I mean that I would like to say a prayer to bless you, your IT leader and the project. Would you be willing to have me pray such a prayer?" Dr. Stern agreed, and I placed my hand on his arm and blessed him and his position as the city's Secretary of Health. I also blessed his IT leader and the pilot project for the installation of the InfoCare software in the prototype hospital. I finished my prayer with the words, "I pray all of these things in the name of Jesus Christ." When I finished praying, I looked up to see a broad smile spreading across Dr. Stern's face. He escorted us to the door and said that my prayer was a great act of kindness. If I ever witnessed God's favor, it was then.

We didn't let things rest there, though. I urged Niel to work with José Sanz to develop a strategy to implement a prototype hospital contract. But José told me that Argentine business leaders were uneasy about investing in Argentine projects and that the funds for the prototype would have to come from outside the country. He also suggested that the Argentine prototype hospital should be in the province of Córdoba.

MIRACLE IN PROGRESS

In 2005, I joined a number of Christian partners to form a healthcare trading company called TriMed International, located in Minnesota. Then we formed operating divisions in China, South Africa and Argentina. The TriMed International board of directors decided to raise the capital necessary to fund the prototype hospital project in Córdoba, Argentina, with Niel Stegmann and InfoCare International. Once the prototype has proven successful, we will then begin the rollout of the strategy for all of the other 34 public hospitals in the province of Córdoba. We continue to establish positive relationships with hospital administrators and government health officials and believe that God will use the vision He gave a doctor in South Africa to bless Argentina and many nations beyond.

Do you have a vision for your business? Are you concerned that adopting a Kingdom-centered business plan isn't financially feasible? Fear no more. If you are convinced that God has given you a vision, step out in faith. As you follow the Lord's leading and do His will, you will be a vehicle for transforming not just a business but perhaps even an industry—and in the process, touching countless lives with the gospel.

GOD'S BUSINESS PLAN

Finding the faith to step into God's "business plan" isn't always easy. The process is often intense, challenging and action-packed. Sometimes it can even be depressing. But the key is to remember, amid the ups and downs of following God's marketplace directives, that He is in charge—He's got the details worked out. Our part is to remain committed. God will bring the success.

I was reminded of this fact in my own life, after Rachel and I left our 25-year business career to become city transformation missionaries to the Twin Cities. It was a difficult transition, and at one point I was in bed for three days straight, suffering from clinical depression. One day, while the depression was upon me, Steve Wirth came over and told Rachel that the Lord had placed it in his heart to bring us a check for $1,000. He didn't understand what was going on, but he knew he had to obey the Lord's directive. When Rachel brought the check up to our bedroom and told me what had happened, I felt energy returning to my body. I got out of bed, took a shower and got dressed. God had sent a special messenger, Steve Wirth, to say it was time for the depression to end, and that it was now time to get started with our ministry; to say that I needn't worry—if I was committed to His plan, He would provide.

We lived across the street from Steve and Kathy Wirth for about nine years, often playing tennis with them on their backyard court. We also went on a spiritual retreat with them one year and had a mountaintop experience. The Wirths have remained faithful financial supporters of our ministry ever since the day that Steve brought the $1,000 check to us. In turn, when they have had difficulties in their businesses, Rachel and I have always counted it a privilege to respond immediately to their prayer requests.

THE BIRTH AND REBIRTH OF WIRTHCO ENGINEERING

Steve and Kathy founded WirthCo in 1980. In the early years of the company, WirthCo imported and marketed agricultural pump and valve products. Unfortunately, the business generated significant amounts of debt. They then broadened the business's scope by acquiring a profitable battery-accessory product line. At some point, however, the WirthCo board of directors made the decision to turn over all WirthCo products to another public company. The rationale was that the public company would benefit from both the new product lines and the sales potential. WirthCo, in return, would use the sales commission it received from its products to pay down its debt.

After some time had passed and contrary to contractual provisions between the two companies, the public company ceased paying sales commission to WirthCo. Steve also learned that the public company was looking to sell off the former WirthCo battery-accessory division. Because he was a stockholder in both businesses, Steve didn't want even the appearance of impropriety or conflict of interest. He certainly had no interest in litigating against the other company.

WirthCo, then still a tiny family business with mounds of bank debt, took extraordinary measures to retrieve its former product line. WirthCo agreed to pay the public company a sizable amount for its own former battery-accessory division. WirthCo even forgave past royalties that were due to them. These were steps of faith because WirthCo was not an operating company at the time. However, Steve was determined not to repeat former mistakes with the rebirth of WirthCo. One cornerstone principle was that Jesus Christ would be the CEO of the new company. The mission of the new WirthCo was to bring glory and honor to God.

WirthCo hired a manager, but sales continued at a modest rate. No progress was being made toward debt reduction. The situation came to a head when Steve met with other family shareholders. Many were startled to learn the amount of debt Steve had personally guaranteed on WirthCo's behalf. Everyone recognized something had to be done. Nevertheless, the other shareholders were understandably reluctant to co-sign bank guarantees.

One family member suggested he would turn over his ownership to Steve for one dollar in order to eliminate his proportional responsibility for the bank debt. The other shareholders felt this approach made sense for them as well. Even though the company was technically worthless, and Steve and Kathy remained personally at risk for all of the bank loans, their consolidated ownership created a more streamlined structure, one that was well-positioned for future growth.

In time, the manager proposed that he buy the company and move it to his home town. After prayerful consideration, Steve turned down his request. What if the manager failed to turn a profit? What if he failed to make the sales commission payments? Steve and Kathy decided that they had little choice but to terminate the manager and move the company to their home. This arrangement offered the lowest overhead and provided a safe harbor for the company.

Just Surviving

Miraculously, over a period of four or five years, WirthCo generated enough income to pay down the bank debt of between $150,000 and $200,000. During that period, the Wirths also paid salaries to employees and to themselves. They also respected their suppliers as valued team members. They developed this company motto: "Understanding and fulfilling customer needs."

They also had a goal to grow the business so that they could move out of their home and into more typical business facilities. Having the company in their home was a sacrifice for their children, Andrew, Dave and Jenn. It was a sacrifice for Kathy, too, to share her home with the company. The living room was an office for first one, then two, then three employees, while the garage was a warehouse. Family life and office life continued simultaneously with the children's piano lessons heard in the background of business calls, while the family dog barked at the UPS man when he came with his deliveries. After six years working out of their home, the Wirths were able to move the company to rented facilities.

Aspiring to God-Given Destiny

WirthCo is now over 25 years old and owns some 25 patents. Steve and Kathy formed a real estate company and purchased their own building to house WirthCo and to incubate other businesses.

Rachel and I joined Steve and Kathy in a time of on-site prayer right after they closed on this building and moved in. We prayer-walked the building and anointed every doorway and piece of furniture with anointing oil. Steve and Kathy stood at the entrance to their work area and, as in Revelation 3:20, declared they heard Jesus Christ knocking at their door. And as the owners of the building and of the business, they heard the Lord's voice, opened the door for Him and invited Him to come into their facilities.

WirthCo has been profitable nearly every year since the first typewriter was moved into the Wirths' home in 1987. It is debt free—and that is truly a miracle!

Another miracle occurred recently when WirthCo, owners of the Battery Doctor registered trade name, acquired the Battery Doc registered trade name and its line of 12-volt battery maintainers and chargers, a line that complements the existing WirthCo product line. The Battery Doc owners had made a strategic decision to exit their own brand of battery maintainers and chargers, while WirthCo was looking to expand its product line in this particular category. Steve and Kathy are now looking at other strategic acquisitions to foster additional growth.

And it's not just their own growth that they are concerned about. Steve and Kathy are always looking for opportunities to help other companies that are looking to adopt a Kingdom-centered business plan. In fact, WirthCo's conference room, at one time or another, has been made available to a number of other start-up entities, primarily medical companies, including Cytogenesis, InterRad Medical, Inc., TriMed International, LLC, and Curing Solutions, LLC.

All in all, WirthCo is a model for other businesses. Nowhere is this more evident than in their management meetings, which always commence with prayer and dedication, keeping in mind Proverbs 16:3: "Commit to the LORD whatever you do, and your plans will succeed" (*NIV*).

If you're looking for the kind of success WirthCo has found, make it a priority to invite Jesus to your next business strategy meeting. Seek His will—He will make a way.

CHAPTER 11

SHOPPING FOR MIRACLES

Sometimes we miss our divine appointments because we're looking in the wrong places. Often this is due to the fact that we have preconceived notions about the miraculous, as if God is unable to sanctify certain people, places or things. Fortunately, God is much bigger than our ideas about what is "holy." He can transform and make holy whatever He chooses, in order to bring men and women to Himself.

Case in point: a shopping mall called The Summit. Owned by Jim Anthony and located in Niagara Falls, The Summit is more than just a shopping center. But it didn't start out that way.

On a trip to Niagara Falls, my wife and I met Jim Anthony. From him, we learned that the mall's history has been similar to the city's history: Great economic prosperity in the 1970s and 1980s was followed by great economic decline. Jim became involved with the mall when his company made a loan to the mall's former owner. When the owner couldn't make the mortgage payments, Jim's firm foreclosed on the loan and was forced to take possession of the mall. Initially Jim tried to sell it, but he found that few people wanted to own a mall in a city in such economic distress. After nearly two years of bizarre happenings around the property, Jim and his partners made a strategic decision. Rather than try to unload this economic albatross, they would seek to operate and redevelop the mall themselves.

They showed up for their divine appointment on the day they decided to approach the resurrection of the mall from a spiritual point of view, rather than purely as a business exercise. They were compelled to acknowledge that God is able to do exceedingly abundantly beyond all that they could ask or think according to the power that works within them. They had no choice but to believe and trust God, or walk away from millions of dollars and a great opportunity.

TUSCALOOSA SPARKS

Jim's shift in understanding actually began when he attended a workplace ministry event at the Billy Graham Training Center in North Carolina in April 2003. Desperate to see God move more powerfully in his work and life, he listened to Ed Silvoso, Rich Marshall, Os Hillman and many others teach that business people are called to be full-time workplace ministers. Immediately he began to implement what he learned, taking prayer walks around his properties with his company teams.

Almost a year later, Jim and Sirus Chitsaz, another Christian businessman from Raleigh, North Carolina, met with Ed Silvoso and me during a marketplace conference in Tuscaloosa, Alabama. The four of us had lunch together during the conference. I remember that lunch well, because after the waitress took our order, I told her that we were about to pray over our meal and asked her if we could pray a blessing over her as well. She agreed, shared her prayer needs, and held hands with us as we blessed her and prayed for her specific requests. Toward the end of our lunch, another waitress came to our table and said she wanted to see who we were. It turned out that the waitress who had served us had been horribly depressed when she came to work that day, but when we had prayed for her, the depression had lifted. She was now full of joy and was telling all the staff in the restaurant about us. Jim, Sirus, Ed and I all believed that this was a sign from the Lord that there was something special about our relationship.

Two months later, in April 2004, I visited Raleigh, North Carolina. I spent the first hours of that trip with Sirus Chitsaz, but eventually Sirus took me to Jim Anthony's office to pray for his business. After a walking tour through Jim's building, we ended up in Jim's office, praying over a huge file related to The Summit, his dysfunctional mall in Niagara Falls, New York.

When I finally visited the mall in October 2005, Jim told me something had shifted in the heavenly realms when we had prayed over the mall's file in his office.

EXPERIENCING A BREAKTHROUGH

In May 2004, less than 30 days after the prayers over the file in Jim's office, an increasingly desperate Jim Anthony received a phone call from Lou Zon, whom he had met when Lou had worked with another group to open a Christmas Wonderland park in The Summit. During that phone call, Lou shared his idea to convert the mall into a huge market-place for small vendors to sell their products and services.

About that same time, Dominic Salamone, a security guard at the mall, wrote Jim a letter asking if he could lease space at the mall. Jim granted his request on a trial basis, and Dominic became a catalyst for the re-leasing of the mall.

In September of that same year, Dominic met Georgia Brannan and, shortly thereafter, introduced her to Jim Anthony. After discovering Georgia's tremendous networking and pastoral skills, Jim asked Georgia if she would serve as a pastor in the mall and to the community. She agreed to do so, and soon afterward, The Summit Life Outreach ministry was founded to operate in the mall.

In December 2004, a local team of intercessors met in the Vineyard church in the mall and prayed for deliverance and revival in the mall and the city. God had begun to build an onsite and offsite team to prepare the way for the King of Glory to come to the mall and the city. And that was just the beginning. In March 2005, Lou Zon introduced Jim Anthony to Anthony Nanula. Anthony's family owned a chain of convenience store/gas stations throughout upstate New York. Anthony had also served in the New York State Senate and as Buffalo City Comptroller. He was a relative-ly new Christian who was drawn to Jim Anthony—he had never before met a businessman who so openly declared *and* lived his faith in Jesus Christ.

Anthony, in turn, introduced Jim to Al and Deb Warner (friends of mine) in April 2005, one year after the prayer for breakthrough in Raleigh. Jim began spending time with Al and Deb and a close friendship devel-oped. In June, the Warners began introducing Jim to intercessors and pas-tors who were part of their regional network of relationships. Al and Deb urged their friends to begin praying in earnest for Jim Anthony and for The Summit.

About the same time, Jim began taking a team on prayer walks at the mall and ministering to the store operators who leased space from him. He also began renovations in faith that tenants would come. That was when a significant breakthrough occurred: In September 2005, Steve & Barry's University Sportswear signed an anchor store lease for 62,000 square feet of space. In November they opened at the mall with a sales volume that shattered projections. Through the Christmas season, the mall traffic reached its highest in more than 10 years!

DEDICATING THE SUMMIT TO THE LORD

On Friday, October 7, 2005, I was one of 80 who attended a dinner meeting held in The Summit's Community Room. Some of the participants were pulpit ministers, but most were marketplace ministers. Jim Anthony introduced two of his tenants, who testified about how significantly Jim had ministered to them. Anthony Nanula spoke as well, describing his positive and life-changing experiences with Jim Anthony since he had come to Niagara Falls.

Then Jim spoke; he challenged the pastors in the room to equip and commission their marketplace ministers. Given the dire economic situation in Niagara Falls, he argued that the marketplace ministry strategy was not optional and must be pursued vigorously. Jim spoke as a man of great authority. Although he had deeply challenged the pastors, when he finished speaking, they embraced him with smiles on their faces. I realized that Jim had imparted hope to the entire audience. I thought to myself, *A man who commits millions of dollars to resuscitate a mall in the midst of a city in economic distress has great spiritual authority to speak to the city's leaders.*

The following day, The Summit was to be dedicated to the Lord. Pastors from all over Niagara Falls, Buffalo and even as far away as Rochester responded to the invitation to participate in this unusual dedication. A multicultural team led the audience in wonderful praise and worship. Several pastors read Scripture and prayed over The Summit. Again, Jim Anthony spoke about restoring the mall as a means to bringing Kingdom transformation and prosperity back to the area. He also introduced Niagara Falls's mayor and led the audience in praying for him. I then spoke about the transformation of Elk River, Minnesota, and encouraged the audience to see the restoration of Niagara Falls as primarily a spiritual transformation, to be followed by physical, social, cultural and economic transformation.

In his address at the dedication, Jim Anthony proclaimed that The Summit belonged to the Lord Jesus Christ. At a time when retailers, businesses, schools and governments are trying to distance themselves from anything with "Christ" in the name, The Summit is defining itself through its relationship with its Owner, the Lord Jesus Christ.

TRANSFORMING NIAGARA FALLS

Intentionally associating the mall with the Lord has allowed mall leaders to innovate and advance in the areas of business, economics, community involvement and spiritual victory. The Summit has become a beacon and example of what those dedicated to transforming the world through the marketplace may accomplish.

For example, Jim hired Rev. Al Warner to create an original staff-training program using biblical core values and a biblical code of ethics. The program has resulted in a surge in employee applications and a dramatic rise in employee satisfaction. Employees are attracted not only to a management system that trains and challenges them, but also to the rapidly growing and improving possibilities at The Summit. More than 200 jobs have been created, with many more to come. Cash flow is rising due to store sales. Generations Music, Niagara Emporium, Niagara Furniture Emporium, The Magical Land of Oz, Summit Pharmacy and Summit Life Outreach are new organizations that have been created or grown through The Summit. The Summit has also assisted more than 40 individual enterprises to increase and improve their retail and service businesses.

Economic advancement is not limited to tenants and employees. The growing profitability of The Summit has had a great impact on the Niagara Falls community. The mall has already paid more than $1 million in property and school taxes. Local officials have begun to take notice, and politicians who previously opposed the mall redevelopment now support it. Local and state legislators, economic development officials, and regional business leaders are impressed at the property and community transformation flowing from the property.

A mall with leaking roofs, physical deterioration, and ugly, dark interiors has become transformed. The skylit interiors invite visitors. A place of persistent litigation has become an area of peace. A symbol of community destruction has become a sign of resurrection.

The Summit has also developed an internship with Niagara University. The Summit and Buffalo Historic Society installed historic exhibits that point to a new, hope-filled future. These exhibits help to create a meaningful, educational center for the community.

Then there's "Downtown Niagara Indoors," an indoor environment that simulates a downtown; anchored at The Summit, it has united fragmented communities. Unification is not limited to the secular world. The Lord is breaking down walls between churches and denominations as God's people serve side by side, without regard for institutional identities. Aside from transdenominational ministry partnerships, individual church groups come to perform music, dance and drama in the mall concourses.

The new strategies and tactics for transformation have not only rebranded the 33-year-old mall, but they also are bringing spiritual nourishment to the city. At Christmastime, two men act as Santa Claus and offer a blessing over each child with whom they are photographed. Before each child leaves Santa's lap, Santa's last words are "Merry Christmas" and "May God bless you," thus pronouncing a father's blessing over each child.

A "greeter" program is also being implemented, in which intercessors and prayer warriors not only greet and bless the mall guests but also provide them with literature that includes a flier describing The Summit leadership's vision and direction, as well as offers of prayer.

Behind the scenes, Jim Anthony and his team work to maintain the lordship of Jesus Christ. They walk and drive and pray over the 80-acre site and 800,000 square feet of buildings. Spiritual warriors declare and establish God's reign—overthrowing principalities and powers—at the site, in the city and throughout the region. They are commencing a spiritual-mapping project to identify the heavenly, spiritual and physical significance of local landmarks, events, buildings, people, neighborhoods, geography, geology and history.

Leaders routinely pray with and for staff, tenants, employees, guests, contractors, service providers and all prominent community figures. When they are allowed to, prayer warriors pray openly with staff and managers at each store. When they are not allowed to, the warriors pray discreetly.

Further, those with whom they pray are not abandoned after the spiritual experience. The Summit is committed to training and discipling employees, guests, educators and government leaders. Christian leaders from the community offer counsel. A spiritual Dream Team has been established and includes two paid chaplains. They even bring children in to lead worship in music during the Christmas season.

Additionally, The Summit conducts seminars on community transformation through marketplace ministry and is constantly working to cast vision for new businesses and ministries. Serving the practical needs of the community, The Summit is establishing a life outreach center that will feature healing rooms, weekly lectures and worship events. The Summit sows financially into ministries, nonprofits, businesses and individuals, and has supported disaster relief funds.

FOLLOWING THE KING

Certainly no one can doubt that God has used Jim Anthony and his colleagues in a mighty way. And who has been better suited for transformation than those who have been tried in the furnace of affliction during the mall's depression, and who then have learned to trust the Lord and pursue His plans without reservation? What could be better evidence for the validity of trusting God than the community transformation demonstrated by The Summit? Niagara Falls may be forever enriched by the tireless efforts of a team of believers who followed their King.

Can God use a dilapidated shopping mall and a few faithful followers of Jesus to perform an extraordinary miracle that transforms a community? Much work still must be done. The battle with evil and the destroyer will never be completed until the Lord returns, but miraculous headway has been made in a city where few believed it possible. The miracle at The Summit has happened because some desperate people had no choice but to take God at His word and to trust Him. Our God is an awesome God, and He reigns at The Summit!

If God can use a shopping mall to bring positive community transformation, be assured that He can do anything! He can work with whatever business-related challenge you are dealing with at the moment. He can use you and your difficulty to build faith and motivate change. But you must first take God at His word—believe Him, trust Him and follow Him!

CHAPTER 12

CREATIVITY—HOLY SPIRIT-STYLE

Are you willing to listen to God's voice and follow His lead, but worried that He won't even take a step inside your office? Maybe you think that your line of business isn't exactly "godly." Well, perhaps that's what makes it the perfect opportunity for God to "do His stuff."

Richard Gazowsky, pastor of Voice of Pentecost Church in San Francisco, considered the television and film industry to be just such an opportunity. He founded the film studio WYSIWYG Filmworks on Treasure Island in San Francisco—"WYSIWYG" means "What You See Is What You Get!" Today, Richard has arranged for intercessors to have access to a room within the Treasure Island Studio so that they will be able to have 24/7 intercession going on in San Francisco. His ministry has definitely come a long way since its inception.

BIRTHING GOD'S VISION FOR WYSIWYG

It was April 9, 2002—a rare sunny day in San Francisco—and WYSIWYG had just signed a contract with Sky Angel, a Christian television station. This would be WYSIWYG's first over-the-air programming schedule. Since it was WYSIWYG's birthday—their seventh anniversary to be exact—Richard and his staff were planning a big celebration. And Richard was starting the day with a miracle: A donor had given him $2,500 to replace a stolen computer. The devastating events that occurred later, however, changed Richard's life forever.

A short time after arriving at work, Richard got a call from his nephew Titus, who leads the grip department. "Richard, can you pray for our baby? The baby has turned breach." From the tone of Titus's voice Richard knew this was serious.

Before he could pray, Richard received word that his oldest sister, Pam, had been taken to the hospital. She had been vomiting uncontrollably for several hours. The doctors had tried everything, but they could not stop the vomiting.

Minutes after he hung up the phone, it rang again. This time it was the principal of his children's school, who said, "One of the students in our school committed suicide at home during the night."

It was as if someone had taken a sledge hammer to Richard's heart. He fell to his knees in the office and began questioning God. "Why did all of these things happen on our seventh anniversary? Have we gotten outside Your will? Haven't we stretched our finances beyond the breaking point by going on television?"

In the stillness of Richard's anguish, the Lord spoke to him with incredible simplicity and crystal clarity. The Lord impressed on Richard that he was birthing the vision backward—breach. The Lord made it clear that He was serious about Richard birthing the vision the right way and about Richard producing only high-quality Christian films. Richard sensed that the Lord was warning him that the vomiting bout his sister experienced was a picture of how the Lord would reject his low-quality films, and the unfortunate death of the 10-year-old boy was a picture of how the Lord might allow Richard's ministry to die within 10 years.

Richard went before his congregation and repented publicly for failing to seek leadership within the Hollywood motion picture industry. He confessed to having made the following excuses: *I don't have the money. My congregation is not wealthy. I don't have Hollywood connections. I don't have enough experience—I'm just not qualified.* But somewhere in his heart he knew that someone with the Holy Spirit dwelling within should be capable of doing even better than the world does. He felt that he would have only one chance to test God's word. He declared that his studio had set a new goal—to lead Hollywood in technology.

SPIRIT-FILLED TECHNOLOGY

After three months of prayer, Richard realized he needed to develop a camera that would change the industry. He dreamed about a digital chip for a 70mm camera that was capable of shooting at a very fast speed. He knew that Hollywood epics such as *Lawrence of Arabia* were shot in 70mm film, but the film for that camera had become very expensive. As a result, filmmakers had changed to the smaller 35mm format.

Richard now knew what God wanted him to do. He went to Sony, JVC and other large camera manufacturers to discuss his idea for a digital chip for a 70mm camera. They laughed at him. They told him it was impossible to build a camera of this type. The technology did not exist.

Yet Richard knew God had spoken to him. He persevered and discovered a new kind of chip called CMOS. This chip was going to be used in future cell phone cameras, but it had never been used in a commercial video camera. He discovered that nine companies were exploring this technology. He finally got a positive answer from a Dutch company called the Fill Factory. The engineers there told him they had just made a technical breakthrough with multi-stamped chips. They said the 70mm chip was now feasible.

Vision Research, the camera manufacturer, told Richard that developing his new camera would cost $5 million. Richard reflected on this for a few moments before the Lord told him to give the camera idea to Vision Research. Their representatives were stunned at Richard's decision and asked if there was anything they could do for him. He said if they really wanted to help they could tithe to his congregation from the sales of the camera. They agreed to the tithing arrangement.

And so the Abraham camera came into existence, the first of many inventions Richard has created. In fact, Richard now has 14 patents on inventions the Lord has given him. The Holy Spirit has definitely worked through Richard's creativity—and glorified God in the process.

A CONFIRMATION—AND A VICTORY

In April 2006, I called Richard to ask him for an update. He told me he had just returned from the National Association of Broadcasters (NAB) meeting in Las Vegas, Nevada. The Abraham camera had been released at this meeting. Interestingly, at this same meeting, Sony announced that on July 15, 2006, they would release a 70mm projector. Without this projector, there would have been no way to show the 70mm output from the Abraham camera. Richard told me this validated that his idea for the camera was indeed from the Lord. He also told me that he is currently working on a biblical fantasy action film called *Gravity*.

Ideas are flowing that are exceedingly, abundantly beyond all that Richard could ask or think, because of the power that is at work within him. He submitted himself to the Lord's desires, and now mighty miracles are being worked through him.

God wants you to experience amazing things that are exceedingly, abundantly beyond all that you can ask or think. But He can't work through you unless you invite Him to do so. Pray a prayer today, asking Jesus to be Lord of your life and Master of your work. He'll do the rest.

CHAPTER 13

THE LORD'S SALESMAN

Do you sometimes feel like the Lone Ranger in your town? Do you think you might be the only Bible-believing Christian in your neighborhood? Even if you are, that's no excuse for staying on the sidelines. Because, after all, you are not alone—the Lord Jesus is always with you. Further, He calls you to be salt and light—to be His salesperson to the rest of the world.

And if you don't think sales skills are your strong point, no need to worry. I'm sure Randy Peck didn't either. A board-certified anesthesiologist, Randy wasn't into selling—and at the time of His calling, he wasn't even that "into" the Lord. Before his calling, he was self-centered, looking to retire early and enjoy "the good life." Because he had not built his life on Jesus the Rock and the Bible was not his source of truth, he nearly lost his wife, his children, his career and his retirement account—everything for which he had worked so hard. He was on the path to destruction, but he didn't know it because he couldn't recognize sin in his life.

But God began to work in Randy when, in February 2002, he began reading *The Greatest Salesman in the World*. That book, by Og Mandino, tells a fictitious story about the greatest salesman in the world, who is now retired. Before this salesman dies, he knows he will be given a sign to let him know who is to receive the 10 scrolls that have been the secret of his success. Ultimately, he gives them to the apostle Paul, the greatest salesman in the world for the Word of God.

Randy didn't just read the book once. From February until November 2000, he read each scroll 90 times per month (3 times a day for 30 days). That is something Randy had never done before. When Randy privately said, "Jesus, I commit my life to You" on January 6, 2001, he immediately knew his life purpose was to be a great salesman for the Word of God.

After making Jesus the Lord of his life, Randy began experiencing the abundant life Jesus promises, and miracles became a regular part of his life.

TRANSFORMING RANDY

Since committing his life to Christ, Randy's life-theme verse has been the Greatest Commandment: to love God and to love people (see Matt. 22:37-40). Randy says the best way to show our love for God—and people for that matter—is with our time. His daily theme verse has become Matthew 6:33: "But seek first the kingdom of God and His righteousness, and all these things shall be added to you." According to Randy, his life verse is useful for guiding every decision that he makes, and helps with long-term planning, while his daily verse is essential for shaping his daily habits, particularly how he starts each day and what he thinks about during the day. When Randy dies, he wants his tombstone to read, "He loved Jesus. He loved people." That is how he wants to live his life.

In early 2002, Randy wrote down his 10-year goal of gradually increasing his daily quiet time with the Lord from one hour to four hours. Randy knew God had called him to be a great salesman for God's Word, and that to accomplish his life purpose he would need to give God more time. Through a series of progressive steps of abiding, faith, obedience and miracles, Randy reached his "quiet time" goal in just two years.

In September 2003, God rewarded Randy with his highest paying job ever, at Giles Memorial Hospital—a place he hadn't even known existed. Randy now works two-and-a-half days a week in this spiritually vibrant hospital, located in one of the most beautiful areas of the country. His twice-weekly, four-hour drive between Culpeper and Giles County allows him to spend more quality quiet time with God. He listens to Bible recordings, sermons and other godly messages, all while driving through beautiful parts of Virginia.

Randy's new part-time work schedule allowed him to start a local Christian radio ministry in Culpeper. He also created a website for his

A Life of Blessing ministry (see www.alifeofblessing.org) and declared that his ministry would include all types of media, including television. He prayed for God to open the door to regular Christian programming on a local secular television station. Six months later, local television station owners asked him to start *A Life of Blessing* television show.

This television program has opened many new doors. For instance, Randy's February 19, 2005, interview of Virginia Morton about her Civil War novel, *Marching Through Culpeper,* created the opportunity to make Virginia's book into a full-length feature film.

The journey of faith for Randy continues. In early 2006, the Holy Spirit gave Randy the instruction that 2007 was to be a year of Jubilee for him—a year of rest. Randy asked God to provide clarification as to what that meant in regard to his anesthesia practice. After a few months, Randy received confirmation that he was not to practice anesthesia in 2007.

In obedience to the Holy Spirit, Randy is stepping away from his favorite anesthesia job. Uncommon obedience always results in uncommon blessings. God has placed a heavy burden on Randy's heart to see Virginia become the healthiest state in the nation by the end of 2007. Randy believes the three keys are to (1) transform marriages by multiplying Jack Serra's Marketplace and Marriage course, (2) ignite prayer evangelism in Culpeper that will rapidly spread across Virginia, and (3) transform healthcare systems using the three-pronged approach of TKC-InfoCare. He realizes that his work has just begun.

Randy is a person who exemplifies the truth that God can do exceedingly abundantly beyond all that we ask or think. He has had an enormous influence on my life and believes that by blessing me, he and his family will be blessed. He truly treats others the way he would want to be treated, and I pray that God rewards him for the blessing he is in the lives of so many people.

TRANSFORMING CULPEPER

A huge part of Randy's ministry has been all about transforming the city of Culpeper, the cradle of religious freedom for the world—it's where the

First Amendment to the U.S. Constitution was birthed. Randy Peck believes Culpeper is a detonator city—a small explosion that will ignite a larger explosion of renewal in our country.

In June 2005, when I arrived in Culpeper, Randy had arranged a series of meetings for me to speak about nation transformation through marketplace redemption. Randy's TV interview with me brought an understanding of the biblical principles of prayer evangelism to a wide array of people in Culpeper. As a result of those meetings and Randy's relationships in the city, a movement called Pray Culpeper has begun. Now, each Monday at noon, pastors, marketplace ministers and intercessors gather in the Culpeper Library to pray for their city. Their objective is to ignite an explosion of prayer evangelism in Culpeper that will rapidly spread across Virginia to transform the state by 2007.

In October 2005, Randy Peck, Michael Stay, Cindy Stay and Doug Wilcox, all from Culpeper, participated in the Harvest Evangelism Institute in Argentina called Nation Transformation Through Marketplace Redemption. Then, in November 2005, Randy represented Culpeper in Elk River, Minnesota, at the Harvest Evangelism meetings called Transformation USA. Three hundred people from 60 U.S. cities attended these meetings and committed to implement the Harvest Evangelism strategic path in their cities.

I went back to Culpeper in February 2006, this time with my whole family. We met Virginia Morton for the first time (read her story in chapter 14). She took us on a number of driving tours of the Civil War battlefields and historic antebellum homes in Culpeper. A few months later, she went to New York City, together with Randy Peck and Michael Stay, for Harvest's International Transformation Network meeting. While there, she received the instruction from the Holy Spirit to invite Josh Orndorff, a 17-year-old high school student from Culpeper, to go to Argentina the following summer for Harvest Evangelism's summer mission trip.

Josh is the son of Randy Orndorff, senior pastor of Culpeper's United Methodist Church. An anonymous group of donors raised funds so that Josh could participate in the Harvest Evangelism Overseas Training Mission in Argentina from June 30 to July 10, 2006. When Josh arrived in Argentina, I introduced him to Daniel Chinen, from Honolulu, and the two spent quite a bit of time together during the two weeks in Argentina. Daniel told Josh about how he had seen God transform his high school through prayer evangelism.

When Josh returned home, he made a presentation at Pray Culpeper's Monday noon meeting. Josh told the participants that God had led him to Argentina so that he could bring the Lord's transformation to Culpeper. Many of the pastors in that meeting, including his own father, invited Josh to preach at their churches.

TRANSFORMING VIRGINIA

But the transformation of Culpeper is just the beginning. It is Randy's sincere belief that Culpeper is a detonator for the transformation of Virginia. Virginia is a very important state. During 2007, the attention of America and the world turned toward Virginia when the four-hundredth anniversary of the city of Jamestown was celebrated. Jamestown is the birthplace of English-speaking America.

I think it is of particular interest that Virginia was home to three of the first four U.S. presidents: George Washington ("father of our nation"), Thomas Jefferson (primary author of the Declaration of Independence) and James Madison (primary author of the U.S. Constitution). Further, when Dutch Sheets and Chuck Pierce spoke at the 50 State Tour gathering in Virginia in March 2004, it was declared that Virginia is the "covenant root state." They declared that Virginia has a governmental anointing and assignment. And certainly Randy Peck would agree with that assessment.

If you think such transformations are outside your sphere of influence, think again. God wants to use you for just such work in your city, in your state. But first you have to be transformed as well. You must complete your "sales" training in the Lord's Word. Take time daily to seek Him first, and find in His Word the grace to love God and neighbor.

CHAPTER 14

LEAP OF FAITH

Most marketplace miracles shared so far are about businesspeople working within their "native" sphere of influence. But sometimes God takes us out of our comfort zone and into a new career. He often desires to show us something amazing about ourselves that we never knew—and in the process bring about miracles we never could have envisioned.

Such was the case with Virginia Morton, who not so long ago was an empty-nester whose spouse, Roger, was working at his dream job while she found herself feeling useless and wondering what meaningful endeavor she should pursue. Meanwhile, she was striving to promote local tourism and to preserve Culpeper, Virginia's Civil War battlefields. About that same time, Virginia and her family took a Southern vacation, which included a tour of Savannah, Georgia. During that visit, she witnessed the enormous impact the book *Midnight in the Garden of Good and Evil* was having on Savannah's tourism.

She concluded, with a little prodding from God, that Culpeper needed a book. It would have to be an entertaining and educational historical fiction book that would transport readers back in time and make them part of the action. As a Richmond native, she had always loved Civil War history, but she had never before had the time to research it thoroughly. Now that she had time, she immersed herself in the project, believing that a successful book would help the local economy through tourism, and convince residents their history must be preserved. This would be her opportunity to give back to the community.

But Virginia had another goal in writing her book: She saw this as an opportunity to weave Christianity into a riveting story. While she wanted her book to be historically accurate, she wanted a love story whose characters were inspiring Christians. A tall order, but she moved ahead in faith.

Now, God knew Virginia needed this all-consuming intellectual challenge to pull her out of the "empty-nest syndrome," but family and friends concluded that this math major had lost her mind: Virginia had no writing experience. But that fact had not escaped her, so she planned to do the research, come up with a story and convince a real writer to take it from there.

A few years passed, and her efforts to find a "real writer" were unsuccessful. Still, the story in her head wouldn't go away. In fact, like Kevin Costner in the popular movie *Field of Dreams*, a voice in her head kept whispering, "Write it and they will come." God had her cornered, and she knew the book would never be written unless she wrote it herself.

Yet, here she encountered another roadblock: She didn't have any computer experience. So God told her to put the story on paper and not to worry about each word or punctuation mark. She could go back and edit later. For 18 months, Virginia wrote away, spending her days and nights in the hearts and minds of her characters.

And then it was finished. She wondered what she should do next. She hadn't let anyone else read it. She knew that one negative word would cause her to give up. But here again, God intervened. He sent her the right person at the right time: A friend in Richmond reluctantly agreed to read her gargantuan manuscript. When her friend finished the book, she convinced Virginia she had to publish it. Her friend said she had enjoyed Virginia's book more than she had enjoyed *Gone with the Wind*.

Since publishers rarely accept long books by unknown authors, Virginia concluded she would have to self-publish the book. This meant she would have to supply the funds to have the book printed; she would have to take the financial risk that enough people would buy the book to cover those costs. She couldn't afford to pay someone to format the book for printing, and the technology was way over her head. But then, she met a friend on the street who suggested several ladies who could format, do the cover artwork and design the cover. These heaven-sent angels got her through the ordeal, and the book was finally printed.

A SUCCESS STORY!

The first 500 copies of *Marching Through Culpeper* sold in less than a month. Women and men alike loved the book. And Virginia was off and running! Despite being a total introvert, she learned to promote the book through speaking engagements and conducting tours. Never did she dream that God would open so many doors. Positive reviews poured in, and soon she had gained a reputation in the male-dominated Civil War community.

Civil War Interactive's review said, "Margaret Mitchell, John Jakes, and Michael Shaara, move over and make room for Virginia Morton. Her gift for weaving fact and fiction has given us a haunting master-piece that depicts the true South better than *Gone with the Wind* and provides rich material for a dynamite movie."[1]

Southern Partisan magazine added, "Best of all, Morton offers char-acters whose steadfastness, faith, and courage make them models of emulation."[2]

Her one-woman tourism campaign also included conducting tours of the town and the Brandy Station and Cedar Mountain battlefields. *She had written it and they were coming!* More than 4,500 people have enjoyed her tours, which have been featured on Richmond and nation-al public television. Her speaking engagements have taken her from New Jersey to Florida. She drives thousand of miles yearly, with God as her copilot. HistoryAmerica Tours honored her by asking her to be the first lady historian to conduct a solo tour aboard the *American Queen*. This tour, called Petticoat Power: Women in the Civil War, journeyed from New Orleans to Vicksburg in 2004. She conducted a second tour, Love and War: Great Love Stories of the Civil War, in September 2006.

Enthusiastic word-of-mouth publicity has propelled sales. Her readers formed the "Fans of Marching through Culpeper" and held a celebration of 5,000 books sold, with J. E. B. Stuart IV, the great grand-son of one of the Confederate Army's most famous generals, serving as master of ceremonies.

Through events she has organized as well as her tours, and by donat-ing book proceeds, she has generated $15,500 in income for historic and preservation organizations. Yet she would tell you that the greatest blessing to come from her book has been encountering so many wonderful folks on her literary journey and making new friends in the process.

Virginia began praying for ways to gain national publicity in order to expand the market for her book. Dr. Randy Peck invited her to tell her story on his Christian television program. She was nervous and apprehensive about baring her soul to the public, but she asked her church study group to pray for her. Giving God the glory was an exhilarating experience that has given her the courage to serve Christ by sharing her faith more openly.

She continued praying about ways to expand the market for her book. Then she heard God tell her to go to *The 700 Club*. She had sent Pat Robertson a copy of the book several years earlier and although she got a thank-you note, she had no way of knowing whether he'd actually read it. She decided to attend a taping of the show in early August 2005, though she wasn't sure why.

Prior to going into the studio, she bought one of Robertson's books, and the hostess told her she would seat her up front so that she could get him to sign her book. At the conclusion of the program, she approached Robertson before he could leave the studio. While he was signing her book, she introduced herself and told him she had sent him a copy of *Marching Through Culpeper*. He looked up and smiled and told her he had read the book and he had thoroughly enjoyed it—especially the meticulous research. Her spirit soared, but she was so tongue-tied she could barely respond.

She then took a tour of the CBN facility and saw the round worship area in the heart of the building. A large, round, hollow pedestal stands in the center and prayer requests from visitors are written and placed inside. She left her written request for *Marching Through Culpeper* to be made into a movie, and the CBN staff has prayed over the request daily.

Upon returning home, she decided to write to Pat Robertson and ask him for a written endorsement of the book. Before mailing the letter, she laid her hands on it and prayed fervently that it would reach him and that he would respond. Three weeks passed and she heard nothing. However, she continued to pray. She felt the letter had been misplaced and asked God to get it to Robertson's desk. Another week passed and then another. She knew God had sent her to *The 700 Club* to learn that Pat had read her book, so she couldn't understand why God would disappoint her now. Finally, after five weeks, the letter came! Pat's secretary apologized for the delay and said it had taken three weeks for the letter to reach them. God had answered her prayers.

Here is what Pat wrote: "I thoroughly enjoyed *Marching Through Culpeper*. This meticulously researched novel upholds Christian values and offers inspiring Christian characters—both real and fictional."

THE MOVIE

I met Virginia Morton on my first visit to Culpeper, Virginia, in June 2005. Randy Peck and I were walking through several buildings in downtown Culpeper when we came upon Virginia and her husband, Roger, who were entering a restaurant to have dinner. Randy introduced me and told them about our interest in transforming Culpeper and the state of Virginia.

Shortly thereafter, in July 2005, I was in Mar del Plata, Argentina, for the Harvest Evangelism Overseas Training Mission (OTM). I was one of several speakers who spoke about nation transformation through marketplace redemption. When I returned to my seat, Pastor Jorge Viamonte, vice president of the pastors' council, told me the Lord had told him I would make a successful movie that will transform many for Christ. This was the first time I had ever heard anything from the Lord about making a motion picture. I asked the pastor if he knew that I have a son, Derek, who is a screenwriter in Hollywood. He did not.

I returned to Culpeper in late August. During this visit, Virginia Morton gave me a copy of her book, *Marching Through Culpeper*, with the idea that I would pass it on to my son to see if he would be interested in reading it and writing a motion picture screenplay based on it.

"You are not going to believe this," I told her. "I just received a word from a pastor in Argentina that I would make a successful motion picture that will transform many for Christ! I believe that this word relates to the motion picture that will be made from your book."

I took off the whole month of December, so I had ample time to read *Marching Through Culpeper*. As I read the book, I was struck by how the Southern perspective contained in the book is dramatically different from what I was taught in Northern schools. Could it be that there is still a huge rift between the South and the North? Could it be that this love story between a Southern lady and a Union soldier might be a catalyst to bring reconciliation between Southerners and Northerners and between European Americans and African Americans?

I discussed this with Virginia, and she said the movie would also demonstrate that God strengthens those who love Him so that they can face any adversity. In addition, she felt the movie would show the importance of character: Even though the Southerners in the story lost their material possessions, they still maintained their character, which sprang from their faith in God through Christ. The movie would also show that God answers prayers—and that passion can be controlled and sex reserved for the sanctity of marriage.

The next phase in the development of the movie came during our family's trip to Culpeper in February 2006. Rachel and I and our two adult children, Derek and Arleigh, spent four days there, and I spoke to several pastors about my vision for transformation. I also met with Virginia Morton to brainstorm about the movie with Randy Peck and Michael Stay, as well as the rest of my family. We beseeched the creative, omnipotent God of the universe to produce and direct a box-office smash hit—*Marching Through Culpeper*. The air crackled with excitement and lightning-fast ideas.

We decided to raise funds from Christian investors to allow my son, Derek, to write the screenplay. After we raise the money, marketing efforts will begin, using our slogan, "Oh, do we have a story to tell." We know God has answers where we have questions. He will connect us with the right people at the right time. The question is not *if* the movie will be made, but *when*.

During that meeting, Virginia shared some Internet research she had located. Among a number of other facts, Virginia told us that in most cases when a movie is successful, it's because a woman took an interest in it and worked diligently to see it made. (As soon as she said that, I thought of Suzy Crowell who, just a month earlier, had been elected to the Harvest Evangelism board—but more on that later.) As providence would have it, Virginia felt the Lord leading her to attend the Harvest Evangelism event being held in New York City in April 2006. Even though she did not have a roommate and wasn't sure how she would get there, she trusted the Lord, and He worked out all the details. At the conference, when we prayed in small groups, Virginia prayed with Ken and Carrie Beaudry, prayer warriors from Elk River, Minnesota (see chapter 7). After they prayed, Ken told Virginia he had a vision of her book on a pedestal, with Jesus standing beside it. She was elated to hear of this vision and began to ponder how to interpret it.

Then Bob, a gentleman from Austin, Texas, introduced himself to Virginia and said he had some experience in the film business. As they talked, he told Virginia the Lord was pleased with everything she had done, but she needed to rest for the next few months. Virginia knew that God was using Bob to speak into her life. She sent him her book, and since then he has become a spiritual mentor and prayer warrior via email.

Soon after the conference, another important meeting took place. I had emailed Suzy Crowell and told her what I had in mind regarding making Virginia's book into a movie. She replied, "I have just the person for you." She said she had served on a committee with a friend from the television industry to promote the Billy Graham Crusade in the Rose Bowl. On May 1, 2006, Suzy hosted a meeting at the Pasadena Country Club with that friend and her husband (both prominent Christians in the entertainment world), Virginia Morton, my son, Derek, and me.

We received two critical suggestions as an outcome from that meeting—that we make the book into a 13-part miniseries that could be aired over HBO, and that we prepare a convincing document that contrasts Virginia's book with *Cold Mountain*. While we had not previously considered the series concept and after considerable research feel a six-hour series is probably more feasible and flexible, we have gone ahead with preparing the document that compares *Cold Mountain* and *Marching Through Culpeper*. We are now having weekly one-hour conference calls with people all over the United States to pray for this book to be made into a television miniseries. Also, my son, Derek, has begun to work on a part-time basis on the screenplay for the premiere episode of the miniseries. I am also reading many other books to understand the nature of the issues that led to the American Civil War.

EXPECTING EVEN GREATER THINGS

Virginia marvels that since she turned the book promotion and movie production completely over to God and gave Him the glory for every achievement, miracles have been happening regularly. She has been praying and receiving messages from the Lord that indicate the pedestal in Ken Beaudry's vision is the pedestal at CBN where she left her prayer request.

Amazingly, people who were strangers several months ago are now bonding together to make all of their dreams—and God's vision—a reality.

And where is that depressed housewife with empty-nest syndrome? God has taken her life in an unexpected direction and showered her with the blessings of countless new friends, challenging opportunities, self-confidence and unwavering faith. Virginia says she awakens each morning tingling with excitement and anticipation of the extraordinary miracles our awesome God is orchestrating.

Doesn't that sound like a great way to wake up every morning? You can, too. It's all about making yourself available to the Lord, praying for His guidance and waiting for His leading. And while there may not be a book or a movie deal in your future, there's certainly an exciting adventure in store.

Notes
1. Mary Bogen-Kuczek, review of *Marching Through Culpeper*, Civil War Interactive, June 2003. http://www.civilwarinteractive.com (accessed November 2007).
2. Randall K. Ivey, review of *Marching Through Culpeper, Southern Partisan* magazine, Columbia, South Carolina, December 2004.

CHAPTER 15

INVESTING IN THE LORD'S WORK

As you seek to enter into God's will for your work life, you need to know how to listen for His voice. You can't advance Kingdom priorities without knowing what your marching orders are. So learn to be still and wait on His word. Then when He speaks, you'll recognize Him—and do His will.

I am very well acquainted with a husband and wife who do hear God's voice—and heed His words: Dave and Gayle Garven. They live their lives in obedience to Him and run their business according to His plan. He, in turn, blesses their work—and all those who have contact with them.

Once on my way to the airport, I asked the Lord for a new car—my car had quit, again. It was time for a replacement. When I arrived at my destination, the Garvens picked me up. As we drove to their home, Dave said the Lord had told them that they were to give me their car! What an amazing moment that was! I then shared with them that I had prayed just six hours earlier for the Lord to give us a new car, and here was the answer to that prayer.

BUSINESS CHALLENGES

Dave and I first met at a church function and agreed to attend an upcoming men's retreat together. Even though that was years ago, I can still remember riding in Dave's car on the way to the men's retreat; we shared our life stories. At the time, Dave owned an independent sales organization that had an exclusive agreement to represent a well-known consumer products company. Dave told me this company had just terminated all its independent agents, so he faced an uncertain future. He had been unemployed before, and he was concerned that he was heading back into another period of unemployment—along with the depression and self-doubt that accompanied it.

Many of the independent agents had hired lawyers and filed a class-action lawsuit against this consumer products company. Dave anguished in trying to decide whether to join the lawsuit. His human logic said yes, but there was an uncertainty in his spirit that made him cautious. Dave prayed for wisdom and did not feel led to join the class-action lawsuit. The group that filed the lawsuit won that case, but they were tied up in the appellate process for many years.

Shortly after Dave decided against joining the suit, he and Jim Lohmiller, another Christian independent agent who had been terminated, prayed for wisdom about what to do. They filed their own lawsuit, independent from the other lawsuit, which was then under appeal. The Lord instructed them to pray with the faith of a mustard seed for a positive result. Amazingly, in contrast with the first lawsuit that went to court and lingered, the defendant company offered an out-of-court settlement on Dave and Jim Lohmiller's lawsuit—a settlement that was 25 percent higher than their own estimate of the maximum amount that might be awarded! Dave had heard the Lord's voice and, because he was obedient, God had performed an extraordinary miracle for him.

But now what should Dave do? He searched for a job as a manufacturer's representative. He found a few clients, but those did not generate enough income to pay his bills. One of his clients, though, was a tarp-importing company with headquarters in Seattle. Dave developed a very good relationship with the owner, Don Johnson, who taught him the business. Dave decided that working for Don was not the career path for him. After much prayer, Dave asked Don if he would mind if Dave started his own tarp-importing company. At first Don was opposed to the idea, but later changed his mind and helped Dave get started. Dave and Don remain good friends.

CSM QUALITY TARPS

Dave founded CSM Quality Tarps as a Kingdom company, dedicated to the Lord. Since Dave had experienced God's favor in the lawsuit settlement, he wanted his new company to demonstrate his gratitude. He declared that Jesus Christ would be this company's CEO. A good portion of the profits would be used to expand God's kingdom.

Once Dave located a South Korean company to manufacture the tarps in a Chinese facility, he had to establish a line of credit to implement international letters of credit as the foundation of the business relationship with the South Korean firm. Dave used his lawsuit settlement to finance the company. Later, he was able to use the inventory to finance the tarp purchases. When Dave ordered tarps, they were shipped to a warehouse facility that kept the inventory records and fulfilled purchase orders. Dave set up a computer system and a fax machine in his house, and he obtained mailing lists and faxed inquiries to the purchasing agents of companies that regularly bought tarps. He asked the agents to consider purchasing their tarps from CSM Quality Tarps.

Orders started coming in, and the warehouse filled the orders. Many adjustments had to be implemented in order to fine-tune the company's operations. For instance, Dave went through several warehouse companies before he found one that met his specifications.

Dave did very little marketing and did not make long, detailed marketing plans. Instead, contrary to Dave's previous business experience, he depended on God to provide customers. Dave has told me repeatedly, "If God wants this business to be successful, He will provide the customers—and He has!"

GULL LAKE

Four years after Dave started CSM Quality Tarps, he and Gayle considered buying a lakefront home on Gull Lake, near Brainerd, Minnesota. They wanted to know if God wanted them to purchase this property. They went for a walk together on Paul Bunyan Trail in another part of the city of Brainerd. They asked God for wisdom, according to James 1:5: "If any of you lacks wisdom, let him ask of God, who gives to all liberally and without reproach, and it will be given to him."

They learned that a woman might bid on the property, so Dave and Gayle agreed that if the woman bought the property, then that was

God's answer. On the other hand, when the woman declined to purchase the property, they saw that as their sign to purchase it. God led them to make an offer on the home and on the lot next door. The purchase of the second lot proved to be an extremely good decision, and was definitely an example of God giving them wisdom liberally.

In the summer of 2003, the Garvens sold their home on Gull Lake. The home sold for nearly double what they had paid for it in 1997. But they did not sell the adjacent lot. Instead, they built a new home on that lot. Their new home on Gull Lake has the same waterfront they loved so well in their first home.

PERSEVERING THROUGH LOSS

Yet embracing God's will has not always been an easy, joyful task. At times, what the Lord has asked of the Garvens has cost them dearly. And they have had to walk in faith, trusting the Lord.

On December 27, 1997, Dave called me on the phone and asked me to pray because his son Jeffrey was missing. At the time, Jeffrey was a sophomore at Bethel College in Arden Hills, Minnesota. While in a neighboring town with friends, Jeff and his friend Matt went for a snowmobile ride. But after that, their friends couldn't find them; both young men were missing. Matt's father called Dave and Gayle at 3 A.M. and suggested they return to Shorewood. He told them the county sheriff was forming a search party to go out on Lake Minnetonka, and they were going to send divers to look under the lake ice.

The divers found Jeffrey's body under the ice late the next afternoon.

Needless to say Dave and Gayle were devastated. Their son's death seemed an insurmountable tragedy. Through the love and grace of God, however, Dave and Gayle persevered through this horrible experience. They still walk in faith and obedience to the Lord.

A SEASON OF GROWTH

In 2005 and 2006, major hurricanes hit Florida and the Gulf Coast, including Katrina's infamous blow to New Orleans. After these hurricanes did their destructive work, people began ordering tarps to cover all sorts of things that needed to be protected. Dave could hardly keep up with the demand. While these hurricanes were tragedies for most Americans, they provided extraordinary opportunities for Dave's business. Dave sold so many tarps during these crises that CSM Quality Tarps came to the attention of the government, which asked him to become a regular government supplier.

In December 2005, FEMA requested the first of three price quotes for special tarps and packaging to conform to strict FEMA specifications—there are serious consequences for contractors who do not produce according to those specifications. None of the first three quotations produced a sale. In July 2006, FEMA requested a fourth price quote. Reluctantly, Dave had gone through the motions of providing a bid, thinking this would be just another dead-end. Working through a special General Services Administration (GSA) sales agent in Boston, Dave learned that FEMA was very serious about his bid.

However, according to FEMA specifications, all products had to be manufactured in a U.S.-approved trading-partner country. This would be a serious problem for Dave because, even though most of his importing relationships are with South Koreans, their tarps are manufactured in China. In fact, most of the tarps produced in the world are produced in China, Vietnam and other countries that do not comply with U.S. trade policies. The only option would be for Dave to purchase the tarps from South Korean factories.

Then Dave learned that South Korea has very little capacity to produce tarps. Nearly everything produced in that country is for its own domestic use. After a number of days of negotiations with the South Korean factories, it appeared that CSM would definitely not be able to meet its quote. Meanwhile, the sales agent sent an order to CSM for 200,000 each of the special-order products for FEMA.

Dave told the sales agent he would try one last desperate appeal to the South Korean manufacturers. He suggested the sales agent pray for a miracle. The agent said, "As a matter of fact, I am going to church on Sunday." The following Monday, Dave received some potentially positive news, but still did not have a final deal. He reported this to the sales agent, who said, "I guess I must have wasted my time going to church on Sunday."

Then on Tuesday, Dave received emails from two South Korean manufacturers, saying they had found new subcontractors and materials and would be able to produce the quantities required according to the FEMA specifications. They would also meet FEMA delivery schedules, and all parties would be able to make a reasonable profit. Dave told the sales agent, "See, our prayers were not wasted."

Throughout this process, Dave was able to witness to the sales agent and also to his South Korean contacts. And, as it turned out, the general manager of one of the South Korean factories is a Christian. Dave has built a solid relationship with this manager, who told Dave that one of the subcontractors' workforce was made up entirely of Christians, and they would be doing a majority of the manufacturing.

With the FEMA contract now signed, CSM's business will double in the coming year, increasing the amount of God's gifts that can be reinvested in His kingdom. Truly the Lord has rewarded this good and faithful servant.

Are you ready to walk in the blessings God has prepared for you, and your business or workplace? Then listen for His voice, heed His Word and invest in the Kingdom. Trust me, the return will be out of this world!

CHAPTER 16

DOING BUSINESS FOR THE MASTER

How many of us consider that we are doing business for the Lord, working as His agents? As Christians we must allow our faith to inform our work. We can't be just Sunday Christians—that's not what God asks us to be. What He asks us to be is good stewards—faithful stewards who are investing wisely, aware that they are doing business for the Master.

Ryan and Pam Kubat are just such stewards. God gave them a little—and they were faithful servants, investing wisely. Now God has increased their measure; they run a very successful business.

In 1996, Ryan and Pam were, like many couples, struggling financially—they were looking for a way to supplement their income. Pam had a full-time job as a sales and marketing manager for a jewelry manufacturer. Ryan had part-time self-employment mowing lawns in the summer and blowing snow in the winter. Ryan was also taking care of their three preschool-aged children at home.

The church they were attending gave them $50, inspired by the parable of the ten minas. Along with the money, Pam and Ryan were given instructions to put the money to work for the Master, just as the servants in the parable were:

> Now as they heard these things, He spoke another parable, because He was near Jerusalem and because they thought the kingdom of God would appear immediately. Therefore He said: "A certain nobleman went into a far country to receive for himself a kingdom and to return. So he called ten of his servants, delivered to them ten minas, and said to them, 'Do business till I come.' But his citizens hated him, and sent a delegation after

him, saying, 'We will not have this man to reign over us.' And so it was that when he returned, having received the kingdom, he then commanded these servants, to whom he had given the money, to be called to him, that he might know how much every man had gained by trading. Then came the first, saying, 'Master, your mina has earned ten minas.' And he said to him, 'Well done, good servant; because you were faithful in a very little, have authority over ten cities.' And the second came, saying, 'Master, your mina has earned five minas.' Likewise he said to him, 'You also be over five cities.' Then another came, saying, 'Master, here is your mina, which I have kept put away in a handkerchief. For I feared you, because you are an austere man. You collect what you did not deposit, and reap what you did not sow.' And he said to him, 'Out of your own mouth I will judge you, you wicked servant. You knew that I was an austere man, collecting what I did not deposit and reaping what I did not sow. Why then did you not put my money in the bank, that at my coming I might have collected it with interest?' And he said to those who stood by, 'Take the mina from him, and give it to him who has ten minas. (But they said to him, 'Master, he has ten minas.') For I say to you, that to everyone who has will be given; and from him who does not have, even what he has will be taken away from him. But bring here those enemies of mine, who did not want me to reign over them, and slay them before me'" (Luke 19:11-27).

They had prayed previously about a business they thought they could start, and now they considered that opportunity in light of verse 13: "Do business till I come." In essence, the Kubats aligned their thinking with this Scripture and committed to "do business for the Master." Once they aligned their thinking with the Lord's thinking, they knew they could expect some level of multiplication of the $50 given to them. They knew that the Lord's thoughts were higher than their thoughts. They understood that He is able to do exceedingly, abundantly above what they could think. So they set their minds on things above and not on things of this earth (see Eph. 3:20).

GETTING STARTED

Pam grew up working in a family business. Then she worked 12 years in accounting before becoming a sales and marketing manager for a jewelry manufacturer, where she had her first exposure to the promotional products industry. She saw great potential for this type of business, so she and Ryan decided to launch their own promotional products distributing company, assisting businesses in their marketing efforts through imprinted products. They came up with the business name "Corporate Recognition." Once they had their letterhead and business cards printed, they were ready to go!

Nothing happened for a while. Pam and Ryan now look back at that time as the birthing process—it was a full nine months later, in April 1997, before the business actually got off the ground.

The first order came from Pam's sister, who worked as a marketing director for a Nevada shopping center. This order ignited the sales process. The shopping center's corporate offices in Chicago soon noticed Pam and Ryan's excellent work. That led to more orders— this time coming from the Chicago office's corporate events department—which was a significant step in moving them closer to becoming a viable business.

During 1997 and 1998, the business continued to grow, though both Ryan and Pam were still working part time. Ryan made sales calls and gathered information from vendors during the day. Pam worked evenings, doing research and handling the accounting.

In January 1999, because of poor working conditions and lack of affordable insurance, Pam quit her full-time sales job with an industry supplier. The Lord was moving her into position to accelerate Corporate Recognition's growth. She took a new job working for an accounts payable department. This new job allowed her more time to be home with her family.

In the summer of 1999, Pam learned that her new employer was going to move the accounting department to Raleigh, North Carolina. She wondered whether this was the Lord moving her into Corporate Recognition on a full-time basis.

Ryan and Pam prayed and waited upon the Lord. They got their confirmation in October, when one of their clients placed a large order and asked Corporate Recognition to assist them in preparing for their upcoming conference. A second confirmation came in the form of a severance-pay package from Pam's former employer. These two factors assured the Kubats that God was telling them to move forward with their business on a full-time basis.

During this time, they expanded and upgraded their home office. They added sheetrock, carpeting and storage cabinets to their corner nook, cement-floor-and-block-wall office in the basement. They even obtained a second desk and a computer. However, by July 2000, the "joy" of being entrepreneurs had begun to turn into sadness. The costs of the filing cabinets, computer and traveling had outpaced their income, and they had run out of money.

By mid-August, Pam's dad, Dean, came for a two-week visit. Dean had owned his own business for 30 years. During that time he had also worked as a hardware salesman. He was full of plans and ideas to help Pam and Ryan find clients. He re-energized Ryan and Pam by teaching them his sales techniques. He chauffeured Ryan and Pam around south-central Minnesota, demonstrating his methods. They were able to build on the local contacts they made during that time. They also became a preferred vendor for their Chicago client, which meant they were able to work with all of the company's offices around the country.

In the spring of 2002, a college student called. She was looking for a business that would take her on as a summer marketing intern and had picked Corporate Recognition because, alphabetically, their name put them at the top of the phone book list. This was another of God's divine provisions for their company. They'd been thinking about hosting a client show in Owatonna in an effort to expose more local businesses to their company and product line, but they were unsure if they would have enough time to prepare for such an undertaking. That's when the intern came on the scene, and they realized that she could be God's provision for their show.

The preparation for the show took about six weeks, but with the intern's assistance they successfully pulled off their first annual client show. It was a huge success! Their clients now eagerly anticipate the event each year. The first show demonstrated that they could use part-time help to make their business more efficient, so they hired a regular part-time employee.

Next, the Lord showed them that the company's growth had been inhibited by the constraints on Pam's time. They needed more staff. But how would they find someone willing to work in their home? Where would they find a person who was teachable, had business savvy and was trustworthy? Talk about a tall order! After more prayer, God led Pam to ask the company's top local client for a referral. In October 2003, they hired the client's referral—their first full-time employee.

About this time, their house started feeling very cramped. Ryan and Pam had a 1,080-square-foot rambler, plus a basement. Their company was occupying about 600 square feet in the basement. They had three computers, three desks, two printers and ten filing cabinets. In addition to all that equipment, they had one part-time and three full-time employees. Their workspace was very limited, and it was challenging to keep their home presentable for friends, employees and customers. They knew it was time to move the business outside their home. God wanted them to step outside their comfort zones again.

In 2004, the Lord showed Ryan a building in one of the best locations in downtown Owatonna. The building had been vacant for six months, but at that time the owner wasn't willing to rent it out. He wanted to sell the building, but the price was very high. So Ryan and Pam waited on the Lord. A year later, in August 2005, the building was still vacant, with no offers to purchase it. Ryan talked to the owner again, and this time he agreed to rent it to them. Ryan surprised Pam when he called and said he'd signed a lease—they could move in 10 days.

God brought everything together perfectly. They wanted to replace the carpeting; a local carpet-layer had just the right color and type of carpet, and had time to install it. On the day they were supposed to move in and set up the computers, phones and other equipment, they had a trade-show to attend. While Pam and Francie, one of their full-time employees, were at the trade-show, Ryan coordinated the move. He had everything moved in and up and running by 10 A.M. the next day.

MORE THAN A BUSINESS

If you think again about the parable of the minas, you'll remember that as the servant was faithful with his master's goods, the master increased his authority. In the same way, as Corporate Recognition grows, the Kubats have increased spiritual authority in Owatonna, Minnesota. They are committed to transforming their city, but their increased spiritual authority could actually cover multiple cities. We have often heard people say that a particular ministry is "good soil"—Corporate Recognition certainly is!

What does this mean for you? That as you seek God's will for your job or business, you consider yourself to be "in business" for the Lord. Follow Ryan and Pam's example: Align your thoughts with God's thoughts. You will see yourself lifted up by His grace—He will take you from where you are today to where He wants you to be.

CHAPTER 17

FINDING CHRIST IN PRISON

We don't usually associate the light of Christ with the darkness of a prison cell. But remember, God is bigger than our limited ideas—and He can work wonders anywhere, even a prison yard. More than that, though, He desires to save sinners, not only the righteous. He desires His followers to be willing to go places where they can find and reach those sinners.

Pastor Juan Zuccarelli is a faithful believer who has answered the call to save lost prisoners—and to transform prisons. Twenty years ago, he heard the Lord say that he was to minister in the infamous Olmos Prison in La Plata, Argentina. The Lord told Juan to apply to be a prison guard. Juan obeyed, but he was told it would take eight months to process his application. He thought to himself, *Maybe in eight months God will forget about it*. To Juan's surprise, it only took eight days for him to be approved as a guard at Olmos.

Once inside, he began working to obtain permission to hold an evangelistic crusade for the inmates. When he finally got permission and held his first crusade, 100 of the 300 inmates gave their hearts to the Lord during that service. Now he had a dilemma: What was he supposed to do with these new Christians? Juan decided to plant a church, with elders, a pastor and members. For more than 20 years, Juan has held evangelistic crusades, and today over 60 percent of the current inmate population are born-again believers in Jesus Christ. Also, as Christian inmates have been transferred to other prisons, Juan worked with those inmates to plant a congregation in each of the 40 prisons within the province of Buenos Aires. It is important to note again that these are not ministries from the outside to the inside of each prison—each prison is being transformed by Christian inmates from the inside out.[1]

In 2003, the governor of the province of Buenos Aires came to Juan and said that for 20 years he had watched the changes at Olmos. The governor exclaimed, "Christ is the only thing that works." He meant that, after their release, most non-Christian inmates soon re-offend and end up back in prison. However, Christian inmates released from Olmos contribute positively to society. The recidivism rate among the Christian inmates of Olmos is less than 5 percent, compared to Argentina's general-inmate-population recidivism rate of approximately 80 percent.

The governor asked Juan if he would be willing to operate a completely Christian prison. Juan agreed. The governor turned over Prison Number 25 to Juan and suggested that Juan rename it "Christ the Only Hope Prison." This would be a low-security prison, with a Christian warden, Christian guards and Christian inmates. The inmates would not have bars on the doors of their sleeping quarters, and they would have great freedom to move around the prison. Their days would be filled with Bible study, worship and prayer. They would also participate in career-development training and would have access to hand tools that would never have otherwise been allowed in a maximum-security prison.

At first, around 270 of the best Christian inmates from Olmos were transferred across the street to Christ the Only Hope Prison. Juan told the governor that he had to have a Christian warden for the prison—he asked for Daniel Tajeda, a Christian who was sub-director of another prison. According to the government, Tajeda was not ready to be promoted. Nevertheless, Juan stood his ground and Tajeda became the warden.

Then in 2005, something quite unexpected happened. Ariel, one of the most notorious mass-murderers in all of Argentina, was captured and sentenced to prison. The warden who had responsibility for Ariel was concerned that Ariel's crimes were so horrendous and so well publicized that the other inmates would kill him. For this reason, Ariel was kept in solitary confinement. That warden contacted Daniel Tajeda, the warden at Christ the Only Hope and asked him if he would be willing to accept Ariel. Warden Tajeda agreed.

In July 2005, I was in that prison with a Harvest Evangelism group, and Warden Tajeda introduced us to Ariel. He explained that Ariel lives at Prison Number 29, but that every other day armed guards bring him to Christ the Only Hope, arriving in handcuffs and shackles. As he stood before us, however, he had no handcuffs and no shackles—he was treated like every other inmate there. Ariel has accepted Jesus Christ as his Lord and Savior—his life has changed dramatically!

The word is out in the Argentine prison system that Christ the Only Hope will accept the most hardened of cases. Warden Tajeda also introduced us to Hector, who has a history similar to Ariel's. I don't want to sensationalize Hector's crimes, but he was among the worst of the worst (Hector's story is now featured on the *Transformation of the Marketplace* DVD, produced by Harvest Evangelism). Yet now, Ariel and Hector are both extraordinary miracles, living abundant lives in Christ.

LINO LAKES PRISON

During one of my early visits to Olmos Prison, Juan Zuccarelli called me to the front of the service. I knelt as he prayed. He prayed that I would take the anointing for prison transformation back to my own country, beginning in my own home town. I eventually met with a local prison ministry in Minnesota, and they arranged for me to minister at Lino Lakes Prison, just north of St. Paul, Minnesota.

Since then, for six years, I have been leading a Bible study at Lino Lakes each Monday evening. This prison ministry has become one of the most important forms of ministry in my life. I am teaching these men about prayer evangelism, and they have become marketplace ministers in Lino Lakes Prison. I have laid hands on them and prayed for God to give them His heart of compassion for unbelievers.

On a later visit to Olmos Prison, I had a chance to address the inmates. I told them that Pastor Juan Zuccarelli had prayed for me at Olmos, and that I had carried his vision and ministry back to Minnesota. I knelt in front of the inmates, and the prison pastors joined Pastor Juan Zuccarelli in laying hands on me and asking God to take the Lino Lakes Prison ministry to a higher level.

EXTRAORDINARY BREAKTHROUGHS AT LINO LAKES

One Monday evening, when I was ministering at Lino Lakes Prison, one of the inmates asked me how to pray for a breakthrough in one's life. He meant that he wanted to know if there was a special kind of prayer that was required when there are areas of a person's life in which he or she is not experiencing complete freedom—something spiritual is holding that person back. He didn't seem to have a problem himself; he just wanted to know how to pray for people with these kinds of problems. I responded that we should see if there was someone in the group who needed a breakthrough. A guy named Bill raised his hand right away.

Bill explained that his wife was getting into trouble and running away from him and from the Lord. He said he was concerned for their two children, and the situation seemed hopeless. He felt it was time for him to consider getting a divorce. I told him that Malachi 2:16 tells us that God "hates divorce." I said he should repent of considering divorce as an option. He agreed and allowed me to lay hands on him and ask God to bring a breakthrough into his marriage.

The next week I left on an international ministry trip. Three weeks later I returned home, and just as I was beginning the class at Lino Lakes Prison, the same guy who had asked me how to pray for a breakthrough asked me another question. That reminded me of my prayer for Bill, so I asked him to give us a report.

Bill said his wife had come to visit him in the prison the preceding day. "Wait a minute," I responded. "Didn't you say your wife was running away from you?" He confirmed that up until the previous day his wife had not come to the prison to visit him. "Would you say that her coming to visit you was a breakthrough?"

"Yes," he replied. Then he told us that during his wife's visit on the preceding day, she had said their problems were spiritual in nature and only the Lord could solve them. I reminded him that three weeks earlier he had said his wife was running away from the Lord. "Would you say that her comment that your problems are spiritual and that only the Lord can solve them represents another breakthrough?" He agreed this was indeed a breakthrough.

But then he went on to tell us that his wife had also told him that three weeks ago, at precisely the same time I laid hands on Bill and prayed for a breakthrough, a neighbor knocked on his wife's door and invited her to a Bible study. "Wow," I said, "another breakthrough!" He agreed this was indeed another breakthrough. I commissioned the other men in the group to keep lifting up Bill and his wife in prayer.

During another Monday evening meeting at Lino Lakes, I asked the guys if they had any testimonies. Jim raised his hand and told us that 15 years earlier, his best friend, Pete, had asked him for some drugs. Jim sold him those drugs, and Pete embarked on a life of habitual drug use and crime that had spanned 15 years. Jim then said that Pete had been transferred to Lino Lakes Prison and had been put in Jim's cell. A big smile came over Jim's face as he shared how he had recently had the privilege of leading Pete to accept Jesus Christ as his Savior and Lord. "Wow," I interjected, "you messed up his life 15 years ago, and then the Lord gave you a second chance to repair the damage and lead your friend to Christ."

Then I asked if anyone else in the class had similar experiences and had led other inmates to faith in Christ. I almost fell out of my chair when half the inmates raised their hands. I remember thinking to myself, *I wasn't even at the prison when this was happening.* I told the guys this was a sign that God is bringing a spiritual change to Lino Lakes Prison.

BELIEVING FOR TRANSFORMATION AT DULUTH FEDERAL PRISON

And my experience at Lino Lakes is not an isolated instance of prison transformation. My friend Pastor Bob Aspling has preached about spiritual transformation on several occasions at the Duluth Federal Prison Camp. He has also shown the Harvest Evangelism DVD, with the testimony about Olmos Prison in Argentina, and challenged the inmates to believe that the Duluth Prison could become the first Christian prison within the Federal Bureau of Prisons. Other U.S. prisons are based on Christian principles, but the federal system is definitely not based on a Christian model. Currently Duluth Federal

Prison has a core group of about 60 inmates who are believing for transformation to come to the prison.

After watching the Olmos DVD, a couple of inmates felt that God was telling them to list the names of the inmates, guards and other prison officials. This is consistent with 1 Timothy 2:1-2, which says:

> Therefore I exhort first of all that supplications, prayers, inter-cessions, and giving of thanks be made for all men, for kings and all who are in authority, that we may lead a quiet and peace-able life in all godliness and reverence.

Bob then suggested these 60 inmates each pray for 16 other individuals by name. In this way they would pray for all 960 people connected to the prison. Much to Bob's amazement, the inmates had already assembled the names so that they could pray in this manner. They continue to pray for everyone in the prison on a daily basis.

The men at Duluth have a Sunday night Life Application Bible Study from 6:30 to 8:30 P.M.—two uninterrupted hours of in-depth study that sometimes includes guest speakers who give them direction for reaching their goal: a federal prison for Christ. Imagine 60 men dedicated to seeing a spiritual climate change in their institution. In addition to this, Bob is one of the leaders of the transformation project going on outside the federal prison in the Twin Ports of Duluth and Superior. These Christian inmates agreed to pray for the success of the Twin Ports transformation process.

During the first week of May 2006, Harvest Evangelism mobilized a prayer launch in many communities across the nation. Twin Ports' congregations prayer-walked neighborhoods in Duluth and Superior, while at that same time, the inmates of the Duluth Federal Prison Camp prayer-walked their compound, declaring God's peace and blessing over the compound.

GOD IS CALLING US TO A HIGHER LEVEL

In early 2007, the new director of the local prison ministry who had brought me to Lino Lakes Prison contacted me and said that they had redesigned their ministry at Lino Lakes and that I was not part of the new plan. At first I was disappointed at this news, but later the Lord helped me to see this from a different perspective. As rewarding as the ministry at Lino Lakes Prison has been, the results there are not even close to what has been accomplished in Argentina. My sense is that the Lord had to remove me from the Lino Lakes strategy so that I could be available to receive His higher vision—to plant a church in a prison. I have aligned my thoughts with that vision and trust Him to move me from where I am to where He wants me to be.

Note

1. Ed Silvoso, *Transformation in the Marketplace* DVD (San Jose, CA: Harvest Evangelism, Inc., 2006).

CHAPTER 18

A PERSONAL CALLING

At this point in the book, I'd like to share about the personal calling that God has placed on my heart for ending systematic poverty. While I never would have envisioned myself as one of God's instruments for this cause, He has decided to use me in this way for His glory. And that's enough for me. I have moved into my calling—praying, listening and waiting for the Lord's leading.

My journey began on January 27, 2006, when God led Ed Silvoso to lay hands on me and to declare that my primary mission was to pioneer the elimination of systemic poverty. He asked Rachel and Kathy Pinson (who is married to Ray Pinson, chairman of the Harvest Evangelism board of directors) to stand with me as he made this declaration. He also referred to the first few phrases of Luke 4:18, which say, "The Spirit of the LORD is upon Me, because He has anointed Me to preach the gospel to the poor."

Ed pointed out that the best news for poor people is that they don't have to be poor anymore. He said this doesn't mean there will be no more poor people. It just means that systems that have kept people in poverty would be eliminated.

Now, this is a goal that is exceedingly, abundantly above all I can ask or think.

In order to understand my calling, you need to know one of the core teachings of my colleague, mentor and team leader, Ed Silvoso. This teaching relates to the paradigms necessary to see communities and nations transformed, particularly the fifth paradigm, "Nation Transformation Must Be Tangible, and the Premier Social Indicator Is the Elimination of Systemic Poverty":

> Didn't the Lord say the poor will always be with us? Yes, but we are not talking about poor people here; we are talking about

the system that makes people poor. Poverty is a social indicator, not a spiritual indicator. There are five biblical reasons that point to systematic poverty as a crucial paradigm.

1. In the Garden scene, in Genesis 3, we see that poverty became the first visible sign of deterioration in the Garden, as illustrated by the thorns and thistles, and the land's lack of cooperation in yielding plentiful fruit. When a city or a region experiences transformation, its economy improves and systemic poverty is either eliminated or significantly alleviated.

2. In Luke 4:18, Jesus opened His first recorded speech with the statement that the Spirit of the Lord was upon Him and had anointed Him to give good news "to the poor."

3. In Acts 4:34, in one of the first snapshots of church life, we read, "Nor was there anyone among them who lacked."

4. In Galatians 2:10, Paul explained that the only requirement for apostolic work the Jerusalem leaders placed before him was this: "They desired only that we should remember the poor," something he said, "I also was eager to do."

5. Finally, in Acts 20:35, Paul explains to the church in the first region ever transformed (Asia) that he made it a specific point to emulate Jesus; teaching them to work hard with their own hands to take care of the needy (see v. 35).[1]

PROTOTYPES FOR ELIMINATING SYSTEMIC POVERTY

While Ed's teaching on this subject provided me with a beginning, I had to wait awhile before the Lord began showing me where He wanted me to begin developing prototypes for eliminating systemic poverty. Now that I believe I have heard His word on this matter, I believe there are to be five initial places where transformation needs to occur.

1. Khayelitsha

In December 2004, my friend Dr. Niel Stegmann and his wife, Rina, took me to worship at Church Without Walls, which is a Christian congregation in the Harare section of Khayelitsha. Khayelitsha is a township within Cape Town, South Africa, that is inhabited by more than one million people. They do not have clean drinking water. They do not have permanent bathroom facilities. They do not have proper electrical connections, and electrical wires even run across the streets. During that visit, I met the congregation's pastors, Thom and Thembie Thamaga.

When I returned to South Africa in September 2006, I asked Dr. Stegmann to take me back to worship at Church Without Walls in Khayelitsha. Because of my interest in Khayelitsha, Dr. Stegmann and the Thamagas arranged for me to meet a group of local pastors. During that same trip to Cape Town, I was invited to participate in the launch of the African chapter of the International Transformation Network (ITN). I hope to work together with the Thamagas, other pastors and the Stegmanns to define a project to eliminate systemic poverty in Khayelitsha.

2. The Khoi People Group

I met AyJay Jantjies during the Harvest Evangelism Institute in Argentina in November 2004. During my visit to Cape Town in 2006, AyJay and I participated in the planning meeting for the launch of the ITN chapter in Africa. During a lunch at that conference, AyJay shared about the Khoi, a first nations people group within South Africa. A day later, AyJay gave me a document describing in great detail the history of the Khoi people group. In the future, I hope to work with AyJay to define a project for eliminating systemic poverty from the Khoi people group.

3. Karaba, Rwanda

A few years ago, World Vision asked a few Elk River pastors to visit Karaba, Rwanda. The Elk River pastors returned home and set a goal: They would utilize the World Vision strategy to see that every child in Karaba orphaned by AIDS is adopted by someone in Elk River. Five hundred children have been adopted through this program. Because there is already a partnership between Karaba and Elk River, there could be an expansion of the current strategy to include the elimination of systemic poverty in Karaba.

4. The Red Lake Indian Reservation

History has taught us that sweeping changes in sociopolitical and economic structures accompany the spiritual transformation process. When God's Word is activated in people's lives, they are awakened to God's heart and begin to have real compassion for the poor. The result is that many people are inspired to confront systemic poverty in a city, region or specific people group.

At a conference in September 2006, I met Darrell Auginash, a Native American from the Red Lake band of Ojibwe in northern Minnesota. Darrell, founder of All Nations Ministry, shared from his heart about his people's needs—needs that extend beyond the spiritual (the Red Lake Indian Reservation is one of the poorest Native American reservations in the United States). Darrell shared that for his people to experience true and lasting transformation, it is necessary to address the economic issues at his reservation. He's seen how economic oppression fosters all sorts of crime and generally holds a people in bondage.

The Red Lake Indian Reservation gained national attention in May 2005 when it was the site of the nation's second-worst school shooting. Nine people were killed, and many others were wounded. One seriously wounded student was Darrell's own 15-year-old nephew. Since that time, Darrell has spent much of his time ministering healing prayer to scores of individuals affected by the tragedy, and proclaiming the message of life transformation through Jesus Christ. Still, he knows that true freedom does not address just the soul, but also the bondages people live with.

I pray we will be able to explore possible economic opportunities with Darrell and the Red Lake Reservation through the transformation process.

5. North Minneapolis, Minnesota

My friend Hattie Horne is the senior pastor of True Love Church Ministries of Arts. She lives and ministers in one of the most difficult parts of the Twin Cities—North Minneapolis, where there has recently been a significant outbreak of crime, including murders. Hattie has agreed to help me establish a prototype project to eliminate systemic poverty in North Minneapolis.

ELK RIVER: "DETONATOR" CITY

In November 2006, while Rachel and I were at the Harvest Evangelism Institute on nation transformation through marketplace redemption, I spoke with Carrie Beaudry from Elk River. She told me a minister had recently been in Elk River and told the group the Lord was releasing Solomon's crown upon the church there. He explained that the release of God's glory would be combined with the release of wealth in that city.

Just then, a pastor from Khayelitsha in Cape Town, South Africa, joined our conversation, so I shared with Carrie that I had visited Khayelitsha and that I had been stunned by the poverty that I had seen there. I then told the pastor about the recent revelation about Solomon's crown in Elk River. The pastor became very excited by this revelation. Just then Ken Beaudry showed up and joined the conversation. He too expressed great interest in developing prototypes to eliminate systemic poverty.

I told Ken and Carrie that it was very significant that all of the delegates from Elk River were so interested in projects to eliminate systemic poverty. I suggested that in addition to being a "detonator city" for city transformation, Elk River might also be a detonator city for the elimination of systemic poverty.

When the break was over, I told Graham Power about the revelation I had during the break. Graham asked me if I would be willing to share this revelation with the delegates who were just returning from the coffee break. When everyone was seated, he called me forward. I told the group that in January 2006, Ed Silvoso proclaimed I would have a major role in the elimination of systemic poverty. I said I had been in Khayelitsha on three occasions and that those visits had changed me. Further, I told them that during the coffee break I had a revelation about Elk River (most of the participants knew I had been involved

with the founding of Elk River's city transformation process and many
had read *The Elk River Story*). But I stated that Elk River is now being
taken to a higher level, as it becomes a detonator city: Together we
would work on projects to eliminate systemic poverty.

SUCCESSES IN UGANDA

At lunchtime on the same day, 400 to 500 of us were gathered in a large
ballroom. I noticed that Ken and Carrie Beaudry were seated at the head
table with Ed Silvoso, Graham Power and Janet Museveni, the First Lady of
Uganda. The First Lady was the keynote speaker for this lunch gathering.

During her talk, the First Lady, Mrs. Museveni, shared with us that
Uganda had died and been buried about 20 years ago. She said the
name of the country at that time was synonymous with war, bloodshed
and violence. Her family had lived in exile during the reign of Idi Amin,
and during the exile, she met and married her husband—the man who
would become the current president of Uganda. Twenty years ago she
began to pray that Uganda's curse of poverty would be broken—that
the country would give to others and not borrow.

Then she shared with us that the name of the country has a more
positive meaning now. Ten years ago, the government implemented universal primary education. Since the implementation of this program,
the number of children involved in universal education has grown from
2.5 million to 7 million in 2006. She told us that in 2007, Uganda will
begin to implement universal secondary education.

She also told us about the implementation of a universal immu-
nization program. This strategy has significantly reduced the rate of
infant mortality. She also told us that the HIV/AIDS infection rate has
dropped: Once 30 percent of the population was infected; today only 6
percent test positive for HIV/AIDS. She said that the country has a
population of 28 million, and 80 percent of the people live in rural
communities. Then she shared with us their goals for the country:

1. Provide access to clean drinking water.
2. Make medical care available in the villages.

3. Enable households to produce enough food to survive.
4. Restore human dignity (poverty cripples the human spirit).
5. Develop income-generating projects (don't give fish; teach how to fish).
6. Raise the standard of living.

She said about 200,000 people live within her district and she wanted to make sure each of them had a pair of shoes.

Following Mrs. Museveni's statement, Graham Power took the microphone and said that people at their table had expressed interest in purchasing shoes for the 200,000 people who live in the First Lady's district. As they discussed this idea, however, they concluded that buying 200,000 pairs of shoes would be equivalent to giving the people fish—rather than teaching them how to fish.

Just then Ed Silvoso took the microphone and said we should do two things: (1) commit to praying for Uganda on a daily basis for the next 12 months; and (2) pray for the International Transformation Network (ITN) as it establishes an investment company to eliminate systemic poverty in Uganda.

Ed Silvoso suggested that we each prepare our hearts to fund an investment company in order to eliminate systemic poverty in Uganda, focusing on the district the First Lady represents in Parliament. This would allow us to turn it into a prototype with the potential to impact, progressively, the rest of the nation. Then the First Lady stood at the podium and wept as 400 to 500 people brought their investments forward and laid them at her feet. This was one of the most joyful spiritual experiences of my life—and gave me great insight regarding how to answer my own call to eliminate systemic poverty.

A VISIT TO UGANDA

In March 2007, I joined a team from Harvest Evangelism and ITN Africa on a visit to Uganda. The night of our arrival in Kampala, we had dinner with President and Mrs. Museveni. On the following day, we took a six-hour bus ride to visit the First Lady's district.

Although there were multiple components to the strategy of eliminating systemic poverty, I was personally drawn to the component of improving the health of the First Lady's constituents. During our two-day visit to the district, we stopped at a medical clinic where we encountered hundreds of women holding infants in their arms. We were told that most of the children had malaria and that the mothers were seeking medical attention at the clinic. However, although there were buildings in the clinic compound, there were no physicians or nurses to treat the children, and no medicine to treat the malaria.

Just before this trip, I had read a book about poverty that stated there was a strong correlation between malaria and poverty. Therefore, one component of the project to eliminate systemic poverty within the First Lady's district could be to dramatically reduce the incidence of malaria. This would include upgrading the medical clinic to treat existing cases of malaria (professional medical practitioners and medicine) and implementing preventive measures (mosquito nets, insecticide sprays and educating people on how to prevent the disease).

EMBRACING MY VISION

As I reflect on the situation in Uganda and think about my own prototype cities, I realize that I have no idea how to eliminate systemic poverty from any of these places. I wonder, *Couldn't I start with something less challenging and work my way up to these more challenging places?*

Although my weak humanity wants to say yes, God's grace in me gently replies no. To do anything less than seek a miracle for these cities is not the vision that the Lord has given to me. So I will continue to seek His wisdom and guidance—I will continue to believe that God can use me to do exceedingly, abundantly beyond all that I could ever think or ask.

So how about you? Are you struggling with a vision that seems far beyond your ability to achieve? Remember that God will equip you to achieve that vision—He will work in and through you. So have no fear; step forward in faith. And see amazing things begin to happen!

Note

1. This material was compiled from Ed Silvoso's Anointed for Business syllabus, his books *Prayer Evangelism* (Regal Books, 2000), *Anointed for Business* (Regal Books, 2002), and my notes on his messages and on his newest book, *Transformation* (Regal Books, 2007), which I am using with his permission.

CHAPTER 19

USING FAITH AS CAPITAL

At this point you might be wondering how your financial situation will affect your sphere of influence—you might think you need a lot of cash to effect transformation in the marketplace. And while new business endeavors normally require cash upfront, your business venture—if it's God ordained—can get up and running using a different kind of capital: faith in God.

That was certainly the experience of Michael and Aderonke Mordi, Nigerians who immigrated to the United States. One year after their marriage, in the summer of 1998, they attended African Christian Fellowship's (ACF) Midwest Regional Conference at Bethel College, just north of St. Paul. One of the sessions featured a Christian couple in the healthcare business whose testimony sparked in the Mordis a strong desire to own their own business—they began to believe that God was calling them to just such a venture. Around the same time, the Mordis attended a conference hosted by a Twin Cities church. As an act of faith, the Mordis sowed a $500 gift into the offering as a seed for their business. This act of faith demonstrated their obedience to the Lord and their commitment to the vision the Lord had given them.

In 2000, with little cash but a great deal of faith, the Mordis started their first business—International Quality Healthcare Corporation—a home healthcare agency that provides services for the elderly, the sick, the handicapped and children and adults in need of personal care in the comfort of their homes. They send out personal care assistants (PCAs) to each client, based on a physician's order. During the summer of 2002, the agency was Medicare-certified, with a Class-A license. The Medicare certification has allowed for the company's phenomenal growth.

In 2000, the Mordis also founded the Alpha Services Company of Rochester, a group home for medically fragile, mentally retarded and/or mentally ill patients. The clients live in a single-family home setting. Some of the clients are in wheelchairs and need to live in a house that has handicap accessibility.

In 2003, the Mordis formed International Properties LLC to manage all the properties they own. Then, in 2004 the Mordis formed Omega Medical Supply LLC, which supplies medical equipment to their clients. They also formed International Quality Interpreting Services, LLC, to respond to the unique requirements of the international community in Rochester, Minnesota. Through the International Quality Interpreting Services unit, the Mordis provide assistance for their clients who do not speak English. The Mordis are fulfilling the need to serve their customers in Rochester who are of Somalian, Arabic, Cambodian and Spanish origin.

In 2005, the Mordis founded International Quality Transportation Services, LLC, which provides specialized services to clients who need transportation to their medical appointments with their primary physicians.

GOD PROVIDES

The Mordis had little cash with which to start their businesses and, because of their lack of business experience, no banks would lend them working capital. That caused them to rely more on the Lord—they prayed diligently. They also sowed financial seeds through offerings, because they believe it is more blessed to give than to receive.

Prior to May 2006, the Mordis started all of their businesses with very little cash in the bank. The Lord gave them many divine appointments along the way, bringing people into their lives who provided help to them at just the right time. For instance, a real estate agent cold canvassing for condominium sales dropped his brochures at their office. At the time, their lease was about to expire, and they were already contemplating a new location for their business. They talked with the man and found that he had 22 years of banking experience. He ended up helping them fix their accounting process by moving from a cash basis to an accrual basis of accounting. He also introduced them to the president of a bank, who gave them their first working capital loan. With this loan they were able to pay off most of their debts.

The Mordis' businesses are growing at a very positive rate. More importantly, their companies—and their lives—are bringing change and transformation to the medical industry, to the clients whose lives they touch each and every day, and to the communities they operate in. And still the Mordis are looking to God for more of what He is about to do in their businesses and in their lives. They believe He will do exceeding, abundantly more than they can ask or think. They are poised for action and are looking forward to a great overflow of His blessings.

Now, what about you?

CHAPTER 20

RELEASING THE JOSEPH GENERATION

While you may never have heard the term "Joseph Generation" before, let me assure you that it has everything to do with transforming the marketplace. Remember that in the Old Testament, Joseph is a Jewish boy who grows up to be Pharaoh's right-hand man. He is true to his faith—and true to his position of leadership in the country. He recognizes that he has been uniquely positioned by God to do good among the people of Egypt—and thus testify to the power and goodness of the Lord.

I was first introduced to this concept by Pablo Abeleira, who, with his wife, Monica, has a long-term working relationship with Harvest Evangelism. Pablo defines the Joseph Generation as a generation of leaders God has chosen for influential positions in fulfilling His plans on Earth. God gives these leaders revelation and supernatural guidance. They can translate this revelation in a way other marketplace leaders can understand. The Joseph Generation is bilingual: Its members can speak the language of their brothers (family, church, and so on), and they can also speak the language of Egypt (marketplace).

It was in June 2003, in San Jose, California, where he had temporarily relocated his family to work with Harvest Evangelism, that the Lord first told Pablo He was raising a Joseph Generation for Argentina, and that He would raise Argentina's flag among the nations as an example of restoration. Then in July, Pablo and Monica and their three boys were in Argentina, visiting family and attending a youth conference where Pablo was to be one of the speakers. During his talk, Pablo revealed what the Lord had told him about the Joseph Generation and Argentina's restoration, and while he was speaking, the Lord told Pablo it was time to return to Argentina permanently.

BACK TO ARGENTINA

In November 2003, Pablo participated in a Harvest Evangelism market-place luncheon in Buenos Aires. At this meeting Pablo met Alicia Vazquez, who is a government official who serves as the main connection between the Buenos Aires government and all its religious organizations. He also met Stephanie Klinzing, mayor of Elk River, Minnesota (Alicia was moved by Mayor Klinzing's testimony and the two became friends).

With Monica's agreement, in June 2004, Pablo moved his family back to Argentina—to Buenos Aires. They had a sense that even though many other Argentine cities were experiencing spiritual awakening, Argentina would not be transformed as a nation until its most populous city, Buenos Aires, was transformed.

They entered Buenos Aires, this time not as pulpit ministers, but as marketplace ministers. They gathered a team of marketplace leaders around them. This team included Pablo's brother, Pepe (a youth pastor and businessman), Tony Serrano (a financial advisor), Daniel DiPaolo (a lawyer) and Jorge Veglia (an engineer). They began meeting together at Tony's house to pray and discuss how to implement marketplace ministry in Buenos Aires.

Not long after their return, an Argentinean Federal School of Government official—let's call him José to protect his identity—called Pablo. José said that he was gathering people between 30 and 40 years of age to "dream" about the new Argentina. Pablo met with José, who said he was writing a book entitled *Choose Your Own Argentina*. José's book envisioned young people being elected to the national congress and other influential positions in order to bring heaven to Earth. Pablo marveled that even non-believers were writing books about the Joseph Generation.

Each year at the beginning of spring (which is September in Argentina), there's a holiday called Students' Day. On that day, high school-aged youth gather in Palermo Park. Pablo and Monica saw a great opportunity to organize a fun Christian event in the park to keep the young people entertained.

Pablo told Alicia about his vision, stating that his only objective was to demonstrate to the city government that he and Monica wanted to serve. Alicia responded that the city had no interest in planning and operating a youth rally on this holiday. Pablo told her he would do the youth rally at his own risk. She said the government would authorize Pablo and Monica to plan and supervise the event.

In September 2004, Pablo and Monica had the first youth rally. It was a great success, and the teens were well behaved. The event—and Pablo—got a lot of media coverage. It was a great success!

A few months later, a band used a pyrotechnics display as part of its show in the Cromanion Republic nightclub in Buenos Aires. The pyrotechnics ignited stage decorations and then engulfed the entire nightclub in flames—198 young people died in the fire.

Much to his amazement, Pablo received a phone call from a government official saying that, because of his excellent work in the Palermo Park youth event, they wanted him to assist them in comforting the grieving relatives of the nightclub fire victims. Pablo agreed to help and made his way to the morgue to extend Christ's love to those who mourned.

MIRACLES!

Over the next several months, Pablo was invited many times to pray in different prayer meetings throughout the city. During one of those prayer meetings, Pablo saw a magazine article describing the pediment on the façade of the National Cathedral. He was amazed to read that the pediment was a depiction of Joseph being reunited with his father, Jacob, in Egypt. This was a sign about the Joseph Generation. Right there, while Pablo was reading the magazine article, he asked God to allow him to pray in that place to release the Joseph Generation.

A few weeks later, Ed Silvoso was visiting Argentina, and during a dinner with pastors, Ed was led by the Lord to declare over Pablo that in the next five days extraordinary miracles were going to happen. Pablo received this declaration from Ed Silvoso with faith.

On his fifth day in Mar del Plata with the Harvest Evangelism team, the Catholic bishop's office called Pablo about a memorial service at the National Cathedral and said that because of Pablo's ministry at the morgue, the bishop wanted him to join him in leading the memorial service. Pablo accepted the invitation, and he and Monica departed immediately for Buenos Aires. They had to travel 250 miles to get to the cathedral, and when they arrived, the Mass had already begun. The bishop was presiding and the president of Argentina, Nestor Kirchner, and his wife, and several national ministers were seated in the first row of seats.

Surprisingly, at the end of the Mass, the bishop introduced Pablo and invited all the people to go outside so that Pablo could pray for them. Receiving an invitation from the Catholic bishop to join him in the service was one miracle. Having the bishop invite an Evangelical to pray for the people was a second miracle. Praying that prayer in the doorway of the National Cathedral, right below the image of Jacob being reunited with Joseph in Egypt, made this an extraordinary miracle! This was the answer to Pablo's earlier prayer that God would allow him to pray at this site, thereby releasing the Joseph Generation.

That day at the National Cathedral was just the beginning of divine appointments for Pablo and Monica.

Meeting with Oil Executives

One morning Monica was having coffee with a group of women who were the mothers of her children's classmates. Monica felt God directing her to "pray for the woman at your side." Though Monica didn't really know the woman, at the end of the meeting, she asked if she could pray for her. The woman, Elena, agreed, not understanding that Monica meant *at that moment*. In spite of her surprise, Elena agreed again, gratefully. While Monica was praying this simple prayer, God's presence came upon them in a very powerful way—right there in the coffee shop! God used this divine appointment to establish a wonderful new relationship between Monica and Elena. They began to meet once a week to pray and fellowship together. During one of those meetings, Monica learned that Elena was the wife of a high-level executive of one of Argentina's petroleum companies. Elena then invited some of her friends, who also were married to petroleum company executives, to join the meetings, which grew into monthly meetings in Elena's house.

Monica's obedience in praying for Elena at the coffee shop opened a new world for Elena and Monica. Now they understand that together they have keys to open doors in order to establish God's kingdom rule in places where it had never been established before.

Sometime later, Elena hosted a dinner party and invited Monica and Pablo and the couples from the oil company. At the party Pablo met Steve, an American man who serves as the CEO for a privately owned Argentine oil company.

In July 2006, Pablo invited me to a lunch meeting with Steve. We had a wonderful time, even learning that our waiter was a Christian from Pablo's hometown of Adrogue, Argentina. We all laid hands on the waiter and prayed for him.

At the end of our time together, I asked Steve how we could pray for him. He told us his company has operations in four countries, and this provides him with access to the presidents of those four countries. He told us that one of those presidents had recently asked him to help solve a problem in his country. So we laid hands on Steve and asked the Lord to give him wisdom about how to minister to the needs of this country's president. I told Steve that this is a good example of a marketplace ministry, and that his business is his ministry.

Meeting with the Lujan Group

The Lujan Group is a collection of young Roman Catholic politicians Pablo got to know in the year 2005, while he was working on a project for the city. They are from different political parties and have joined together to dream and work for a new Argentina. As Pablo got to know them, he understood that the Lujan Group was another part of the Joseph Generation.

In July 2006, Pablo's associate Tony Serrano took three of us to visit with the Lujan Group. It was there that Werner Swart of South Africa explained how the church worked with the president of Uganda to end nearly 20 years of civil war in that country. Hawaiian pastor Cal Chinen told about how his state's lieutenant governor has assumed a leading role in transforming Hawaii. I described Mayor Stephanie Klinzing's leadership role in the transformation now underway in Elk River, Minnesota.

At the end of the meeting, one of the participants introduced himself as chief of staff for Esteban Bullrich, a member of Argentina's House of Representatives. The chief of staff promised to speak to Representative Bullrich about a meeting with the three of us in his office. We actually got to meet him later that same day!

Representative Bullrich met with Werner Swart, Pastor Cal Chinen and me in his office. We repeated our stories about Uganda, Hawaii and Elk River, and then Representative Bullrich told us that, as a member of the Roman Catholic Church, he is very interested in integrating his faith in Jesus Christ into his career. He told us about eight projects he hopes to complete throughout the country. We told him about the nation transformation process now underway in Argentina and offered to put him in touch with our network of evangelical pastors in each of the provinces where he wants to implement his projects.

Meeting with the Chief Executive of Buenos Aires
In July 2006, right after the meeting with the Lujan Group, Pablo Abeleira took 120 of us to meet with Jorge Telerman, the chief executive of Buenos Aires. The office of chief executive is similar to a mayor of a city, except that Buenos Aires is one of the biggest cities in the world. After exchanging gifts, Dave Thompson of Harvest Evangelism and Pastor Cal Chinen joined Pablo in laying hands on the chief executive and praying blessings over him. All of us could see that the chief executive was deeply moved by these prayers.

On the day following the meeting with Jorge Telerman, the French ambassador to Argentina invited Pablo to a special ceremony at the French Consulate to honor Mr. Telerman. When Mr. Telerman spotted Pablo, he greeted him and thanked him for the previous day's prayers. He then introduced Pablo to his wife and children.

ONWARD!

Just as Pablo and his wife are working to release the Joseph Generation in Argentina, many others around the world are also working and praying for transformation and restoration to occur in their towns and their countries. We have all been called to be a part of this renewal. It's time for each of us to claim our vision and pursue its fulfillment. Let's not delay a moment longer!

CHAPTER 21

MAKING A DIFFERENCE

This marketplace miracle is very dear to my heart, because it's all about my sister-in-law and my nephew. They are two people who have taken disappointment and turned it into a divine appointment. A disability has become an ability to transform the lives of children—and to show a heart of compassion in the healthcare marketplace.

"Wow, where are all the people?" I asked my sister-in-law, Patti Herbst. My family and I had driven from Bloomington, Minnesota, to Western Springs, Illinois, for our nephew's high school graduation party. Earlier in the day, caterers had brought enough food for an army—or several dozen voracious high school seniors. Actually, Patti was expecting more than 100 guests, and it was time for the party to start—but no one was there yet. We were becoming a bit concerned: Justin's graduation held special meaning because he has cerebral palsy (CP).

Then the doorbell rang, and the first guests arrived. Soon the entire backyard was filled with friends and family—all there to celebrate Justin's high school graduation and wish him well as he prepared to attend Southern Illinois University in the fall. Several of us were in the family room, viewing senior prom pictures taken just a few days earlier. It seemed that Justin, in his bright-red sports coat, had had his picture taken with many of the girls in his graduating class.

Just then, Justin, adorned in his red sports coat, steered his electric-powered wheelchair through the family room and out the back door onto the concrete patio, where most of the crowd was gathered. We set aside the prom-night photos, sensing something was about to happen right there in the backyard. Without any announcement, every eye turned and focused on Justin, and in a loud and confident voice, he addressed the crowd:

First of all, I want to thank you all for your support. I want you to clap your hands for yourselves. You are an amazing group of people. First, I went to the elementary school across the street. With my mother's help, I was able to move successfully around the school. Then I went to McClure Junior High School, where I met Nicky in the sixth grade. I feel very blessed to have Nicky in my life.

Then I would like to introduce my brother and my sister. My brother, Clay, has kept me in line all of these years. He has a lot of qualities that I would like to have. My sister, Kacie, is my other mother. I love her so much. She always keeps me in line. She is so smart!

Then I went to Lake Ontario and met Gyorgyi Ezsias. She was my European mother. She helped me to understand that I needed to correct my body. She helped me see that I need to be stronger. Through her assistance I learned to love my disability. I would like to thank her for making me stronger.

I love my mom for putting it all together. I can't talk about my mom without talking about my dad. My dad is like a big kid. I love to see him dance. I love to see him playing video games. He gave me a love for sports that I can never relinquish—we all know how much I love watching professional wrestling. He gave me a passion for life that I can never relinquish.

My Aunt Rachel and my Uncle Rick are here. They found God and they are big believers in the "Big Guy Upstairs." My Uncle Rick was successful in business and he gave it all up for God and to help others find God.

There's a guy holding the camera right there—my Uncle James. He is a true free spirit and a true heart. He used to be a hippie. He embraces nothing but peace and love.

Then I moved on to Lyons Township High School. I became a more mature individual. I also developed a greater sense of creativity. My creativity has really come out in the area of rap music.

I would also like to introduce my Aunt Kathryn and her daughter Lauren. My Aunt Kathryn is also such a great individual. And Lauren has grown to be such an energetic young lady.

I know that she will make such a positive impact on this world.

I have embraced my disability. My disability has helped me to understand the world in a bigger way. I have begun to understand that it is so difficult to achieve what you want. You could give up. But you just have to keep going. You have got to keep striving.

I would also like to thank my grandfather, James Herbst, also known as Poppi, and my grandmother, Rachel Kirn Herbst, also known as Bama. First of all, Poppi, you are a wonderful man. You have a great sense of humor. You have filled me with such wisdom. You are such a great man. You served bravely in the war back in the 1940s. You are the wisest man that I know. You have such a grasp of history. You have such vigor for life. You both have such an amazing vigor for life. You are still young at an old age. Whenever I come to your house, I always feel welcome. I always feel loved and appreciated.

THE CAMPAIGNS

In 1987, my brother-in-law Chuck and his wife, Patti, had just begun their baby preparation classes and were excited about welcoming their first baby. But Justin came 11 weeks ahead of schedule and weighed just 2 pounds. His circulatory system was not fully developed, which led to cranial hemorrhaging, similar to a stroke. This hemorrhaging resulted in his cerebral palsy.

Patti and Chuck lived in the neonatal intensive care unit for six weeks, waiting for their child to gain enough weight to go home. Imagine bringing your first child home attached to a monitor with alarms that blare in the middle of the night. That was just the beginning of many challenges the family would face in raising a child with severe physical disabilities. Justin was six months old when the family learned he would be a quadriplegic—he would need a wheelchair to get around and would require therapy for the rest of his life.

When Justin was five years old, the family learned he would have to leave the elementary school where he had attended kindergarten in order to attend first grade in the "only accessible elementary school" in the area. That school was miles away. Instead of busing Justin across town, the Herbsts sold their home and moved their family across town so that all of their children could attend the same school.

I remember stories about Patti's campaign to persuade school officials to provide a sidewalk for Justin's safe passage into the building. Later, Patti and Chuck went in front of the school board, well in advance of Justin's entry into middle school, to alert them about Justin's need for accessible passage throughout the school. The board wanted to provide a lift, but after much discussion with the Herbst family and others, the middle school now has an elevator. That elevator served Justin and, many years later, continues to serve other students, grandparents and others with physical disabilities. Patti realized throughout this process that by making an effort to accommodate her son in schools, she could also positively impact the lives of others with disabilities.

From the time he was six months old until he was seven-and-a-half years old, Justin received one-on-one physical, occupational and speech-therapy services. However, due to financial pressures from physicians and insurance companies, CP patients get only enough therapy to avoid potential contractures (shortening of the muscles causing deformities) and other CP-related ailments—but not enough therapy to promote independent functions.

In early 1996, when Justin was nine years old, Patti pulled him out of physical therapy. Although he never had any contractures, the therapy didn't seem to be helping him progress. Patti was really frustrated, and the therapist wasn't listening to her.

During that period of frustration, Patti had a conversation with her friend Jean. Jean and her husband, Steve, have two girls, Katelyn and Lauren—both of whom have CP. When Jean attended an expo in Chicago for disabled people, she found out about Kevin Hickling's Ability Camp in Picton, Ontario. The camp is based on the principles of conductive education for children with CP. Kevin founded Ability Camp because his daughter has CP.

Conductive Education is the formal name for an intensive motor-training program for children with physical disabilities. Created in 1948 in Budapest, Hungary, it is a unique group-method of teaching children how to be more physically independent. Unlike traditional one-on-one therapy, conductive education is provided in a group setting, typically with a ratio of three children to one conductor/teacher/therapist. Group education, with its peer support, interactive setting and competition, motivates the children to complete tasks, encourages accomplishments and supports confidence and effort. In addition to promoting improved motor function, the program stresses self-direction and self-advocacy.

During the school year, children spend between 8 and 15 hours per week working on developing physical independence. During the intensive summer training, they receive 30 hours of therapy per week, which is far more than most other programs offer.

ABILITY CAMP

So, in July 1996, Jean and Patti and their children made the 13-hour trip from Western Springs, Illinois, to Picton, Ontario, just over an hour's drive east of Toronto. Every time she stopped to rest or eat, Patti had to lift nine-year-old Justin out of the car seat and into his wheelchair. More difficult still, Patti had to be away from her husband and other two children for an entire month.

When they arrived at Ability Camp, they found the facilities were like a Jewish kibbutz. There was one large, communal living room, one kitchen, and 10 to 12 bedrooms. Many other families were there, each with one or more children with CP. Over the course of the month, they grew to love and support one another as they went through this strenuous yet wonderful experience together.

Justin still refers to Ability Camp as "boot camp." It was the first time he had been expected to do so much physically and mentally. He was away from Patti for six hours each day, Monday through Friday, working independently with the Conductive Education teachers (conductors). The conductors had high expectations for each child. For the first time in his life, Justin had to muster the strength and determination to get through these exercises—there was no one to help him. But that was the plan.

Gyorgyi Ezsias, a woman from Budapest, was the lead conductor. When Patti came to pick up Justin at the end of the first day, Gyorgyi told Patti he had fallen off his stool. Patti's initial instinct was to protect her child, but Gyorgyi convinced her to give the process time to work for Justin.

On the following day, when Patti came to get Justin, she noticed he had a lump on his head. In answer to her question, Gyorgyi said, "He fell off the stool again." Gyorgyi could see Patti was struggling. "Listen, Patti," she said, "it's Justin's job to learn how to sit on a chair. It's not your job! By the end of the week, he will have the opportunity to fall down and to pick himself up again."

Patti then realized how overprotective she had been. It's easy for a parent to be overprotective of a child with a disability. She never would have allowed Justin to risk falling and hurting himself. She thought to herself, *Every two-year-old has to fall in order to learn how to walk. We have to allow our son to fail—otherwise he will never progress.* It felt as if a huge boulder had been lifted from her shoulders.

During the last week of camp, Chuck drove to Ability Camp to replace Patti, who had to go back to work. She had kept Chuck informed throughout the first four weeks of the camp, so he was aware of how much Justin had progressed, but he was still amazed when he finally saw it with his own eyes. One day as he looked through the one-way glass, there was Justin, sitting in a regular chair, feeding himself! A bit later, Justin walked independently with the help of a walker. It elated Justin to watch his dad's response to his progress. He told Chuck he couldn't wait to go back to school in Western Springs and show the other kids what he could do. When he got back to the school, his friends applauded his accomplishments.

THE SUMMER CAMP AT ST. JOHN'S

Before he and Justin left the camp, Chuck had a conversation with Gyorgyi, who said she wanted to start a summer camp in Chicago. Later, Chuck and Patti wrote many letters and made many phone calls between Western Springs and Budapest as the discussions progressed.

Gyorgyi kept mentioning a man named Zsolt, who eventually became her husband. It was finally settled—Gyorgyi and Zsolt would come to Chicago and run a conductive education camp the following year.

In March 1997, Patti went to her church, St. John of the Cross Catholic Church, and asked a priest if she could use the church's parish center for the summer camp. The priest declined because of the potential liability for the church. Patti went home and told Chuck about her conversation. "How can they say no to us?" she asked.

Within three weeks, that priest had been replaced by another named Richard Hynes. Patti introduced herself to Father Hynes, and after she explained what she had in mind, he looked at her and said, "Of course you can use our parish center."

Patti rushed home and phoned Gyorgyi and Zsolt in Budapest and told them the good news. They came to Chicago and made preparations for the six-week summer camp that was to begin in July. Patti says she doesn't know how the initial group of children found out about the program. They never advertised it in any way, but still, six children signed up for that first camp. One of those children, Kyle, has been Justin's best friend ever since.

As the program continued, many parishioners who had been wary of the program changed their minds. They enjoyed the songs the children sang, and many told Patti they were blessed to have the program in their church. Visiting priests and nuns told Patti they could see how the children were progressing. All the priests stopped by to pray for and bless the children, sharing with Patti how visiting the children was the best part of their day. They observed how the children laughed and enjoyed life. The children loved one another; many people commented that they learned what real love was from watching them.

Patti led a second summer camp at St. John's the following year. The number of children enrolled doubled to 12. But Patti observed that the kids who returned from the prior year's summer camp had regressed during the school year. Inactivity eroded their progress, and Patti couldn't stand to watch the effects this regression had on the children. She determined then to begin a year-round program.

CENTER FOR INDEPENDENCE

Justin wasn't the only one in the family making progress: Patti told me how significant it was that I had invited Chuck to attend the 1993 Promise Keepers gathering in the Twin Cities. I flashed back to the scene in the Minneapolis Metrodome. When the altar call was given, Chuck got out of his seat and headed for the platform. Patti says that when he came home from Minneapolis, he was different—he was interested in spiritual things. Patti said he became the spiritual leader of their family.

After that, in 1995, Chuck enrolled in the Christ Renews His Parish program or CRHP (pronounced "chirp") at St. John's. The CRHP program solidified Chuck's decision to make Christ the number-one priority in his life. This was extremely important, because if the Conductive Education program went from summer-only to year-round, Patti would have to sell her accounting practice. This was a huge decision because of the amount of money she earned from her business. Selling it would be a leap of faith for the whole family.

But Chuck and Patti eventually decided to sell the accounting practice and lead their new Conductive Education organization. In 1998 they obtained a 501(c)3 tax exemption and incorporated the Center for Independence. But they had no money. In a creative move, they started running golf-outings and eventually discovered other unique approaches to fund-raising. Today they have a substantial mailing list of donors who are committed to the financial health of the Center for Independence. At that point, keeping the year-round program at St. John's was not an option, so they went on the search for a new site. Patti's friend Pat Johnson, who had joined the board of directors, asked Patti if she had thought about the nearby Presbyterian Church in Western Springs, Illinois, as a possible location. The church was six blocks from the Herbst home and was in the process of adding a large addition to the building. So Patti phoned Pastor David Jones and arranged to meet with him, together with her friend Pat.

Patti told Pastor Jones about the progress they had made at the Catholic Church facility over the past two years. But now they had outgrown that space. Thirty-six children were signed up for the third-year of the summer camp. Each of these families had learned about the program through word of mouth.

Pastor Jones invited the two women to accompany him on a tour of the new facility. When they got to the second floor, they entered a large room. "Will this work for you?" Pastor Jones asked. "Yes, this would be perfect," Patti responded. In addition, Pastor Jones showed them a second large room they could use.

When they returned to his office, Pastor Jones said he wanted to tell them a story that dated back 33 years, from his seminary days. Each day when he walked to his seminary classes, he passed a young man in a wheelchair—let's call him Larry—and each day the two of them would talk. They had meals together and became close friends. When it was time for Jones to be ordained as a pastor, he invited Larry to the ordination service. After the service, Larry gave Pastor Jones a small canoe he had whittled from a block of wood. He told the new pastor it had taken him three weeks to whittle the canoe. The pastor thought to himself, *A person without a disability might have taken only a few hours to whittle the canoe—that's what makes it an even more precious gift*.

Larry had CP.

Just then, Pastor Jones reached into his desk drawer and pulled out the canoe. He said, "I've been waiting 33 years to see what this canoe would bring me. Now it has brought me to you. I hope you will move the Center for Independence into our church." With that, all three of them broke into tears—and Patti and Pat were convinced God had led them to this facility.

At this point, Patti saw the true meaning of this prayer that is attributed to Mother Teresa:

> *The fruit of silence is prayer.*
> *The fruit of prayer is faith.*
> *The fruit of faith is love.*
> *The fruit of love is service.*
> *The fruit of service is peace.*

They moved the center to the Presbyterian Church in the spring of 1999. Again, some of the parishioners were concerned about this program in their new church building. Just like at the Catholic Church, however, the parishioners were blessed by the presence of this dynamic program. During the next three years, the program's enrollment grew from 36 to 62 children. At the end of those three years, Pastor Jones retired.

HOMES OF THEIR OWN!

In 2001, the Center for Independence applied for funding from the Coleman Foundation.[1] With those funds and finances from other sources, the center's staff was able to raise enough money to purchase their own building, which includes three large classrooms, a parent waiting room, staff offices and a beautiful playground that has been adapted for use by disabled children.

Three years later, however, the center had outgrown its own building—100 children were now enrolled at the Center for Independence. Patti and Chuck discussed the idea of purchasing an even bigger building, but Patti was adamant that they were not to pursue that strategy. She told Chuck she wanted to go to where the children live—especially children from poor families.

In 2001, Patti met Dr. Vincent Allocco, Ph.D., the executive director of an organization called El Valor Corporation. El Valor is a nonprofit community-based organization that was founded in 1973 by the late Guadalupe A. Reyes. A visionary leader and mother, Mrs. Reyes dreamed of a community in which all members, including her son with special needs, could live, learn and work. She and several others took out a small bank loan and borrowed a church basement in Pilsen where they started the first bilingual, bicultural rehabilitation center in Illinois. They named it *El Valor*, which means "courage."

From its roots in the Latino community, El Valor has grown into a multicultural, multipurpose organization that reaches thousands of families in the Chicagoland area, and millions throughout the nation. El Valor's mission is to support and challenge urban families to achieve excellence and participate fully in community life. Their programs exist to enrich and empower people with disabilities, the disenfranchised and the underserved.[2]

When Patti and Dr. Allocco met, they sensed they would work together to help the disabled children of poor Latino families in the Pilsen neighborhood. By 2005, the Center for Independence and El Valor Corporation jointly sponsored a summer program of Conductive Education for 14 disabled children in the Pilsen area. Patti and the Board of Directors of the Center for Independence added these new program costs to their budget and promoted this new program to affluent donors in suburban Chicagoland. As a result, the summer camp was provided free of charge to each family with a disabled child. They were able to serve some of the most financially disadvantaged children in the area by bringing the Conductive Education program, equipment and staff from the suburbs right into the heart of urban Chicago. This allowed the children to stay in their own neighborhoods, thereby increasing attendance and strengthening each family's connection to the community. The camp held during the summer of 2005 was a huge success.

In the summer of 2006, the Center for Independence and El Valor Corporation expanded into a second El Valor site—South Chicago. This second summer camp for disabled children in another part of urban Chicagoland was funded by donations. So, again, the camp was provided free of charge to participating families.

A TRUE MARKETPLACE MOVER

In 2000, *Chicago* magazine named Patti Herbst as one of the top eight outstanding Chicagoans for work in improving the lives of children with disabilities. This came as no surprise to those of us who know and love her. And to the God she serves—whose work she does out in the world—it was an echo of His own thoughts, I'm sure.

Perhaps you feel that God doesn't have plans for you to do anything as exceptional as what Patti has done. But you're wrong. Whatever the scope of your work, whatever your abilities, God has a plan for you to transform your job, your workplace, your city. He wants to work miracles through you—in fact, He can't do it without you!

Notes

1. Check out the Coleman Foundation website at www.colemanfoundation.org.
2. See the El Valor Corporation website at www.elvalor.net.

CHAPTER 22

CITYWIDE TRANSFORMATION

Though we've already taken a look at citywide transformation, it's worth revisiting—it's impossible to overemphasize the importance of the need to work for revival in towns all across America, including your own. But right now we're going to take a journey to Raleigh, North Carolina—to see the amazing things happening there.

It was Saturday, July 29, 2006, and I was staying with Sirus and Kaye Chitsaz at their home in Raleigh. I had just showered and dressed. Downstairs was quiet as I descended the stairs. I hopped onto a stool at the breakfast bar and began talking with Sirus. The television was on behind me, and I heard something about Raleigh. I turned, and focused on the TV, and heard a reporter talking about the grand opening of Fayetteville Street to automobile traffic. For 30 years, the street had been a pedestrian mall. The people in the center of the picture shouted out in unison, "Good morning, America!" Suddenly, I realized that the opening of this street in Raleigh was being broadcast to the entire country. Just a couple days earlier, my friend Pastor Les Lawrence showed me a newspaper headline stating that the opening of this new street was the first step toward revival in Raleigh.

TRANSFORMATION BEGINS

I reflected on my first meeting with Sirus Chitsaz and Jim Anthony, two Raleigh business leaders, at a conference in Tuscaloosa, Alabama, in early 2004. During the conference, Sirus, Jim, Ed Silvoso and I had lunch and talked about the process of transforming cities for Christ. I shared about the prototype already established in Elk River, Minnesota. That day, Sirus and Jim each caught the vision for Raleigh's transformation.

Among People Groups

Then in January 2006, Chief Jay Swallow and I were at First Baptist Church in Raleigh to serve as facilitators for a city transformation. God used this event to bring repentance and reconciliation between different ethnic groups, including Native Americans and African Americans. We even had ceremonial foot washings. A powerful moment occurred when a white lady whose ancestors had owned slaves repented and washed the feet of a 91-year-old black lady whose father had been a slave. There was also reconciliation between Christians of Jewish and Catholic origin. Each group repented for the sins of their forefathers, received forgiveness and, as a restoration gesture, washed others' feet. This process facilitated the healing of the land and launched the movement that has become known as Transformation Raleigh.

Now, here I was, seven months later in July 2006, watching the outcome of the reconciliation meeting the previous January. I went first to a prayer meeting in Wake Forest and then to one in Raleigh. Both meetings were amazing in that there was such wonderful unity between African-American and European-American participants. At the second meeting, Pastor Bill Morgan, head of Bethlehem Baptist Church and leader of the Raleigh pastors' prayer group, instructed us to begin the meeting by kneeling or lying prostrate on the ground to seek God's direction for the city. Then we proclaimed the things we heard in prayer for all to hear.

In the Schools

During the July 2006 Raleigh visit, 16-year-old Adam Walton picked me up from the home of Sirus and Kaye Chitsaz. I hardly recognized him because he had shaved his long, curly hair in order to be more comfortable in the heat and humidity at Millbrook High School's summer football camp. Adam is the team's starting center.

We drove to a nearby sandwich shop to grab a bite and chat. Adam and I had really gotten to know one another during our July 2005 trip to Argentina. During that trip, I had observed the strong relationship between Adam and his father. When they returned home, they worked as a team to transform Millbrook High School. Even Adam's mom,

Leslie Walton, was swept into the revival fire that her husband and son had brought back from Argentina. After years at home raising her five children, all of the excitement of seeing God at work in Adam's high school had prompted her to go back to work as a teacher at West Mill-brook Middle School.

As Adam and I enjoyed our deli sandwiches, I asked him when he first became aware that he was part of God's strategy to transform Raleigh. He said it began in Argentina, but that it became crystal clear when he returned home and saw the DVD documenting how teenager Daniel Chinen had worked to transform his Honolulu high school. When he saw that testimony, Adam knew that God could bring about the same kind of transformation in his school.

Adam went on to explain that during the trip to Argentina, he had realized he was all wrong about the concept of evangelism. He used to think that as a Christian, his job was to tell his friends they were going to hell if they did not know Jesus. He did not see this as a very enjoyable task. But during the trip to Argentina, he heard an expression about prayer evangelism that stayed with him: "Talk to God about your neighbors, before you talk to your neighbors about God." He said he became much more positive about prayer evangelism than he had been about trying to scare his friends into faith.

Just before the new school year began in September 2005, Adam and his dad began Campus Light. I was there when they introduced this new strategy at Millbrook High School. Using the Millbrook student roster, they made up 3x5-inch cards with the names of 10 students on each card. They also put the principal's name on each card so that she would be blessed each time one of these intercessors prayed blessings over the 10 students on their card. Then one Saturday Doug and Adam invited 100 people to the Millbrook cafeteria and asked each person to take a card and commit to praying for each name on the card. After a few instructions, the group prayer-walked every square inch of the school.

About that same time, Adam began preseason football practices in preparation for the 2005 season. Almost immediately he began to see manifestations of a changed spiritual climate among the students.

One friend asked Adam why he didn't use foul language like others did. Adam responded that God had filled the void inside him so that his speech reflected the peace and security he feels. He asked his friend if he could pray that he would stop using foul language and start feeling that same peace and security. The next day, that teammate told Adam he hadn't used foul language during the entire 24 hours since Adam had prayed for him.

Later that year, Adam felt led to take a Bible to school with him, which he read in his free time during first period. A girl in the class asked Adam about it, and said that she needed to read the Bible. When Adam asked her why, she said her life was riddled with sin. Adam responded that we are all sinners, but the girl indicated that her sins were much worse than most. Adam asked if he could pray for her. She responded by confessing her sin to Adam. Adam thought to himself, *I can't believe she is telling me this.* Then he prayed for the girl to be free of this sin and to be able to live a healthy life.

About a month later, in the same first-period class, Adam saw that same girl. He asked her how things were going, especially in the area for which he had prayed for her. "I'm doing a lot better now" was her response. Adam asked if she needed prayer for anything else. She said she was really concerned about her upcoming final exams. Without waiting for Adam to initiate prayer, the girl said, "Let's pray right now." She gathered all the other students in the room and instructed them to hold hands while Adam prayed for them—right in the middle of the first-period class. Adam began by blessing them. He asked the Holy Spirit to be with them and give them peace. He also prayed for the teacher who was sitting in front of the class, watching this impromptu prayer meeting. When he prayed for her, the teacher began to weep. The Holy Spirit was visiting that classroom. When he finished praying, the class went wild. They said they could not believe they had just prayed in school. Everyone thought praying in class was "cool."

At this point in the conversation, Adam shifted my attention back to the present—and the football summer camp now underway at Lenior Rhyne College. When Adam checked in at his dorm room, his roommate was already there. Adam knew that some of the guys watched pornography on the DVD players in the rooms, so Adam made it clear to his roommate that pornography was not acceptable in their room. All of the team captains came to their room and talked about the pornography situation. One teammate told Adam he knew watching pornographic movies was wrong, but he blurted out his fear that if he gave up watching pornography, he would have to become a Christian. He was concerned that if he became a Christian, he wouldn't be able to have any fun.

Adam responded dramatically. "Look at me. Do I look like I'm cooped up in my room all day—not having any fun?" Adam continued, "God doesn't want to make your life miserable; He just wants to bless you." The room was silent. Just then the coach came by and urged them to get down to the practice field.

During a scrimmage on the practice field, a player used foul language. One of the captains said, "Hey, watch your tongue!" Adam knew his behavior was having a positive impact on the other guys. He felt he was becoming a spiritual captain for the team.

After the football camp ended, Andy George, the youth pastor from Crossroads Fellowship, offered to let the Millbrook football team use the Crossroads Fellowship facility as a retreat center on game days. The head football coach, along with his assistant coach, Pastor George, and three booster club mothers—one of whom was Adam's mother—met to discuss the team's game-day meetings at the church. The head football coach liked the idea of having the team sequestered on game days. Additionally, he asked Pastor Andy if he would lead the team in devotions before each game.

Toward the end of the school year, Doug Walton, Sirus Chitsaz and Andy George met with Millbrook High School principal Dana King to ask how they and local churches could bless and serve the school. Ms. King suggested that men from various congregations could come to the campus during lunchtime to encourage the students. She said many students are lonesome, lacking both positive role models and a positive male presence in their lives. Doug, Andy and Sirus agreed to work with local Christian congregations like Crossroads Fellowship and others to bring that male presence on campus during lunchtime.

Further, Adam and his family's involvement at the school is having a positive impact on their church. Adam recently met with a group of friends from Crossroads Church. At lunch, he told them about God's marvelous works at his school. They were likewise inspired and told him it was their turn to experience God's move.

Adam also told me that in less than a year, the youth group at Crossroads Church had grown from 60 to 210. Thirty-five of those kids attend Millbrook High School with Adam. Another 80 attend Wakefield High School. Adam leads the Crossroads kids at Millbrook in a daily prayer meeting before school starts. A similar prayer group operates at Wakefield on Tuesdays and Thursdays.

When we finished lunch, Adam drove me back to his home to meet with his parents. Doug and Leslie told me they were holding prayer meetings at various schools on the third Saturday of every month. For the first 90 days they were at Millbrook. During the second 90-day stretch they were at Sanderson. During the third 90-day period they were at Wakefield. All three of the Wakefield schools (high school, middle school and elementary school) are located on the same site. God gave Doug and Leslie entry into the middle school first, and from there they prayer-walked the elementary school and the high school. While praying in the middle school on that first Saturday, they heard the Spirit say, "The kingdom of God has come to Wakefield."

Adam's friend Andrea Jones and two other Wakefield students went to their principal at Wakefield High and said, "We wanted to inform you that we are praying before school in the Media Center. Is there anything we can pray about for the school?" They started with 6 kids—they're now up to about 25 kids praying on Tuesday and Thursday mornings at Wakefield High.

SPREADING THE FIRE

In June 2005, in response to a call by Pastor Bill Morgan of Bethlehem Baptist Church, 30 Raleigh pastors signed a Prayer Covenant for Unity. They agreed to pray and fast together every week for one hour from July 1 to September 30. They also agreed to pray individually, obey the Holy

Spirit and avoid promoting their own ministries during this time. They based these covenants on 2 Chronicles 7:14 and Psalm 25. The time proved so meaningful after the initial 90 days that they chose to extend the prayer meetings indefinitely.

A group of 18 North Carolina leaders joined 300 participants from 60 cities at the Transformation USA meeting in Elk River in November 2005. Ed Silvoso and I participated in a special meeting of all of the North Carolina participants. The group was ready to put what they had learned into action. Ed Silvoso told them they were called to transform the entire state of North Carolina. Everyone there felt the weight of this mission from the Lord.

One-hundred forty people from Raleigh and six other cities attended a meeting at the Ezra Center in Raleigh on December 8. About 35 were pastors, and the rest of the attendees were evenly divided between marketplace ministers and intercessors. The group agreed to partner with Harvest Evangelism. They committed to implement the My City, God's City strategy, developed by Harvest Evangelism's Ed Silvoso and Dave Thompson.

In February, Durham businessman Ron Jacobs hosted a meeting in his conference room attended by about 25 people, including Pastor Ron Lewis, Pastor Bill Fuller, Dave Thompson, Sirus Chitsaz, Pastor Bill Morgan, Pastor Jim Sink, Pastor Les Lawrence, Wendy Clark and me. We planned a meeting called Transformation North Carolina, to be held at King's Park Church in Durham, on September 8 and 9, 2006.

In addition to Ed Silvoso, speakers included Chuck Ripka, Mayor Stephanie Klinzing, Pastor Cal Chinen, Daniel Chinen, Jack Serra and me. Transformation Raleigh was presented as a working prototype of transformation and prayer evangelism within North Carolina. Other cities from around the state were encouraged to emulate the Raleigh process.

GENERATIONS OF PRAYER

This move of God did not begin recently. Generations of intercessors have responded to God's call to pray for transformation to come to Raleigh. One minister who has been interceding on behalf of Raleigh for decades is Don Rayno, who leads Concerts of Prayer, a ministry that gathers Christians to cry out together in prayer for Raleigh's transformation. Another minister is Dan Nelson, who has led worship music on the streets of downtown Raleigh for years.

When I think of all who have interceded for the outcome that we are witnessing today, I think of Luke 10:23-24:

> Then He turned to His disciples and said privately, "Blessed are the eyes which see the things you see; for I tell you that many prophets and kings have desired to see what you see, and have not seen it, and to hear what you hear, and have not heard it."

Are you seeing the move of God on your city? If not, perhaps it's because you haven't heard His call—or haven't answered it yet. Begin today to listen for His voice. Ask what He desires of you. Then follow His lead passionately. He will bring the transformation—a vision beyond your wildest imaginings.

CHAPTER 23

FOR GOD'S GLORY

A common thread in these stories I have shared is the idea that our work is ministry—and unless we embrace that concept, we'll never be used mightily by God to transform the marketplace. For that reason, I'd like to close this book with the amazing story of a marketplace minister from Hong Kong, Yuk-Lynn.

I met Roy and Yuk-Lynn Chen and a number of other pulpit and marketplace ministers in April 2006 at a dinner party at the home of Judge Barbara Chan of Hong Kong. After dinner, I showed the group the *Marketplace Transformation* DVD produced by Harvest Evangelism, and Roy and Yuk-Lynn were particularly moved by the presentation. They purchased many copies of the DVD and said they were going to give them to their Christian friends who were marketplace leaders.

Later that same month, Roy and Yuk-Lynn flew to New York City and participated in the International Transformation Network (ITN) meeting led by Harvest Evangelism. They met Ed Silvoso there and were further intrigued by the concept of transforming nations through the marketplace. Then, in October 2006, Ed Silvoso was in Hong Kong to launch the Asian chapter of the ITN and, once again, Roy and Yuk-Lynn were there and found the transformation message irresistibly compelling.

A month later, Roy and Yuk-Lynn joined us in Buenos Aires at the Harvest Evangelism conference on marketplace transformation, and Yuk-Lynn Woo (she has retained her maiden name) gave her testimony at a luncheon for international delegates and Argentine marketplace leaders. As I listened to her story, I felt the Lord was leading me to add her testimony to this book. *What am I doing?* I thought to myself, *I have just a few days before this manuscript is due at the publisher.*

Nevertheless, I told Yuk-Lynn what I was thinking—I said I couldn't guarantee we could get another chapter into the manuscript, but I wanted to try. Yuk-Lynn responded that the Lord had told her four times prior to the trip to Argentina that she should write her story. She told me that in obedience to the Lord's prompting she had written her testimony and could therefore email it to me. By the end of that same day, I was pouring over Yuk-Lynn's written testimony.

THE HEART OF HONG KONG

A friend prompted Yuk-Lynn to see her business as her ministry. Shortly afterward, another friend gave her a tape about the gift of faith. As the tape concluded, Yuk-Lynn prayed to receive the gift of faith. After that prayer, she was filled with such faith that she proclaimed that all 2,000 of the employees in five locations, *and their entire households*, would accept Jesus Christ.

Fifty-three years ago, her grandfather had built a cotton yarn-spinning and denim-fabric manufacturing factory in a desolate area known as Tsuen Wan, in Hong Kong's New Territories. This area is much more populated now. Recently, the city's church leaders showed Yuk-Lynn that Tsuen Wan is in Hong Kong's geographic center. The factory had been placed strategically in Tsuen Wan, even though none of Yuk-Lynn's ancestors knew Christ. Even the company name, Central Textiles, reflects this prophetic significance—they call it "Centre" for short.

Yuk-Lynn and her brother Pat Nie and a few staff members started a prayer group at work. Then they decided the first step toward their objective of evangelizing the work force was to hold an Alpha course—a course to which people can come to learn about Christ—at the factory.

On the day the company started the Alpha program, one of their workers fell from a high place in the factory and went into a coma as a result of his injury. His brain was so swollen that doctors had to remove a portion of his skull to reduce the pressure. The doctors said he would not live. Many of the other employees questioned why such a negative thing would happen when God was moving so strongly within the company. It seemed the enemy was warning Yuk-Lynn that bad things like this would happen if she continued to bring Christ into the business.

Undaunted, she gathered all the Christian workers to pray for their fallen coworker—many of those who prayed were brand-new believers. Some of them visited him in the hospital and laid hands on him and prayed for him. They had faith that the Lord would work a miracle and heal him. After six months, even though he has not fully recovered from the fall, he is alive and his whole family has come to faith in Jesus Christ.

This was also the first month in the company's history when there were absolutely no orders. Yuk-Lynn was sure it was a spiritual attack—she said she could smell fear in the atmosphere around the company. One day the Lord led her to 2 Chronicles 20:21, where Jehoshaphat gives thanks to the Lord and sings that the Lord's love endures forever: "After consulting the people, Jehoshaphat appointed men to sing to the LORD and to praise him for the splendor of his holiness as they went out at the head of the army, saying: 'Give thanks to the LORD, for his love endures forever'" (*NIV*).

Immediately, she stopped working and went home to worship the Lord. On this day that she had chosen to thank the Lord and acknowledge His enduring love, the company gained two new business relationships.

After the Alpha course, the Lord led Yuk-Lynn to reach out to the Body of Christ around Tsuen Wan. After all, how can one person pastor so many employees while taking care of her family? She was hesitant because the congregations in Tsuen Wan had never been unified. Eventually, she remembered the fourth pivotal paradigm shared by Ed Silvoso in his personal presentations.[1] She felt that she was being told, *The Lord is building the Church—you are not.* She opened the company's door to the city's congregations and, to her surprise, those congregations were united. They told her the Lord had given each of them different gifts, and they were meant to help each other serve the community and bring people into the Kingdom.

The pastors' network in Tsuen Wan is called the Love Your Neighbor Network, and it unites 15 ministries and denominations in the district. The Love Your Neighbor Network and Central Fabrics have joined together in a unique relationship that could lead the Tsuen Wan district to be the first of the 18 districts within Hong Kong to enter into transformation.

After attending the ITN meeting in New York, Yuk-Lynn finally understood what the Lord was asking her to do. She began to see the bigger picture: God had called her not only to transform the company, but also the entire community. Because Tsuen Wan is in the heart of Hong Kong, God has given Yuk-Lynn special grace to start Hong Kong's transformation.

On July 19, 2006, the Lord asked Yuk-Lynn to gather all the Christians in the company and ask them to repent for all their sins. She told them they were on an impossible mission—one that only God could accomplish. She told them they had to advance from being a good company to a great one. It was the first time Yuk-Lynn felt the Lord was calling them to become a world-class company that would glorify Him. Competition from other firms and problems maintaining quality on her production line would have to be overcome.

Then the Lord asked Yuk-Lynn to wash her employees' feet. She really struggled, but finally realized it was her pride and fear of men that caused her to resist the Lord's directive. She washed the feet of the department heads. Then her brother Pat Nie and the department heads washed their subordinates' feet. On that day, the company hierarchy was broken. They had finally become brothers and sisters in Christ.

SOLVING THE QUALITY PROBLEM

But their problems were not yet over—Central Textiles was experiencing quality-control difficulties. Still, even here, the Lord provided. He called Anna Poon, a friend, to intercede for Yuk-Lynn. The week after the foot-washing service, Anna and Yuk-Lynn traveled to New York for the ITN meeting. In New York, Anna introduced Yuk-Lynn to her husband, Jim, who is the worldwide chairman of the Six Sigma Quality Council of a multinational electronics company (Six Sigma is the top-level of quality-control systems pioneered by Motorola).

Yuk-Lynn started to tell Jim about the quality-control problems at her textile plants, but before she could finish, Jim surprised her by offering to help solve the company's quality problems *without charge*. He offered to train her staff in the Six Sigma process. Yuk-Lynn was stunned.

Then imagine her surprise when she learned that Jim's head office is in Tsuen Wan, just one street away from her office. The Central Textiles and Central Fabrics employees asked her why anyone would give them world-class training for free. That was Yuk-Lynn's opportunity to tell them about Jesus. The Lord opened up evangelical opportunities for her to reach all her employees through Jim's sacrificial actions.

PREPARING FOR THE HARVEST

Yuk-Lynn's aunt, who has the gift of giving, will now take care of the family foundation. Yuk-Lynn's aunt heard Ed Silvoso speak in her church in Palo Alto, California, about the five pivotal paradigms for nation transformation. This moved her heart to want to give to the poor and needy, especially in Tsuen Wan. Central Textiles and the Woo family will join forces with the united congregations of Tsuen Wan to have a banquet for 1,000 elderly people. Yuk-Lynn cannot wait to see what God wants them to do to break down systemic poverty in Tsuen Wan.

The Lord gave her Isaiah 37:30: "This shall be a sign to you: you shall eat this year such as grows of itself, and the second year what springs from the same; also in the third year sow and reap, plant vineyards and eat the fruit of them."

This is the second year of Yuk-Lynn's amazing walk of transformation. In accordance with the last two lines of Isaiah 37:30, she believes that in the third year they will plant their vineyards and God will grant a huge harvest.

Note

1. The five pivotal paradigms are now published in Ed's book *Transformation* (Ventura, CA: Regal, 2007).

TRANSFORMATION CHURCHES

Rev. Dr. Gregory M. Pagh

I hope you have been encouraged, as I have, by the extraordinary miracles described in this book by my good friend Rick Heeren. As Central USA Regional Vice President for Harvest Evangelism, Inc., Rick has been instrumental in challenging pastors and marketplace leaders in Elk River, Minnesota, as well as others worldwide, to believe God for spiritual transformation in our city, state, nation and throughout the world.

For more than 10 years, committed Christian believers have been gathering every Tuesday at noon at the Elk River Public Library Community Room to pray for our city. This location is no accident. God has anointed this time of unified prayer and allowed us to minister to government leaders, businessmen and women, school administrators, law enforcement officials, and many others.

The Pray Elk River movement is a response to Jesus' passionate prayer for Christian unity in John 17:23: "May they be brought to complete unity to let the world know that you sent me and have loved them even as you have loved me" (*NIV*). When local pastors and marketplace leaders gather to pray, we set aside denominational affiliation and personal theology to lift up the name of Jesus in unity. We believe God "is able to do exceedingly abundantly above all that we ask or think!" We have experienced extraordinary miracles.

The first of these miracles is a noticeable change in our city's "spiritual climate." We have seen a greater openness about spiritual things in every facet of community life. Conversations about Jesus, as well as shared prayer, take place regularly in local restaurants, schools, businesses and even jails. Citywide, new ministries of compassion have opened, ministering to at-risk youth, the poor, the grieving, the homeless and children as far away as Rwanda, Africa. Physical miracles of healing are no longer considered unusual. The church is a welcome partner in the community, rather than a judgmental antagonist. Competition among the churches has given way to an unprecedented level of cooperation. Yet, we believe these signs are just the beginning of the transformation that is coming!

Just as Rick shared with you several "Kingdom Businesses" that are experiencing extraordinary miracles, I want to share with you the beauty of "Transformation Churches" that God is raising up today. As a launching point for further reflection on all that God has just stirred in your heart, let me share four of the key principles that are helping define Transformation Churches today. These principles are being embraced by the pastoral leaders in the Pray Elk River movement as a prototype for others who desire to see Christ transform churches and cities.

First, *Transformation Churches seek transformation!* Perhaps that seems obvious, but evidence suggests that many churches no longer truly believe in God's power to change lives. We talk about it. We preach it. We know the Bible says it's supposed to happen, but reality is another matter. There is very little evidence today of authentic, measurable, spiritual transformation in our personal lives, churches and communities. As a matter of fact, researchers consistently point out that Christians are more likely to reflect the values, worldview and behavior of the culture around them rather than those of a transformed life in Christ.

Several years ago I participated in an interview team that was hiring a marriage and family counselor for Lutheran Social Services of New England. One of my fellow interviewers asked the prospective counselor, "Do you believe that people can change?" The interviewer explained that he would not hire a counselor who didn't expect to see God's power transform his or her clients' lives. This is a fitting question to ask in the Church today: "Do we really believe in spiritual transformation?" After all, if we don't believe individual lives can be radically transformed by the power of God at work within us, how can we possibly expect to see transformation come to cities and nations?

In 2 Corinthians 5:17, the apostle Paul boldly proclaims, "Therefore, if anyone is in Christ, he is a new creation; the old has gone, the new has come!" (*NIV*). Then again, in Romans 12:2 he challenges, "Do not conform any longer to the pattern of this world, but be transformed by the renewing of your mind" (*NIV*). That's transformation! Old things become new! The mind and the heart are changed. Our unholy alliance with the world is broken. We are raised up by God's love and grace to see the world as God sees it. Excellence becomes the norm, and extraordinary miracles happen every day through the power of the Holy Spirit.

Transformation Churches claim these promises wholeheartedly. They not only believe in the possibility of transformation, but they also seek it, they pray for it in unity with other believers and they work together, believing God will bring spiritual transformation to individuals, churches, cities and whole nations!

Many Christians today are praying fervently for revival, but revival is based on the assumption that "life" is already present. You can't revive something that is dead. Too often we just try to put a new face on our church life and pretend that is transformation. That's called a façade. We build new buildings. We change our worship style. We launch new ministries. We hire more staff and develop new programs, but our hearts remain far from God.

For true transformation to come to our churches, this spirit of religion that so easily settles for superficial faith must be broken. Form without substance never leads to authentic spiritual transformation. We must die to self in order to be raised with Christ. The old must pass away in order for the new to come. Unless there is heart-deep, life-changing transformation, the Church will remain ineffectual and have little impact on the world. We must not only believe in the possibility of transformation; we must also earnestly seek it.

That's why Transformation Churches seek transformation! They not only believe transformation is possible. They long for it. They pray for it. They work for it. They earnestly desire the spiritual transformation of individuals, institutions and whole communities, because they know that's what Jesus died for. Transformation Churches believe in the power of the gospel of Jesus Christ to change people from the inside out; people who in turn God will use to change the world! It is this passionate belief that continues to shape the Pray Elk River movement and capture our hearts as pastors and marketplace leaders.

Second, *Transformation Churches see themselves as part of the "Church of the City."* Long before Christians had so neatly, or not so neatly, arranged themselves into dozens of denominations and ministry organizations, the Church of Jesus Christ was recognized by geography rather than church polity. In the New Testament, we read of the church at Corinth, Ephesus, Philippi, Thessalonica, and so on. Although it gathered in many locations, ranging from homes, to the temple, to the marketplace, the Church was understood to include all believers in that location.

If transformation is going to come to whole cities and nations today, we must reclaim the concept of the "Church of the City." We must once again stand united as brothers and sisters in Christ. What does it mean, practically speaking, to act as the Church of the City? It starts when pastors recognize they are called not only to serve their local congregation, but also to serve in partnership with others as "spiritual elders" of their city or geographic area. Just as there is great spiritual authority in unified prayer, there is even greater spiritual authority when brothers and sisters in Christ stand side by side in spiritual agreement for their city's transformation.

Transformation Churches are passionately committed to fulfilling the Great Commission of Matthew 28:16-20, believing Jesus died and rose again not only to redeem individuals, but also to transform cities, nations and the whole world. Jesus said, "Go and make disciples of all nations." This mandate calls us to a vision of the Church that is larger than our own denomination or local congregation. It takes the whole Church to reach the whole city!

The Church Growth Movement of the past 30 years has helped many congregations develop a greater mission focus and passion for reaching the lost. Evangelism efforts have increased and many nonbelievers have been brought into the kingdom of God through a personal relationship of faith in Jesus Christ. Megachurches have brought vitality to the Body of Christ through their vision, teaching and strategic thinking. But in spite of this influence, the Church Growth Movement has not resulted in a single example of a city or region in America that has been significantly transformed by the gospel of Jesus Christ.

The reason for this failure, I believe, is that church growth does not automatically translate to individual or corporate transformation within the Body of Christ. We've grown a lot of big churches, but no single church, no matter how dynamic or successful, can reach the whole city. We must recognize the true Body of Christ—and that includes every believer in our geographical area. We must rise up and be the Church that Jesus has called us to be, acting in unity "so that the world may know." Transformation Churches in Elk River, Minnesota, as well as a growing number of churches around the world, are embracing this paradigm of the Church of the City.

In the Pray Elk River movement, we strive to have our words and deeds convey our deep desire to act as the Church of the City. Therefore, we have agreed in the Spirit to the following commitments:

- We will make Jesus our number-one priority.
- We will build genuine relationships of love and support.
- We will pray and worship and work together in unity "so that the world may know . . ."
- We will sacrifice any claim to individual success as pastors or congregations, for the sake of our unified witness to Elk River and the world, exercising mutual submission within the Body of Christ.
- We will bless instead of curse.
- We will lay hold of our collective spiritual authority as the Church, "binding and loosing" in Jesus' name, and standing together against the Evil One.
- We will expect miracles as a witness to God's power.
- We will work to strengthen marriages and families.
- We will care for the poor and strive to eliminate systemic poverty.
- We will pray for and bless our city leaders and public officials.
- We will remain a "move of the Spirit" rather than a program or an organization.

These commitments have been lived out through years of prayer and partnership. When our Pray Elk River Servant Leader Team is speaking to pastors and marketplace leaders from other communities, I often describe how I used to participate in what I call "drive-by cursings." Many of you know exactly what I mean. A "drive-by cursing" takes place when you drive by another church in your city and, in effect, curse it because its members don't share your theology or your way of doing things. Or worse yet, you subtly curse others from the pulpit by conveying the attitude, "We're the ones who really have the truth! Our church is where the action is!"

Once I really began to understand the implication of the Church of the City, my thoughts and attitudes changed. When I began meeting weekly with my fellow pastors to pray, it wasn't so easy to cast judgment on their ministries. I began to see their heart. I began to see our differences as assets, not liabilities. But even more important, I began to focus on what unites us: our common confession that Jesus is Lord! This trumps everything else, and some day, when we get to heaven, it will be all that matters. Shouldn't it also matter the most to us now?

Today I participate in "drive-by blessings"! When I pass another local congregation, regardless of the Christian denomination, I intentionally bless it, speak peace over it and pray for its success. After all, we are on the same team, working toward the same goal—to see Jesus Christ transform the greater Elk River area and beyond! So, you see, this concept of the Church of the City is not an exercise in superficial ecumenism. It is at the core of what it means to be the Church and live out our mission together in Christ. If you adopt this transformation principle, I guarantee that both your heart and your approach to ministry will change forever!

Not every pastor or church will embrace this city-reaching vision, because denominationalism, individualism, pride and fear are so engrained. Don't be discouraged. Our experience has shown that when a committed core of pastors and marketplace leaders begin to pray in unity for their city, the Holy Spirit is able to do exceedingly abundantly above all that we ask or think. Psalm 133 perhaps captures it best: "How good and pleasant it is when brothers live together in unity! For there the Lord bestows his blessing, even life forevermore" (vv. 1,3, *NIV*). Transformation Churches are discovering a powerful anointing from God awaiting those who are willing to see beyond their local congregation walls and act together as the Church of the City.

Third, *Transformation Churches commission and release their members to reach the marketplace.* For more than 500 years now, Protestant Churches have talked about the theology of "the priesthood of all believers." First Peter 2:9 says, "But you are a chosen people, a royal priesthood, a holy nation, a people belonging to God, that you may declare the praises of him who called you out of darkness into his wonderful light" (*NIV*). At the heart of this Reformation theology is the assertion that "everyone is a minister."

Transformation Churches are actively implementing this theology of "the priesthood of all believers" by commissioning and releasing their members to be ministers in the marketplace where they live and serve every day. The workplace is no longer viewed as a necessary evil. Instead, many believers are discovering that it is their personal mission field. A phrase that has become a part of the vocabulary of the Christian community here in the Elk River area is "My work is my ministry." Christian ministry is no longer defined by what takes place within the walls of the local congregation, such as teaching Sunday School, serving as an usher, singing on a worship team or leading a small group. Christian ministry also happens in the marketplace, in the arena of business, labor, government and education.

In the Pray Elk River movement, we have come to view the marketplace even more broadly. It is anywhere people live, work and play. The marketplace includes our family and friends, neighbors, coworkers, classmates, community organizations and sports teams.

When Jesus commissioned His followers to "Go and make disciples of all nations," He was not only sending them out to the far reaches of the world; He was also sending them out to be "salt and light" within their own circles of influence. While this should be self-evident in our theology, it has not been our common practice in the Christian church. For example, too often pastors have viewed business leaders only in terms of the leadership and financial support they can contribute to growing the local congregation and expanding its programs. Transformation Churches recognize that God also wants to use business leaders to transform the marketplace.

At the encouragement of Ed Silvoso, president of Harvest Evangelism, I have been making regular visits to my congregation members' workplaces. I take them out to lunch and ask, "Can you tell me about your work? What do you love about it? What challenges are you facing? What is a miracle you need? How would you like to see God transform your workplace for His glory?" After we've had a good talk, we go back to their workplace. I get "the tour," and then we pray.

As God answers our prayers in the weeks that follow, their faith grows and a new boldness develops in the lives of these "marketplace ministers." Their attitude changes from, "I'm a Christian just trying to survive in the workplace" to "I'm a Christian beginning to thrive in the workplace!" We can't talk about transformation just within the safe environment of the Church. We must help people begin to experience transformation in the marketplace, where the rubber meets the road!

A member of the congregation I serve, Christ Lutheran, is working in a very tough environment as a highway department maintenance manager for a Twin Cities-area county government. Every day he deals with a corrupt union, lazy workers who steal tools and overcharge for their work, and supervisors who tell him to just look the other way. He has been ridiculed and ostracized for being a man of integrity.

I visited his workplace and we asked God to begin transforming his poisonous work environment into a place of honesty, integrity and respect. Recently, he called to report that the county has hired a consulting firm to evaluate the organization from top to bottom. This has never happened before. Since we prayed, he has also discovered a Christian friend who shares his heart for transformation, and they have begun to pray together for their fellow workers. This friend's attitude about his work has also changed dramatically. He knows God is using him there and so he is actually excited about going to work each day. He no longer talks about quitting! You see, spiritual conversion can happen in a moment, but transformation is usually a process.

For transformation to break loose on a grand scale, church members must be similarly commissioned and released to be marketplace ministers. Transformation Churches are not threatened by this change; they support it and encourage it. Our Pray Elk River movement has been blessed to host numerous Anointed for Business conferences and Faith @ Work luncheons. We have publicly commissioned hundreds of marketplace ministers and encouraged them to recognize that their work is their ministry.

As pastors we have also come to accept our marketplace leaders as full partners in our city-reaching efforts. They continue to share gifts and insights that have led to greater unity, influence and passion for the things of God. We believe the next great move of the Spirit is going to come through the marketplace. Friends, it's already happening!

And fourth, *Transformation Churches commit a growing percentage of their resources to Kingdom expansion beyond the local congregation!* What is the evidence of such a commitment? Transformation Churches make tangible investments in other churches and ministries in their community to strengthen the whole Body of Christ. As well, Transformation Churches launch new ministries in partnership with other churches and the marketplace that help reach the city for Christ. They do this even though they may not get credit for a particular program and the ministry may not result in growing their own congregation. Transformation Churches participate in shared mission partnerships that cross over denominational boundaries and contribute to the expansion of the kingdom of God around the world. Transformation Churches support ministries, organizations and institutions that are committed to the transformation of nations. And Transformation Churches strive to utilize 51 percent or more of their resources to support mission and ministry beyond their local congregation!

It's true that many Christian churches today are faithful in tithing—giving 10 percent of their income—to ministries beyond their walls. A great deal of good has been accomplished through the generous benevolence of Christian congregations and organizations around the world. Where would we be without Christian colleges and universities; hospitals; relief organizations; and those that care for the poor, the erly, and the mentally and physically challenged? Transformation Churches celebrate these gifts but also recognize that a tithe is just the beginning for the spirit of generosity that God desires to see capture the hearts of those who serve Him.

The apostle Paul speaks glowingly of this kind of generosity as he had witnessed it in the Macedonian churches. In 2 Corinthians 8:2-5, he says, "Out of the most severe trial, their overflowing joy and their extreme poverty welled up in rich generosity. For I testify that they gave as much as they were able, and even beyond their ability. Entirely on their own, they urgently pleaded with us for the privilege of sharing in this service to the saints. And they did not do as we expected, but they gave themselves first to the Lord and then to us in keeping with God's will" (*NIV*).

Do you notice the qualities that Paul describes as characteristic of generous giving? They include joy born out of trial and poverty, giving beyond obvious ability, and a deep desire to serve the Lord and others by exceeding expectations. I believe that the day is coming when the hearts of individual Christians will be so transformed by the love of God that they will "urgently plead for the privilege of sharing their gifts with others." Could this spirit of generosity also overcome the Christian Church?

On October 1, 2000, seven congregations representing various denominations here in the Elk River area cancelled our Sunday morning worship schedule and met together for a Celebration of Unity at the local high school. The offering collected that day was $15,600. We pastors felt led to sow this resource back into our city. The entire offering was presented to our mayor, Stephanie Klinzing, to begin a Mayor's Discretionary Fund to assist the poor and needy. That generous gift birthed a spirit of generosity in our city that continues to grow to this very day! As a result, several new ministries have been launched with a vision for city and nation transformation.

Love Elk River is a ministry of caring and support to the poor in our communities, yet it has a unique discipleship component. Its only budget is the generous time, compassion and prayers of the volunteers who serve under the direction of our mayor. When a financial need does arise, prayers go out, and the money just seems to come forth. A unique transitional housing program has also grown out of Love Elk River that may one day become a national model because of its cost efficiency and effectiveness.

Mission Rwanda is a community-wide mission partnership connecting Elk River with the people of Karaba, Rwanda. This "first of its kind" community mission partnership connects churches, businesses and schools in response to the HIV/AIDS crisis in Africa. Today more than 500 Rwandan children are sponsored through World Vision by families in the greater Elk River area. We continue to believe that as we sow into the lives of children halfway around the world, God will give us bigger hearts to see the needs right here in our own community.

Following the devastation of Hurricane Katrina, Elk River businessman D. J. Baaken provided the leadership for a new crisis response ministry called Hope-filled Hands. Two semi trailer loads of relief supplies were sent to Slidell, Louisiana, within the first week after the storm. Since that time, several teams of volunteers have traveled to the New Orleans area to provide ongoing relief, construction assistance and lots of love and support. D. J. is a leading example of an "on-fire" Christian who has discovered that his work is his ministry. Many other missionaries and ministries, both local and worldwide, have received financial support, volunteer assistance and prayer through the spirit of generosity that has become characteristic of our community.

In 2 Corinthians 9, the apostle Paul continues, "Now he who supplies seed to the sower and bread for food will also supply and increase your store of seed and will enlarge the harvest of your righteousness. You will be made rich in every way so that you can be generous on every occasion, and through us your generosity will result in thanksgiving to God" (vv. 10-11, *NIV*).

The Church of the City also continues to discover that a spirit of generosity leads to a harvest of righteousness and thanksgiving to God. About three years ago, Twin Lakes Christian, the Assemblies of God congregation in our community, was building a brand-new facility on a beautiful piece of property east of town. This church had seen some difficult days. Many of the area churches sent financial gifts to encourage them in their growth. These gifts represented far more than dollars and cents. These gifts spoke loudly to the whole community, and especially to the members of that congregation, about our partnership in the gospel. As the foundation of the new sanctuary was completed, the area pastors gathered together on the property, joined hands and asked God to "enlarge the harvest." You see, a transformation mindset unleashes within us a spirit of generosity that is more interested in growing God's kingdom than in building our own.

Here's a humorous postscript to this story. When Twin Lakes Christian was later able to buy a house next door to be used as a parsonage, I met my good friend Pastor Percy Kallevig for lunch and surprised him with a check for $500 from Christ Lutheran to help with the down payment. I didn't think it was a big deal, just a little encouragement. That next Sunday, Percy shared with his congregation that the Lutheran pastor had given him a check for $500 toward their new parsonage. One of his members approached him immediately after the service and said, "Then here's a check for $1,000. I'm not going to be outdone by the Lutherans!" As I said earlier, transformation is a process!

Friends, let me get straight to the point. As long as 90 percent of our resources go to support buildings, staff salaries and local congregational programming, we will never see whole cities and nations reached for Christ. Jesus said, "Where your treasure is, there your heart will be also" (Matt. 6:21, *NIV*). The fact that most Christian churches struggle to give away even 10 percent of their incomes beyond their local ministries tells me that our hearts have not been truly transformed. We have made the floor the ceiling. It's time to turn this paradigm upside down.

Do you know when we will get serious about fulfilling the Great Commission? It will happen only when 20 percent, 30 percent, 40 percent, 50 percent or more of our congregational budgets are invested in mission to our cities and world, because "where our treasure is, there will our hearts be also!"

I have lifted up this vision to my local congregation, as have several other pastors in our Elk River community. We are preparing to implement a process of growth that would allow us to symbolically make God the senior partner in the finances of our congregations, giving away

51 percent or more of our income to transformational ministries in community and world. We acknowledge that "the earth is the Lord's and everything in it." It all belongs to God. This must be a process of grace, not legalism, but we are determined to be faithful in taking tangible steps toward greater transformation in our city, nation and world.

So I believe that these four key principles are foundational to the definition of Transformation Churches. Others will continue to emerge as God gives greater revelation. These principles are being embraced by a growing number of churches around the world that believe in the power of God to change personal lives, institutions, cities and whole nations.

The International Transformation Network serves as a connecting point for those who want to share information, inspiration and revelation. In partnership with Harvest Evangelism, our Pray Elk River Team has hosted delegations of pastors and marketplace leaders from dozens of cities in the United States as well as from countries from around the world, including Canada, England, Argentina, Bermuda, China, Philippines, Hong Kong, South Africa, Liberia, Rwanda, Ukraine, Australia, and many others.

Transformation Churches are committed to realizing a bigger vision of the Church, one that transcends congregation, denomination and personal theology. Transformation Churches act as the Church of the City, recognizing the spiritual authority that derives from believers standing united in the name of Jesus. Transformation Churches are releasing the Church to be the Church 24/7, as every member takes hold of his or her calling to be a minister in the marketplace. And Transformation Churches are exhibiting a spirit of generosity that is resulting in a harvest of righteousness.

Yes, extraordinary miracles are taking place. The Christian Church is discovering in new ways that God "is able to do exceedingly abundantly above all that we ask or think!"

Rev. Dr. Gregory M. Pagh
Elk River, Minnesota
November 2006

KINGDOM COMPANIES

Many years ago, I was driving my old reliable Honda Accord up to the north side of Minneapolis. I got off the expressway and my clutch went out right at the top of the exit ramp. I called Rachel and she brought me home in her car. Later that day I telephoned my friend Steve Wirth (see chapter 10) and asked if he had a tow rope. I wanted to pull the Honda back to the south side of town. Steve said towing a car on the expressway is too dangerous. He said he would hire a towing company to take the Honda to a repair shop and asked if I had a favorite. When I told him I did not, he said he had recently heard about a shop called Undercar that was owned by two Christian men. Steve then had the Honda towed to the Undercar repair shop.

A few days later I borrowed a white Suburban from a friend and drove it to Undercar to see if the Honda had been repaired. There I met Mike Morrone, one of the two owners of Undercar. Mike told me that he and his partner, Ken Malz, had just opened Undercar Services, Inc. He also told me that he had been in the car repair business at an earlier stage in his life, but that he had put the business in front of his relationship with God and in front of his relationship with his wife, Cindy. He said that it almost ruined him—he almost lost his marriage. Then after a few years of counseling and learning how to grow spiritually, Mike had cried out to God, saying, "Lord, I need confirmation that it is Your will for me to go back into the car repair business."

Mike suggested that there would be two signs, first, that Cindy would be at peace with the decision, and second, that God would send him a spiritual mentor. When Mike and Cindy prayed together, she told Mike that she was at peace with him going back into the car repair business. Mike was still very apprehensive, waiting for that second sign. When Mike looked out of the waiting room window and saw me drive up in the white Suburban, the Holy Spirit told him that I was the one who would mentor him. It was in that context that Mike bolted out the door to meet me.

We prayed together right then and there in the Undercar parking lot. Mike and I look back on that day and acknowledge God's sovereign plan for us to meet. It's been years now that we've been meeting and I've been mentoring him, helping him see his business as his ministry. Very early in our friendship, the Lord led me to declare over him that there would come a time when there would be an Undercar Services car repair shop in every state within the United States. At the time, however, Undercar was struggling to stay in business at just one location. It seemed quite preposterous then that Undercar would grow into a national network. Nevertheless, that was the vision that was given by the Lord, and we had to align our thinking with His.

When I first met Mike, Undercar was a six-bay shop. Their whole shop was approximately 3,600 square feet—quite small for a car repair shop. Undercar got involved with truck fleet business, but had to work on the larger trucks under a tarp outside of the building. This was especially difficult during the cold winter months. As a start-up company, Undercar faced many challenges, such as having trouble paying the rent each month. Eventually the landlord agreed to let Undercar out of its lease in order for them to relocate so that he wouldn't have to go though the process of evicting them.

This was a low point for Mike and his partner, Ken, but I reminded each of them of the declaration that I had made over them that some day Undercar would be a national network of car repair shops. Soon God's extraordinary miracles began to happen. Mike and Ken were able to join another businessman in purchasing a large industrial building. Mike and Ken now own over 50 percent of that building. Their new space in that building is 15,000 square feet. Now Undercar is a 13-bay facility, including one lift that is large enough to handle large trucks. The garage door leading into the facility is also very large—now they can work on trucks inside the building in the coldest weather in complete comfort and warmth. This is significant because it enabled Undercar to expand their number of truck fleet maintenance agreements. They see now that having the land-lord force them out of their lease was actually a blessing!

Mike has since told me that many of Undercar's customers bring them cakes, pies and cookies to thank them for their excellent work. This is unique. Most car repair shops do not have good reputations—actually many people think that mechanics are dishonest and charge too much for work that's unnecessary. The fact that Undercar's customers bring them gifts demonstrates that those customers feel that they receive an extraordinary value there. Customer loyalty and trust are being earned. Some business schools refer to this as a "competitive advantage."

Mike and I began to look for ways to accentuate that competitive advantage. The Lord reminded me that Paul did extraordinary miracles by laying his hands on handkerchiefs which were then taken to sick people to heal them, as we see in Acts 19:11-12:

> And God did extraordinary miracles by the hands of Paul, so that handkerchiefs or aprons were carried away from his body to the sick, and diseases left them and the evil spirits came out of them (*RSV*).

Since beginning this analysis of extraordinary miracles, I have concluded that extraordinary miracles are not limited to using handkerchiefs or aprons. However, I reasoned that if Paul could lay hands on handkerchiefs and aprons, why couldn't the mechanics at Undercar lay hands on their customers' steering wheels and pray prayers of blessing over them? Mike agreed to give this new idea a try. Customers immediately began to testify that after Undercar worked on their cars, there was a "good feeling" in the facility and in their cars as they drove away from the Undercar parking lot. What they were actually saying is that they felt the presence of the Lord at Undercar and in their cars.

At one point, I found out that Undercar was not prospering financially. I began to ask more questions. I found out that Mike and Ken had become involved in the management of another business in another industry. They had even made a loan to the other company using the borrowing power available to Undercar. When Undercar's sales fluctuated, they were unable to borrow short-term working capital from the bank and found themselves trapped.

I confronted Mike and Ken in love with the idea that they had abandoned the revelation from the Lord about Undercar and had shifted their focus and their finances to another company. Mike and Ken received this gentle rebuke in a positive way and repented, turning their thoughts back to the original vision for Undercar. They saw immediate results.

In fact, Mike and I spoke by phone about a week later and he reported that Undercar was now generating positive financial results. Those results have continued for multiple weeks and months. After this improved performance, Mike and Ken have agreed to re-declare that Undercar Services, Inc., is a Kingdom company and will continue to do God's will. They're committed to pursuing the 12 components of a Kingdom Company:

1. Commitment to the King of the company—the Lord Jesus Christ
2. Commitment to obey the King's commands
3. Commitment to marriage and family
4. Commitment to a Kingdom ownership structure
5. Commitment to fulfilling the Great Commission through prayer evangelism
6. Commitment to the five pivotal paradigms
7. Commitment to being extraordinary
8. Commitment to Kingdom thinking
9. Commitment high standards of conduct
10. Commitment to Kingdom giving
11. Commitment to a transformation church
12. Commitment to prayer

1. COMMITMENT TO THE KING OF THE COMPANY

Owners of Kingdom Companies have declared that Jesus Christ is the CEO of the company and that the owner is simply a steward for Him. This principle is based on 1 Chronicles 29:10-16:

While still in the presence of the whole assembly, David expressed his praises to the Lord: "O Lord God of our father Israel, praise your name for ever and ever! Yours is the mighty power and glory and victory and majesty. Everything in the heavens and earth is yours, O Lord, and this is your kingdom. We adore you as being in control of everything. Riches and honor come from you alone, and you are the Ruler of all mankind; your hand controls power and might, and it is at your discretion that men are made great and given strength. O our God, we thank you and praise your glorious name, but who am I and who are my people that we should be permitted to give anything to you? Everything we have has come from you, and we only give you what is yours already! For we are here for but a moment, strangers in the land as our fathers were before us; our days on earth are like a shadow, gone so soon, without a trace. O Lord our God, all of this material that we have gathered to build a temple for your holy name comes from you! It all belongs to you!" (*TLB*).

Through this Scripture the Lord told me that everything belongs to Him. The morning that He led me to this passage, I went to my computer and opened an email from my friend Dr. Paul Cox. Here is what he had written:

It appears that when a declaration is made that something "belongs to me" there is an evil spiritual connection formed between the individual and the object. The object may range in size from a small item to a large land mass. Therefore, if ownership is declared over a piece of property it is, in essence, given over to the enemy (i.e., high place), and an ungodly spiritual connection called a dominion is formed between the individual and the object.

Isn't it interesting that God spoke to me through verses of Scripture and then He spoke to me on the same topic through an email from a friend? The Lord owns everything, and in that context, when we claim to own anything, the enemy establishes an ungodly spiritual connection between the individual and the object.

I also remembered Colossians 3:23, another verse the Lord highlighted for me many years ago: "And whatever you do, do it heartily, as to the Lord and not to men."

Owners of Kingdom companies should work for the company as if working for the Lord.

2. COMMITMENT TO OBEY THE KING'S COMMANDS

In the book *Thank God It's Monday!* I wrote about the importance of marketplace Christians knowing God's Word. I referred to Deuteronomy 17:18-20 in that book:

> Also it shall be, when he sits on the throne of his kingdom, that he shall write for himself a copy of this law in a book, from the one before the priests, the Levites. And it shall be with him, and he shall read it all the days of his life, that he may learn to fear the LORD his God and be careful to observe all the words of this law and these statutes, that his heart may not be lifted above his brethren, that he may not turn aside from the commandment to the right hand or to the left, and that he may prolong his days in his kingdom, he and his children in the midst of Israel.

Here is what I said about that passage: "Notice that as stated in Deuteronomy 17:19, reading the Scriptures on a daily basis leads to acquiring the fear of the Lord, 'that he may learn to fear the LORD his God.' You might remember something else that Solomon wrote. In Proverbs 1:7 we read, 'The fear of the LORD is the beginning of knowledge, but fools despise wisdom and instruction.'"[1]

So often I hear marketplace Christians say, "Tell me where to find that Scripture, Rick." The truth is that many marketplace Christians don't know the Word of God. Marketplace ministers must know God's Word if they are to be regarded as peers by pulpit ministers. Joshua 1:5-9 says obedience depends on three things: (1) God's presence,

(2) being strong and courageous, and (3) meditating on the Word of God:

> No man shall be able to stand before you all the days of your life; as I was with Moses, so I will be with you. I will not leave you nor forsake you. Be strong and of good courage, for to this people you shall divide as an inheritance the land which I swore to their fathers to give them. Only be strong and very courageous, that you may observe to do according to all the law which Moses My servant commanded you; do not turn from it to the right hand or to the left, that you may prosper wherever you go. This Book of the Law shall not depart from your mouth, but you shall meditate in it day and night, that you may observe to do according to all that is written in it. For then you will make your way prosperous, and then you will have good success. Have I not commanded you? Be strong and of good courage; do not be afraid, nor be dismayed, for the LORD your God is with you wherever you go.

God's Presence

The kingdom of God is simply the presence of the King. Revelation 3:20 communicates this concept best: "Behold, I stand at the door and knock. If anyone hears My voice and opens the door, I will come in to him and dine with him, and he with Me."

The key to the kingdom of God is to understand that any believer can open the door and invite the Lord's presence in. Marketplace Christians need to see themselves as the "anyone" referred to in this verse of Scripture. They need to open the door and say, "Come in, Lord Jesus," and He will come in.

Being Strong and Courageous

As important as it is to know the Word of God, obeying it by ourselves is impossible. As we see in Romans 8:3-4, the only way to be obedient to the Word of God is to be led by the Holy Spirit.

> We aren't saved from sin's grasp by knowing the commandments of God, because we can't and don't keep them, but God

put into effect a different plan to save us. He sent his own Son in a human body like ours—except that ours are sinful—and destroyed sin's control over us by giving himself as a sacrifice for our sins. So now we can obey God's laws if we follow after the Holy Spirit and no longer obey the old evil nature within us (*TLB*).

Many people have invited Jesus Christ into their hearts as their Savior, but they have not given Him top priority as Lord in their lives. This is especially true of marketplace Christians who so often look to their own resources when they get into a difficult situation in their business lives. Before a person becomes a Christian, he or she lives his or her life according to his or her soul. The soul includes the mind, will and emotions. Even after salvation, the soul continues to demand its role as lord over one's behavior. This is why, in Luke 9:23, Jesus told His disciples that His followers need to deny themselves: "Then He said to them all, 'If anyone desires to come after Me, let him deny himself, and take up his cross daily, and follow Me.'"

This verse has three components: (1) Deny self. (2) Take up the cross daily. (3) Follow Jesus. Let's look at each of those components.

1. *Deny self:* The key word in this first phrase focuses our attention on the word "self." "Self" is another word for "soul." Through years of practice, the soul has grown accustomed to having its own way. There is no way to reform the soul. The soul must be denied.

2. *Take up the cross daily:* It has been easy for me to thank God that He sent Jesus to die on a cross for me. I have had very little trouble accepting the fact that, by faith, I could appropriate His death on the cross as atonement for my sins. Through my studies of Scripture, however, I have become convinced that I too need to have my soul crucified in order to proceed to the next step of following Jesus. My favorite verse for this concept is Galatians 2:20: "I have been crucified with Christ; it is no longer I who live, but Christ lives in

me; and the life which I now live in the flesh I live by faith in the Son of God, who loved me and gave Himself for me."

Taking up our cross means to see our sinful nature as a hindrance to following Jesus. Ephesians 4:22 conveys the same idea: "Put off, concerning your former conduct, the old man which grows corrupt according to the deceitful lusts."

You can't get rid of your sinful nature, but you can deny it, and decommission it—put it off so that it does not influence your daily life. For instance, according to the first few words of Philippians 4:6—"Be anxious for nothing"—when I feel anxiety about a situation, I need to remember that anxiety is contrary to God's will. Anxiety is a manifestation of the sinful nature—the soul.

3. *Follow Jesus:* Led by God's Holy Spirit, an anxious marketplace Christian who has read Philippians 4:6-7 will remember it and be calmed: "Be anxious for nothing, but in everything by prayer and supplication, with thanksgiving, let your requests be made known to God; and the peace of God, which surpasses all understanding, will guard your hearts and minds through Christ Jesus."

How will that person remember that verse? The Holy Spirit will remind him or her of it. Then that person does what the verse prescribes: "By prayer and supplication, with thanksgiving, let your requests be made known to God." That person then asks the Lord to assist him or her with the challenge he or she is experiencing. That person then thanks the Lord for hearing the prayer and receives God's peace, which comforts his or her mind and heart.

Meditating on the Word of God
Cindy Jacobs once encouraged me to read a 365-day Bible. I have done so ever since. Each day I read a portion of the Old Testament, a portion of the New Testament, a Psalm and a Proverb. In this way I meditate on God's Word. I have come to see the process of reading the 365-day Bible

as having my spiritual breakfast—and it's just as important as having my physical breakfast. We can see this concept of eating the Word of God in Jeremiah 15:16: "Your words were found, and I ate them, and Your word was to me the joy and rejoicing of my heart; for I am called by Your name, O LORD God of hosts."

3. COMMITMENT TO MARRIAGE AND FAMILY

We can't take care of our business unless we've taken care of our marriage and family first. Certainly God calls us to run a successful Kingdom business—but not at the expense of our family. They must be our first priority, after our relationship with God.

Connection Between Marriage and Job

In 1999, God gave my friend and colleague Jack Serra a strong word that a businessperson's ministry in the marketplace will only advance to the extent that his or her marriage permits. First Peter 3:7 shows us that when a wife is disconnected from her husband, the husband's prayer life is hindered: "Husbands, likewise, dwell with them with understanding, giving honor to the wife, as to the weaker vessel, and as being heirs together of the grace of life, that your prayers may not be hindered."

Jack also says, "A wife is a revealer of the enemy." This means God gives a wife the ability to hear the Spirit's voice regarding issues her husband faces at work. When a husband has a difficult issue at work, he needs to take it home and discuss it with his wife. Likewise, a professional woman in the marketplace should share her difficulties with her husband. God may have the perfect answer standing in the kitchen or sitting on the couch.

I remember a story Jack told me about hiring a new employee in his company. Just prior to making the employment offer, however, he mentioned his plan to his wife, Alice Jane. She replied, "I don't think that you should hire that guy." Jack asked why, and Alice Jane said, "I don't know." Jack disregarded what seemed to be vague counsel. What happened? The employee turned out to be a major problem at work.

Jack eventually had to terminate him. Jack now reflects upon the intu-
ition he received from his wife and wishes that he had listened to her.[2]

Intimacy

Owners of Kingdom companies must do everything possible to develop
and maintain intimacy in their marriages. Here is my definition of
the concept of intimacy in a marriage: When a husband and wife
reveal their deepest, most private thoughts about themselves to each
other in the context of friendship, trust and longevity of their relationship, they experience intimacy. Proverbs 31:10-12 reflects one
aspect of this concept of intimacy: "Who can find a virtuous wife? For
her worth is far above rubies. The heart of her husband safely trusts
her; so he will have no lack of gain. She does him good and not evil all
the days of her life."

Family

Doug Walton of Transformation Raleigh recently told me that God
revealed to him that a family needs to be in the ministry together. He
said that for a while he had ministered solo in the marketplace. In this
mode, ministry had the tendency to become a wedge between him
and the rest of his family. But now his whole family has joined him, and
ministry no longer brings division—it brings unity.

Ed Silvoso has taught about this concept using Psalm 127:3-5:
"Behold, children are a heritage from the LORD, the fruit of the womb
is a reward. Like arrows in the hand of a warrior, so are the children of
one's youth. Happy is the man who has his quiver full of them; they
shall not be ashamed, but shall speak with their enemies in the gate."

4. COMMITMENT TO A KINGDOM
OWNERSHIP STRUCTURE

Owners of Kingdom companies are committed to the truth of 2 Corinthians 6:14: "Do not be unequally yoked together with unbelievers.
For what fellowship has righteousness with lawlessness? And what
communion has light with darkness?"

If the ownership structure is rooted in real spiritual unity, a Kingdom company can have a mission statement that says its business is a ministry and it can donate corporate funds to non-company causes that extend God's kingdom. These concepts are not possible if part of the ownership does not share a commitment to use the company as an agency of transformation.

I believe the best corporate structure is a sole proprietorship. In other words, if there is only one owner, real spiritual unity is assured. In a partnership, even if both partners are Christians, there is the possibility that one could be walking in the Spirit, while the other is walking in the flesh. In other words, it is possible for two Christians to be unequally yoked in business.

No Exit Strategy

When I was in Cape Town, in December 2004, I met with Graham Power, who is the CEO of The Power Group of Companies. The Power Group is a collection of companies that refers to itself as "the first choice supplier of civil, development and building services and related products in South Africa." In their promotional booklet about The Power Group, Graham writes:

> As we mark the achievements of an eventful 21 years, it is perhaps an appropriate time to revisit our 100-year dream and reflect on the value it holds—for us and for those who will succeed us.
>
> The 100-year dream is a commitment, which our leadership made in 2001 to the prolonged existence of our company. It is an undertaking that this company and its culture and ethics will continue to thrive long after our time. Far from being a fanciful notion or a pipedream, this is an actual long-term business objective, with definite processes and courses of action put in place to ensure its fulfillment in ten, twenty—and even more—decades from this great milestone which we are celebrating this year.
>
> This orientation towards the future underscores the strong spiritual side of the Group, and embodies my personal belief that this is God's business, not ours. We are merely managing

it on His behalf in order to create upliftment, training and growth opportunities for our special people, as well as for the communities in which we operate.

For this reason, people and their well-being are a key motivator in what we do. It is therefore our heartfelt responsibility to train, mentor, empower and identify successors to lead this company into the future.[3]

This is the first company I have seen that has made plans to be in existence 100 years from now. Many companies have the objective of becoming successful and then taking the company public in order to realize and access the market value of the company in the short-term for their own personal benefit.

A Kingdom company, like The Power Group, with its declaration as "God's business," would not want to take the company public. Such a move would jeopardize their mission and goals, and indeed their very identity as a Kingdom company. A Kingdom company that has made a 100-year plan is focusing on the development of people and is planning for succession within the company.

5. COMMITMENT TO IMPLEMENTING THE GREAT COMMISSION THROUGH PRAYER EVANGELISM

I am greatly influenced by Harvest Evangelism's mission statement, which is, "To work with the Church throughout the world to implement the Great Commission in this generation through the biblical principles of prayer evangelism." More about prayer evangelism can be found in Ed Silvoso's book *Prayer Evangelism*.[4] I strongly recommend that owners of Kingdom companies read this book and integrate its principles into their day-to-day operations. Here I've extracted four key principles from the book:

1. *Bless* (see Luke 10:5)
2. *Fellowship* (see Luke 10:7)

3. *Minister* (see Luke 10:9a)
4. *Proclaim* (see Luke 10:9)

Ed Silvoso has also written a book called *Anointed for Business*,[5] in which he reveals how to transform cities and nations by transforming the marketplace—the heart of those cities and nations. This is another must-read for owners of Kingdom companies. Kingdom company stewards need to see their companies as transformation agencies.

6. COMMITMENT TO THE FIVE PIVOTAL PARADIGMS FOR NATION TRANSFORMATION

These five paradigms, developed by Ed Silvoso, are the foundational principles for Kingdom companies:

1. Disciple nations, not just individuals.
2. The marketplace has been redeemed; now it needs to be reclaimed.
3. Everyone is a minister, and labor is worship.
4. Take the kingdom of God to where the gates of Hades are operating so that Jesus can build His Church.
5. Eliminate systemic poverty.

7. COMMITMENT TO BEING EXTRAORDINARY

This commitment can take many forms, though in this context I'm referring primarily to a commitment to pursue extraordinary miracles and a commitment to pursue a strategy of differentiation.

Commitment to Pursue Extraordinary Miracles
This means the company seeks to operate at a level of excellence that is exceedingly, abundantly above the norm. If it is really possible for a Kingdom company to operate at a level of excellence that is exceedingly, abundantly above the norm, then its customers will regard it highly. Remember, for example, Undercar Services, whose customers bring

them cakes, cookies and pies to show their gratitude for the quality service they receive.

Commitment to Pursue a Strategy of Differentiation

Companies follow one of two primary strategies: cost leadership or differentiation. Cost leadership means a company seeks to charge the lowest prices for its products. Examples of this strategy would be Wal-Mart or Costco. A Kingdom company probably cannot pursue a strategy of cost leadership. Pursuing the lowest cost does not reflect the strategy of providing the highest degree of value. Differentiation, on the other hand, means a company seeks to provide products that are superior to its competitors' products. An example would be Mercedes Benz. The whole premise of a Kingdom company is that it provides value that is not available through competitors. In other words, its customers would be willing to pay a premium price in order to obtain the additional value.

8. COMMITMENT TO KINGDOM THINKING

This consists primarily of a commitment to the *agape* way of life, the idea that holiness is not optional, and an anointing for creativity by the Holy Spirit.

Commitment to the *Agape* Way of Life

Sirus Chitsaz of Raleigh, North Carolina has lived next door to Bob Mumford for many years. Sirus and I extracted the following material from the book that Bob authored, entitled *The Agape Road*.

> The Greek language has three words to describe three different kinds of love: *Agape* (unconditional love), *Eros* (conditional love) and *Phileo* (brotherly love). We will focus on the first two. The Father's greatest gift is His intimacy with us. Jesus, Agape incarnate, came to show us the Agape way; the way to the Father and intimacy with Him. Agape satisfies the most important need for anyone, the need for security, identity and belonging. Agape can be shown as a straight arrow of unconditional

love, wanting nothing in return. A person who is intimate with the Father manifests seven godly characteristics:

1. Compassion
2. Grace
3. Patience
4. Mercy
5. Truth
6. Covenantal faithfulness
7. Forgiveness

These seven characteristics are the "DNA" of God, and were manifested in all Jesus did. God's Glory is evident in any believer who spends time with Him on the Agape road. As described in 2 Corinthians 5:14-15, agape is God's way of controlling and shaping our desire: "For the love of Christ compels us, because we judge thus: that if One died for all, then all died; and He died for all, that those who live should live no longer for themselves, but for Him who died for them and rose again."

The opposite of Agape is Eros, which is a selfish and self-centered love that has a hidden "catch or agenda." Eros can be shown as a hook. Eros lays dormant when undisturbed, but rages uncontrollably when exposed or challenged. Eros is capable of horrendous evil and unimaginable manipulation. Eros is the nature of fallen man. We need to recognize Eros and seek to slay it at the foot of the cross. Left unchecked, it results in a cross-less Christianity, as explained in Philippians 3:18: "For many walk, of whom I have told you often, and now tell you even weeping, *that they are* the enemies of the cross of Christ."

Eros can be detected by the following seven characteristics:

1. Looks good   External view vs. internal reality
2. Feels good   Avoids pain at all costs
3. Appears right   Know-it-all

    4. Stays in control   False self-confidence
    5. Hides agenda   False unity
    6. Seeks personal advantage   Self-centered
    7. Appears undisturbed   Personal gain is the end goal[6]

Holiness Is Not Optional

In Ephesians 4:17-24, Paul writes:

> This I say, therefore, and testify in the Lord, that you should no longer walk as the rest of the Gentiles walk, in the futility of their mind, having their understanding darkened, being alienated from the life of God, because of the ignorance that is in them, because of the blindness of their heart; who, being past feeling, have given themselves over to lewdness, to work all uncleanness with greediness. But you have not so learned Christ, if indeed you have heard Him and have been taught by Him, as the truth is in Jesus: that you put off, concerning your former conduct, the old man which grows corrupt according to the deceitful lusts, and be renewed in the spirit of your mind, and that you put on the new man which was created according to God, in true righteousness and holiness.

The essence of this Scripture is that believers need to stop thinking like Gentiles. In the Old Testament, Gentiles were those who were not connected with God. They were alienated from the life of God. But Paul wrote Ephesians 4:17-24 to the Church at Ephesus. This means it is possible for believers to behave as if they are alienated from the life of God. Nothing could be more tragic than to have a relationship with God but not be using it.

Another important point is that Gentiles had futile thinking. "Futile" means serving no useful purpose. Worse still, this Scripture states specifically that a person with this kind of futile thinking will be insensitive, lewd, unclean and greedy.

This Scripture admonishes believers to walk in the Spirit. This is consistent with Romans 8:1: "There is therefore now no condemnation to those who are in Christ Jesus, who do not walk according to the flesh, but according to the Spirit."

We should walk in the Spirit and not in the flesh. Isaiah 64:6 says, "But we are all like an unclean thing, And all our righteousnesses are like filthy rags; We all fade as a leaf, And our iniquities, like the wind, Have taken us away."

Romans 8:5 shows us that holiness is a way of thinking: "For those who live according to the flesh set their minds on the things of the flesh, but those who live according to the Spirit, the things of the Spirit." The next verse shows that fleshly thinking is dead and spiritual thinking is alive: "For to be carnally minded is death, but to be spiritually minded is life and peace." Romans 8:7 demonstrates that when our thinking is carnal, it is the exact opposite of the way that God thinks—it is against God's way of thinking: "Because the carnal mind is enmity against God; for it is not subject to the law of God, nor indeed can be."

Let's look back at Ephesians 4:20, which says, "But you have not so learned Christ." How does one learn Christ? Learning is acquiring knowledge. When we acquire knowledge we often try out the new knowledge, but fail to use it properly. If we keep trying, then eventually we operate according to the new knowledge. Walking in the Spirit is not always accomplished on the first try. When we fail, we simply have to recognize what has happened and try again. The sequence is as follows:

1. *Put off the old man.* This simply means to recognize the soul's influence over your thinking and decide that such thinking is contrary to God's character.

2. *Be transformed by the renewing of your mind.* Find a Scripture that exemplifies the Godly way of thinking.

3. *Put on the new man.* Set your mind on things above and not on things below (see Col. 3:2) so that your thinking will reflect true righteousness and holiness (see Eph. 4:24).

Finally, let's look at 1 Peter 1:13-16, which says holiness is not an option—it is a command!

Therefore gird up the loins of your mind, be sober, and rest your hope fully upon the grace that is to be brought to you at the revelation of Jesus Christ; as obedient children, not conforming yourselves to the former lusts, as in your ignorance; but as He who called you is holy, you also be holy in all your conduct, because it is written, "Be holy, for I am holy."

Anointing for Creativity

If you have the Holy Spirit, and your competitors don't, shouldn't you have an advantage? Of course you should! Exodus 31:1-3 is one of my favorite Scriptures.

Then the LORD spoke to Moses, saying: "See, I have called by name Bezalel the son of Uri, the son of Hur, of the tribe of Judah. And I have filled him with the Spirit of God, in wisdom, in understanding, in knowledge, and in all manner of workmanship."

Just like Moses, when we don't know how to do something, we should ask the Lord what to do. This Scripture shows that God will anoint people with creativity. If we have God's creativity, we should have a competitive advantage.

9. COMMITMENT TO HIGH STANDARDS OF CONDUCT

This commitment is so important for Kingdom companies to stay true to—it will set them apart from their competition and ensure that they give godly witness to the world.

Not Give or Take Bribes

As I have been focused on the paradigm of eliminating systemic poverty, I have learned that systemic corruption is one of the biggest causes of systemic poverty. I have discovered that if corrupt people are taking an unreasonable share of the cash flow, there will be a much smaller amount for ordinary folks. In other words, eliminating systemic corruption is one big step toward eliminating systemic poverty.

It is not enough to eliminate bribery from your business strategy. Kingdom companies must take a stand within their sphere of influence to make sure bribes are not part of their business relationships. It is important to sow the opposite spirit. And it's not just a matter of stopping bad behavior, as we see in Ephesians 4:28. We must press on to give to those in need, to offset societal theft and corruption: "Let him who stole steal no longer, but rather let him labor, working with his hands what is good, that he may have something to give him who has need."

A Kingdom company could participate in a program that rewards customers or suppliers with financial rewards based on outstanding performance.

Pay Appropriate Taxes
In many countries, tax evasion has become a national dilemma. The governments of those countries are unable to balance the budget because of the huge shortfall of tax revenue. Kingdom companies must sow the opposite spirit and look for ways to promote just tax payments in their spheres of influence.

Pay a Competitive Wage to Employees
Colossians 4:1 explains this concept: "Masters, give your bondservants what is just and fair, knowing that you also have a Master in heaven."

Invest in the Workforce and in Families
Kingdom companies will have their well-being of their employees and their families at heart. Ephesians 6:5-9 exhorts us to do this:

> Bondservants, be obedient to those who are your masters according to the flesh, with fear and trembling, in sincerity of heart, as to Christ; not with eyeservice, as men-pleasers, but as bondservants of Christ, doing the will of God from the heart, with goodwill doing service, as to the Lord, and not to men, knowing that whatever good anyone does, he will receive the same from the Lord, whether he is a slave or free. And you, masters, do the same things to them, giving up threatening, knowing

that your own Master also is in heaven, and there is no partial-
ity with Him.

I have listed verses 5 to 8, because they provide a context for verse 9,
which says, "masters, do the same things to them." This means that
Kingdom company employers are to lead as "bondservants of Christ,
doing the will of God from the heart, with goodwill doing service, as to
the Lord, and not to men." In other words, Kingdom company owners
must treat their employees as if they were serving the Lord and not
men. It also shows that "whatever good anyone does, he will receive the
same from the Lord." That means that whatever the leaders sow into
their employees' lives they will receive the same from the Lord.

Then, in the second part of verse 9, we see that employers should
not threaten their employees, but treat them as valuable company assets, remembering that God is looking out for them.

These verses from Ephesians 6:5-9 lead to the conclusion that Kingdom company employers should sow into the lives of their employees
through such programs as performance evaluations, training and mentoring. I believe Kingdom companies should also look out for the families of their workers. For instance, they should assist their employees
in getting out of credit-card debt.

Invest in the Community

Here are three verses that show why a Kingdom company should invest
in the community:

1. Isaiah 62:4: "You shall no longer be termed Forsaken, nor
   shall your land any more be termed Desolate; but you shall
   be called Hephzibah, and your land Beulah; for the LORD
   delights in you, and your land shall be married."

2. Jeremiah 29:7: "And seek the peace of the city where I have
   caused you to be carried away captive, and pray to the LORD
   for it; for in its peace you will have peace."

3. Acts 17:26: "And He has made from one blood every nation
   of men to dwell on all the face of the earth, and has deter-

mined their preappointed times and the boundaries of their dwellings."

Invest in Improving the Environment

In April 2006, I was in New York City for the meeting of the International Transformation Network (ITN). During that conference, we discussed the nature of Kingdom companies. One of the participants at that meeting, Derk Maat of Toronto, commented that a Kingdom company should take responsibility for improving the environment. My wife, Rachel, and I looked at each other and sensed that this was something that the Lord wanted added to the list of components of a Kingdom company. (For more information about how Kingdom companies can lead the business world in this area, see appendix B.)

10. COMMITMENT TO GIVING

If a Kingdom company lacks a commitment to giving, its efforts are likely to fail. God demands that His businesses make a return to Him for the blessings they have received.

Tithing

In a Kingdom company, tithing means giving a percentage of your profits to the Lord. A tithe is customarily thought of as 10 percent, although many have increased the percentage to higher levels.

Fifty-one Percent Strategy

Many Kingdom company owners are committing to give 51 percent of their profits to the Lord. This reflects the fact that God is indeed the senior partner.

Christian Venture Capital

The concept of Christian venture capital is in Acts 4:32-35:

> Now the multitude of those who believed were of one heart and one soul; neither did anyone say that any of the things he possessed was his own, but they had all things in common. And

with great power the apostles gave witness to the resurrection of the Lord Jesus. And great grace was upon them all. Nor was there anyone among them who lacked; for all who were possessors of lands or houses sold them, and brought the proceeds of the things that were sold.

I covered this topic extensively in my book *Thank God It's Monday!* in which I wrote the following:

This Scripture is pointing the way to Christian venture capital financing. In essence, if a Christian in the marketplace has a need for funding for his/her venture, apostles becoming aware of the need should contact other Christians in the marketplace requesting that they send the money without expecting anything in return. There are three motivations for this kind of behavior: (1) the apostles involved will proclaim the gospel with great power, and (2) great grace will be upon them all (i.e. givers, receivers and apostles), and (3) no one among them will lack.[7]

The Lord has given me new revelation on this topic recently. In verse 34 we see a reference to "possessors of lands or houses." Both of these terms are plural. In other words, the possessors owned multiple lands and/or multiple houses. If a person didn't have multiple properties, then when it came time to exercise this concept of Christian venture capital, the person would have to sell his or her home—and be out on the street. Therefore, I believe that Kingdom company owners will own multiple lands and/or houses so that when required by the Lord to sell something and give it away, the owner's primary residence will not be affected.

11. COMMITMENT TO A TRANSFORMATION CHURCH

A Kingdom company owner should be a member of a transformation church. This will insure maximum synergy between the owners of the Kingdom company and their congregational leadership (see Dr. Greg Pagh's Afterword in this book).

12. COMMITMENT TO PRAYER

I don't think it's possible to overemphasize the importance of this commitment. Without prayer, we cannot commune with God. How can we say that we're running a Kingdom business if we're not having regular conference calls with the Guy in charge?

In my book *Thank God It's Monday!* I made the following comments:

In 1989, during a short-term mission trip to East Africa, our microbus was stuck in the mud just outside Nairobi, Kenya. All of the men took off their shoes and rolled up their pantlegs and waded into the water and mud to try to push the microbus. After the men had committed an hour or so of unsuccessful pushing, my wife, Rachel said, "We could pray for help." Each of us looked at each other thinking, "Why didn't I think of that?" We waded over to Rachel and she said that prayer and no sooner had we all said, "Amen," than a four-wheel-drive truck with a winch on the front appeared upon the horizon and pulled us easily from our captivity. No other vehicle had passed by during the entire period that we were stuck. We experience this same phenomenon when called in to intercede for ailing Christian businesses. The owners have tried everything they can think of—that is, except prayer.[8]

Kingdom companies must begin to see prayer as a part of the standard equipment for running their companies. Check out what Jesus Himself has to say about prayer:

Most assuredly, I say to you, he who believes in Me, the works that I do he will do also; and greater works than these he will do, because I go to My Father. And whatever you ask in My name, that I will do, that the Father may be glorified in the Son. If you ask anything in My name, I will do it (John 14:12-14).

And owners of Kingdom companies should not just be praying alone—they should also pray together with other Kingdom company owners and have intercessors who pray for them.

I have taken teams of intercessors into many Christian companies that are having difficulties. The owners of the companies are typically filled with anxiety. Anxiety seems to be an epidemic in the Body of Christ. Kingdom companies should set a new standard—they should pray about everything.

Notes
1. Rick Heeren, *Thank God It's Monday!* (San Jose: Transformational Publications, 2004), pp. 79-84. Copies can be ordered at www.citymiracles.com.
2. Jack Serra, *Marriage, Marketplace and Revival* (Orlando, FL: Longwood Communications, 2001). See www.themmconnection.com.
3. Graham Power, *The Power Touch, Reaching Out, Taking the Challenge, Embracing Change*. Promotional brochure, The Power Group of Companies, Wimbleton Road, P.O. Box 129, Blackheath 7581, Cape Town, South Africa, 2004.
4. Ed Silvoso, *Prayer Evangelism* (Ventura, CA: Regal Books, 2000).
5. Ed Silvoso, *Anointed for Business* (Ventura, CA: Regal Books, 2002).
6. Bob Mumford, *The Agape Road* (Cookeville, TN: Lifechangers, 2004). See www.lifechangers.org.
7. Heeren, *Thank God It's Monday!* pp. 115-117.
8. Ibid., p. 67.

KINGDOM COMPANIES AND THE ENVIRONMENT

IS IMPROVING THE ENVIRONMENT BIBLICAL?

After the Fall in the Garden of Eden, the ground (the marketplace of that time) was cursed. But Jesus Christ redeemed the marketplace through the atonement. Now it is our job to take back what Christ has redeemed. Genesis 2:15 gives us our mandate: "Then the LORD God took the man and put him in the Garden of Eden to tend and keep it." We are also instructed to rule over the earth: "Then God said, 'Let Us make man in Our image, according to Our likeness; let them have dominion over the fish of the sea, over the birds of the air, and over the cattle, over all the earth and over every creeping thing that creeps on the earth'" (Gen. 1:26).

As we seek to be good stewards, we must keep in mind John 3:16: "For God so loved the world that He gave His only begotten Son, that whoever believes in Him should not perish but have everlasting life." Many Christians believe this Scripture speaks only to the idea that God loves the people in the world. While it is true that God loves the people, God also loves the physical world.

OUR OPPORTUNITY

Every marketplace activity or service relies on the earth in some way to sustain its activity. Every service or activity uses energy or some form of resource extracted from the earth. Indiscriminate consumption and degradation of the land and its resources constitutes a violation of the very creation we are called to steward.

North American and European countries have in some areas developed environmental controls to which marketplace enterprises have responded with innovation and ingenuity to protect the environment.

The investment community is advising investors and shareholders to move investments from traditional asset classes to companies developing emission control technologies, the nuclear energy sector, synthetic fuels such as hydrogen, new housing forms and materials of construction, new transportation systems, and environmentally safe commodities.

KINGDOM COMPANIES CAN TAKE LEADERSHIP

Some companies are leading the way when it comes to cutting waste, protecting the environment, improving the longevity of their products and minimizing energy consumption. Kingdom companies need to have an environmental and a creation-based stewardship paradigm that addresses the need to develop the following:

1. New economic financial models that reflect the full cost of resource depletion and environmental impact

2. New energy conservation patterns that will reduce our indiscriminate use of fossil fuels

3. New nonfossil fuel (biomass, solar, wind, nuclear) sources that will replace a portion of our oil consumption and that will limit the emission of greenhouse gases into the atmosphere

4. New sustainable housing and transportation alternatives that limit the impact on the environment, the use of energy and the generation of waste

5. New accounting and auditing practices for public and private companies that fully account for environmental impact, energy use and resource demand

6. New environmental ethics for individuals and corporations

Companies pursuing alternative energy sources are now reaping the fruits of their labor in the form of increased market share, consumer confidence and bottom-line profitability. Some pulp and paper companies that have developed nonfossil-fuel-based energy sources and zero-waste pulping technologies are now in the forefront of profitability. A few oil companies are developing sustainable oil-extraction technologies. Some automobile companies that are developing hybrids and low-fuel and clean-fuel-consuming automobiles are gaining market share and are leading in profitability.[1]

Note

1. Much of the above perspective was gleaned from an email that was sent to me by Derk Maat, CEO of Hobbs, Miller & Matt, Inc., 2651 Fonthill Drive, Oakville, ON L6J 7H5, (905) 829-1749, www.hmmenvirotech.com.

MARKETPLACE CHRISTIANS FEATURED IN THIS BOOK

PABLO AND MONICA ABELEIRA

Pablo and his wife, Monica, are native Argentines. For many years they served as associate pastors at Iglesia Cristo Para Todos (Christ for Everyone Church) in Adrogue, Argentina, a church that has led at least one person to the Lord in more than 99 percent of the homes in that town. Pablo and Monica developed a method of using questionnaires for street evangelism. During our three days in Adrogue, the 162 members of our delegation helped 750 people fill in questionnaires and led 550 of those people in prayers to receive Jesus Christ as their Savior and Lord. In 2001, God led Pablo and Monica to bring their three boys, Gaston, Mariano and Santiago, to live in San Jose, California, to work with Harvest Evangelism, ministering to Hispanic congregations. In June 2003, the Lord told Pablo He was raising a Joseph Generation for Argentina and that He would raise Argentina's flag among the nations as an example of restoration. Pablo and his family then returned to Argentina.

JIM ANTHONY

Jim received his B.A. from Duke University in 1976 and his MBA from the University of California in 1978. Prior to founding Anthony & Company, he served as a consultant with Grubb & Ellis Company in Los Angeles, California, from 1979 to 1983. In 1980, he won the "Rookie of the Year" award at Grubb & Ellis. In 1983, Jim moved to Raleigh to be the Leasing and Management Director for Carolantic

Realty. Jim founded Anthony & Co. in 1987. In 1994, he was named Raleigh Chamber Entrepreneur of the Year. In 1998, he acquired Allenton Commercial in Durham, North Carolina, and four years later project offices were opened in Myrtle Beach, South Carolina; Atlanta, Georgia; and Niagara Falls, New York. Today, the company has opened a project office in Burlington, North Carolina, for the redevelopment of the first outlet shopping center in that state. For more information, visit www.summitniagara.com.

KEN AND CARRIE BEAUDRY

Ken and Carrie Beaudry live in Elk River, Minnesota. They have four adult children whose names are Dana, Lisa, Trevor and Jacob. Ken is the founder and CEO of the Beaudry Companies, which has four divisions: propane, commercial diesel, transportation of petroleum products, and lubricants. They have been in business for 24 years, and during that time Ken gave his life to Jesus Christ. The leadership team of Pray Elk River commissioned Ken and Carrie to serve as leaders of an intercessory group for the team. They have mobilized and trained intercessors in Elk River and they have led citywide strategic intercession for the city.

DR. CLIFFORD DAUGHERTY

Dr. Cliff Daugherty joined Valley Christian Schools as President/ Superintendent in July 1986. Under his leadership, enrollment more than doubled, and the school was able to construct permanent facilities for all three campuses with a current value of more than $100 million. Dr. Daugherty is the founder of Neighborhood Christian Preschools, the Christian Schools Association of Santa Clara County, and the Quest Institute for Christian Education, and he served as the founding principal of Los Altos Christian Schools. Dr. Daugherty received his B.S. in English Literature, Bible and Theology from Bethany College; his M.A. in Public School Administration from San Jose State University; and his Ed.D. in Private School Administration and Special Education from the University of San Francisco. He holds lifetime and ACSI Teaching and Administrative credentials. Dr. Daugherty and his wife, Kris, live in San Jose, California. They have two children and three grandchildren.

DAVE AND GAYLE GARVEN

Dave attended Mankato State College in Mankato, Minnesota, and graduated in 1969 with a Bachelor of Science in Business Education. For most of his career, Dave has been an independent sales and marketing representative for major consumer products companies. Dave is the founder and current CEO of CSM Tarps, which imports and sells tarps. In May 2005, Gayle retired after 36 years as a flight attendant for Northwest Airlines. Dave and Gayle have had two children and now have two grandchildren. During the winter months, they live in their home in Sarasota, Florida. During the summer months, they live in their home in Nisswa, Minnesota.

RICHARD GAZOWSKY

Richard is the senior pastor of Voice of Pentecost Church in San Francisco, California. He is also Director and Producer of WYSIWYG Filmworks. Richard, his wife, Sandy, their two daughters, Misty Dejavu and Rocki Starr, and their son, Sunny, are all involved in the operation of WYSIWYG. For more information, visit the company's website at www.wysiwygfilmworks.com.

JOHN AND SANDY HALVORSEN

John Halvorsen graduated from the University of Minnesota in 1972 with a Bachelor of Arts Degree in Psychology. He also attended two Bible schools prior to entering the ministry. He is currently the senior pastor of Great Lakes Gospel Church in Duluth, Minnesota, a regional representative for Harvest Network International, and also chair of the Lake Superior Pastors' Fellowship in Duluth. John and his wife, Sandy, have four children and live in Duluth. Sandy is a nurse at St. Luke's Hospital and serves as the St. Louis County coordinator for the Minnesota network of the U.S. Global Apostolic Prayer Network (USGAPN).

RON AND LINDA OLSON

Ron and Linda Olson are currently missionaries with the Central USA Region of Harvest Evangelism, Inc. Ron is a licensed minister. They have two children, Melissa and David, and live in Minnetonka, Minnesota.

CHUCK AND PATTI HERBST

Chuck attended Western Michigan University, and in June 1981 he received a Bachelor in Business Administration degree with a major in Accountancy. From 1981 to 1985, he worked in the Chicago office of Arthur Andersen & Company, where he focused on the audit of financial institutions, and then from 1985 to 1989 in the Chicago office of Kenneth Leventhal & Company, where he focused on real estate tax.

Chuck began his real estate career in 1989, working for Combined Properties. He formed Revolution Partners Corporation in 1994 and continues to serve that company as its president. The mission of Revolution is to create value and profit by acquiring, developing, renovating and managing retail, residential and mixed-use real estate developments in primarily urban settings. Chuck is a Certified Public Accountant and a licensed real estate salesperson.

Patti attended Loyola University and in 1983 received a degree in Accountancy. She began her first job on the audit staff at Arthur Andersen & Company. She founded her own accounting firm, called Chamberlain & Herbst, in 1991, and then sold the practice in 1997 in order to found The Center for Independence. Pattie is the executive director of The Center for Independence (see www.center-for-independence.org). Patti is a Certified Public Accountant. Chuck and Patti live in Western Springs, Illinois, with their three children, Justin, Clay and Kacie.

RYAN AND PAM KUBAT

Ryan Kubat, together with his wife, Pam, started Corporate Recognition, Inc., in 1997 as a promotional products distributor in Owatonna, Minnesota. Looking for real purpose for their business, they found the encouragement they needed to step out in faith and bring ministry into the marketplace when they participated in an *Anointed for Business* (Ed Silvoso) Bible study. Ryan and his son, Adam, have traveled to Argentina twice to witness transformation taking place in the cities, churches and prisons in that country. Ryan was also inspired by *The Elk River Story* (Rick Heeren) to bring transformation to his hometown of Owatonna. Ryan is the Steele County coordinator within the Minnesota network of the U.S. Global Apostolic Prayer Network (USGAPN). Ryan and Pam have three children: Kate, Rebecca and Adam.

MICHAEL AND ADERONKE MORDI

Michael and Aderonke were both born in Nigeria. Aderonke immigrated to the United States in 1992 and Michael arrived in 1995. They met in March 1997 and were married on August 23, 1997. Aderonke was a widow with an 8-year-old son named Adeboye (now 17). The Lord has blessed their marriage with three more children, Ify (8), Ekene (7) and Ebube (4). Michael is a pastor. Aderonke is a scientist with a PhD in biochemistry.

VIRGINIA MORTON

Virginia Morton, a Richmond native, has lived in Culpeper for more than 36 years. A former teacher, she became fascinated with Culpeper's vast Civil War history and, after several years of intense research, decided to tell Culpeper's story to the world. Virginia hopes that her historical novel *Marching Through Culpeper*, now in the ninth printing, will promote tourism and preservation of the county's three battlefields.

Virginia conducts Civil War walking tours of the historic downtown area as well as battlefield tours at Brandy Station, Cedar Mountain and Kelly's Ford. She is a frequent speaker at Civil War Round Tables civic groups, libraries, and book clubs, where she presents a dynamic slide presentation that gives an overview of the war in Culpeper. On April 12, 2002, she was named writer of the year at the Richmond Conference of the American Christian Writers. In February 2004, she served as leader of a HistoryAmerica Mississippi Riverboat Cruise focusing on women in the Civil War. She also wrote an article about Confederate scout Frank Stringfellow, which was published in the *Washington Times*.

Virginia serves on the boards of the Brandy Station Battlefield Foundation and the Friends of Cedar Mountain Battlefield, was co-founder of the Academic Booster's Club, and has served as a youth counselor at the Culpeper United Methodist Church and as chairman of the Congressional Award Committee. She and her husband, Roger, have a grown daughter living in California. For more information, visit www.edgehillbooks.com.

APOSTLE JULIUS PETER OYET

Apostle Julius Peter Oyet is the Founder and Presiding Bishop of Life Line Ministries in Kampala, Uganda. He is also the General Secretary of National Fellowship of Born Again Pentecostal Churches (NFBPC), which has more than 10,000 churches and more than 7 million Christians in Uganda (see www.lifelineministries.org).

RANDY PECK, M.D.

Randy received his B.A. in biochemistry from the University of Virginia in 1979 and his M.D. from the Medical College of Virginia in 1983. In 1988, following his postdoctoral training at the Medical College of Virginia, he was certified by the American Board of Anesthesiology. From 1986 to 1987, he served as a private practice anesthesiologist at Washington County Hospital in Hagerstown, Maryland, and then at the Culpeper Regional Hospital in Culpeper, Virginia. From 1994 to 1998, Randy served as the Director of Anesthesia at Culpeper Hospital, and then as a *locum tenens* anesthesiologist for five hospitals and freestanding ambulatory surgery centers in 2000 to 2003. From 2003 to 2006, Randy served as a private practice anesthesiologist at Carilion Giles Memorial Hospital in Pearisburg, Virginia. Randy also founded Peck Webs, an Internet marketing solutions company, in 2001. He went on sabbatical from his medical practice during 2007 and dedicated that entire year to his Internet marketing consulting business. He now feels that the Lord is leading him to devote full-time to that business. Randy and his wife, Julia, and their two children live in Culpeper, Virginia. (For more information, see www.peckwebs.com.)

R.J. AND LEN JOHNSON

R.J. and Len Johnson are pseudonyms. The actual individuals have requested that they remain anonymous for the purpose of this book.

NIEL STEGMANN, M.D.

Niel is married to Rina, and together they have three children: Hubert, Hanli and Alet. Niel became qualified as a dentist in 1974. After 10 successful years in private practice as a dentist, he went back to school at Stellenbosch Medical School in Cape Town, South Africa, and became a Maxillo facial surgeon.

Following four years of private practice, Neil entered the field of hospital management. Soon after, he built and managed his first private hospital. Then he joined Hospiplan, a hospital management company, as operational director. In four years, the company grew from 5 to 17 hospitals throughout South Africa and Namibia. While operating these hospitals, Niel became acutely aware of the shortcomings of the hospital management software available at the time. He dreamed of building a software system that would meet his practical needs as a hospital administrator.

In 1996, the hospital management company was sold to an even larger South African company. Niel purchased the two hospitals in Namibia and started to implement his dream of building a health information system, which he eventually named InfoCare.

GRAHAM AND DIANE VERMOOTEN

Graham and Diane founded Media Village in 1995. They live near Cape Town, South Africa, with their two sons, Shane and Ryan. Graham and Diane have won the admiration of leaders such as Michael Cassidy, founder of African Enterprises; Graham Power, founder of The Power Group of Companies, Transformation Africa and the Global Day of Prayer; and Ed Silvoso, founder of Harvest Evangelism, Inc. For more information, visit www.mediavillage.info.

STEVE AND KATHY WIRTH

Steve is an attorney with a master's degree in tax law, but he is more entrepreneur than attorney. He has always wanted to own his own business, and he has always enjoyed looking for a business opportunity with big potential. Kathy grew up in an entrepreneurial family. A graduate of the University of Minnesota, she has been actively involved in running WirthCo for the past 19 years. The Wirths have three grown children. For more information about the Wirths, visit www.wirthco.com.

YUK-LYNN WOO

Yuk-Lynn Woo earned her Bachelor of Science degree in Engineering in Computer Sciences from Imperial College, London University. After working for Spicer & Oppenheim Consultants in the UK and Singapore for two years, she completed an MBA from Columbia Business School in New York. She worked five years with the Boston Consulting Group (BCG) in their New York and Hong Kong offices, and then entered the family business, where she is currently Executive Director of Central Textiles (H.K.), Ltd. and Central Fabrics, Ltd. She is the third generation of her family to work in this company. Her husband, Roy Chen, is employed by the Sterling Global Group, an asset management firm. Yuk-Lynn and Roy have one son and two daughters.

PASTOR JUAN ZUCCARELLI

Juan is the senior pastor of Christ the Only Hope Church in La Plata, Argentina. He has also overseen the establishment of a Christian congregation within Olmos Prison in La Plata. Currently, 60 percent of the inmates at this prison are born-again Christians. Prisoners transferring from Olmos Prison have planted congregations in other prisons, so that today each of the 40 prisons in the province of Buenos Aires has a Christian congregation. The governor of the province of Buenos Aires has given Pastor Zuccarelli a prison, Christ the Only Hope Prison, which is being run as a Christian prison.

CONTACT INFORMATION

Rick Heeren
Regional Vice President
Central USA Region
Harvest Evangelism, Inc.
c/o Heeren Enterprises, Inc.
P.O. Box 385375
Minneapolis, MN 55438

(612) 840-5813
www.citymiracles.com

Faith Makes a Difference in the Workplace

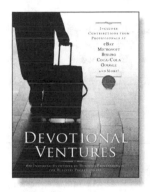

Devotional Ventures
60 Inspiring Devotions by Business
Professionals for Business Professionals
Edited by *Corey Cleek*
ISBN 978.08307.43148

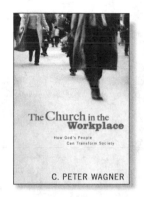

The Church in the Workplace
How God's People
Can Transform Society
C. Peter Wagner
ISBN 978.08307.39097

TGIF: Today God Is First
Daily Workplace Inspiration
Os Hillman
ISBN 978.08307.44794

The 9 to 5 Window
How Faith Can
Transform the Workplace
Os Hillman
ISBN 978.08307.37963

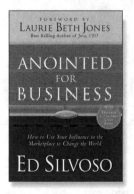

Anointed for Business
How Christians Can Use Their
Influence in the Marketplace
to Change the World
Ed Silvoso
ISBN 978.08307.41960

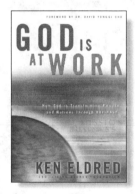

God Is at Work
How God Is Transforming People and
Nations Through Business
Ken Eldred
ISBN 978.08307.38069

Transformation Begins with YOU!

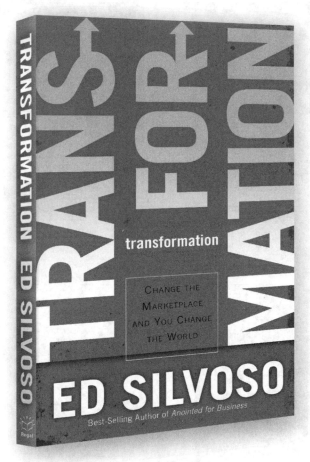

Transformation
Change the Marketplace
and You Change the World
Ed Silvoso
ISBN 978.08307.44756

Are you tired of living an ordinary life?
You were created to do great things!
But how do you begin?

God loves you and has a unique blueprint for your life—but it's up to you to
find it and live it out. Mingling contemporary stories and biblical anecdotes
with practical advice, Silvoso shows
how God intervenes in human affairs
today to transform people and nations.
In these pages, you'll hear extraordinary
stories about the power of God working
through those who discovered their specific purpose.

Learn Silvoso's five critical paradigms
for implementing change: discipling
nations, reclaiming the marketplace, seeing work as worship, using the power of
God to overcome evil in everyday situa-
tions and eliminating systemic poverty.
Then be challenged to transform yourself—and by doing so, transform your
family, school, business and nation.

Just think! You *can* make a difference
in the world. It's time to look at yourself the way God does, as loved and
designed with a unique purpose. You
can aim high, knowing that He has
entrusted you with great things. "God
sees you as a nation transformer," says
Silvoso. God has faith in you!